The Dall Sheep *Dinner Guest*

The Dall Sheep *Dinner Guest*

IÑUPIAQ NARRATIVES OF NORTHWEST ALASKA

Wanni W. Anderson

STORYTELLERS:
John Patkuraq Brown
Leslie Tusraġviuraq Burnett
Flora Kuugaaq Cleveland
Lois Piŋalu Cleveland
Maude Kanayuqpak Cleveland
Robert Nasruk Cleveland
Kitty Qalutchuq Foster
Sarah Qiñuġana Goode
Willie Panik Goodwin, Sr.
Minnie Aliitchak Gray
Beatrice Anausuk Mouse
Nora Paniikaaluk Norton
Nellie Qapuk Russell
Andrew Nuqaqsrauraq Skin
Emma Atluk Skin
Wesley Qauluġtaiḷaq Woods

© 2005 by University Press of Colorado

Published by University of Alaska Press
An imprint of University Press of Colorado
1624 Market Street, Suite 226
PMB 39883
Denver, Colorado 80202-1559

The University Press of Colorado is a proud member of
Association of University Presses.

The University Press of Colorado is a cooperative publishing enterprise supported, in part, by Adams State University, Colorado State University, Fort Lewis College, Metropolitan State University of Denver, University of Alaska Fairbanks, University of Colorado, University of Northern Colorado, University of Wyoming, Utah State University, and Western Colorado University.

∞ This paper meets the requirements of the ANSI/NISO Z39.48-1992 (Permanence of Paper).

ISBN: 978-1-889963-74-7 (hardcover)
ISBN: 978-1-64642-410-8 (paperback)

The dall sheep dinner guest : Iñupiaq narratives of northwest Alaska / [compiled by] Wanni W. Anderson ; storytellers, John Patkuraq Brown . . . [et al.].
             p. cm.
        Includes bibliographical references and index.
        ISBN-13: 978-1-889963-74-7 (alk. paper)
        ISBN: 978-1-64642-410-8 (alk. paper: paperback)
        1. Inupiat—Folklore. 2. Tales—Alaska. 3. Legends—Alaska.
        I. Title: Iñupiaq narratives of northwest Alaska.
        II. Anderson, Wanni Wibulswasdi, 1937–
        III. Brown, John Patkuraq.
E99.E7D324 2005
398.2'089'9712–dc22   2005043085

Cover and text design by Dixon J. Jones, Rasmuson Library Graphics
Dall sheep cover image © 1995 SoftKey International Inc.

Contents

Illustrations

Preface

The collection of Iñupiaq stories in this volume was carried out in conjunction with several of Brown University's archeological and ethnological field research efforts on the Kobuk and Selawik rivers.

I gratefully acknowledge the support of the following organizations: the National Science Foundation for the archeological investigation of Onion Portage (1966–1968); the Wenner-Gren Foundation for the ethnographic research in Selawik (1971–1972); the National Park Service and the U.S. Department of Fish and Wildlife for the Selawik Eskimo subsistence study (1977); and the National Science Foundation for support of the project "Human Subsistence Practices in Response to Environmental Fluctuations in Northwest Alaska" (1991–1996). I appreciate the support of the Northwest Arctic Borough, which jointly funded the translation of stories from Iñupiaq to English with the National Science Foundation (1994).

I am most grateful for the generosity and kindness of the following Iñupiaq storytellers who welcomed me into their homes and summer tents and shared their coffee and stories: Robert Nasruk Cleveland, Maude Kanayuqpak Cleveland, Lois Piŋalu Cleveland, Nora Paniikaaluk Norton, John Patkuraq Brown, Emma Atluk Skin, Beatrice Anausuk Mouse, Sarah Qiñuġana Goode, Flora Kuugaaq Cleveland (Selawik), William Panik Goodwin, Sr., Andrew Nuqaqsrauraq Skin, Nellie Qapuk Russell, Leslie Tusraġviuraq Burnett, Kitty Qalutchuq Foster, Minnie Aliitchak Gray, and Wesley Qualuġtaiḷaq Woods. I appreciate the assistance of Emma Saḷaq Norton of Selawik and Clara Paniikaaluk Lee of Ambler in facilitating my story collecting. Their friendship, hospitality, and fascinating storytelling events are valued memories of my time on the Kobuk and Selawik.

In 1973, Elmer Misruk Jackson of Kiana translated a number of stories. Later, in 1977, I commissioned Michael Qakiq Atoruk to translate another set of stories. To compare differences in the translations, I had Michael Atoruk translate a few of the stories that had been translated earlier by Elmer Jackson. The edited stories in this collection are based on seventy-seven stories that Michael Atoruk translated and nine stories that Elmer Jackson translated. Jonas Aakataq Ramoth of the National Park Service office in Kotzebue, a native of Selawik, translated the two legends told by Wesley Woods. I thank Ruthie Tatqaviñ Sampson, coordinator of bilingual and bicultural education, Northwest Arctic Borough School District, for interesting discussions on the cultural meanings of Iñupiaq terms and for looking over Iñupiaq terms. Her observations on the vocal characteristics of Kobuk Iñupiat versus Selawik Iñupiat were most helpful in establishing locational differences in story deliveries discussed in the introduction. Finally, I would like to thank the manuscript reviewers for their helpful suggestions, Dr. Erica Hill of the University of Alaska Press, and Dr. Alta-Mae Stevens for her editorial assistance.

Wanni W. Anderson
Providence, Rhode Island

Introduction

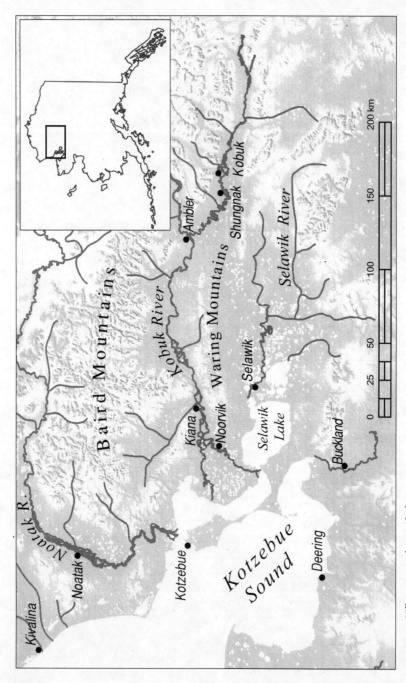

FIGURE 1 ~ *Villages in northwest Alaska.*

Iñupiaq Oral Narratives
Collection History and Narrative Culture

IÑUPIAQ ORAL CULTURE IS KNOWN FOR ITS RICH STORYTELLING TRADITION.
The earliest ethnographic report of this tradition in northwest Alaska appears
in Edward William Nelson's study, *The Eskimo About Bering Strait*. Nelson published two stories, "The Shaman in the Moon" and "The Man-Worm," which
he collected from Kotzebue Sound in 1881 (1899:515–516). The story "The
Shaman in the Moon" gives a rare portrait of the sky world as conceptualized
in Iñupiaq cosmology.

In 1921, Greenland explorer Knud Rasmussen began his historic Fifth Thule
Expedition by dog team, traveling through Inuit villages from Greenland across
Canada, Alaska, and East Cape (Siberia) (Burch 1988:81–100; Ostermann 1952).
Rasmussen arrived in Kotzebue in 1924 and recorded two stories, which are
reported in *The Alaskan Eskimos* (Ostermann 1952). Rasmussen's recorded
stories provide further evidence of the existence of Iñupiaq folktale traditions
in northwest Alaska. Three years later, in 1927, the expedition of the acclaimed
photographer Edward Curtis led him to the Kotzebue Sound area. Curtis's study,
The Alaskan Eskimo (1930), includes thirty folktales that he collected from
Kotzebue, Noatak, Kobuk, and Selawik storytellers. Curtis's folktale collection
points to the salience of the storytelling tradition in various settlements along
the river systems. Ten stories came from the Noatak River, eight stories from
the Selawik, nine stories from the Kobuk, and three stories were collected from
Kotzebue.

During the 1940s, James Louis Giddings conducted anthropological and
archeological surveys of the Kobuk River in conjunction with a tree-ring dating
project. The first two field seasons (1940, 1941) led to the collection of twenty-six
tales and legends told by five Kobuk storytellers: Kahkik (Kobuk Mike), Pegliruk

(Charlie Custer), Niyuk (Charlie Johnson), Nasruk (Robert Cleveland), and Noonagak. The stories appeared in *Kobuk River People* (Giddings 1961), the first substantial collection of folktales from the Kobuk River. In 1951, while at Elephant Point, Eschscholtz Bay, anthropologist Charles Lucier (1954) collected sixteen stories that he called "Eskimo myths" from Buckland. His Buckland storyteller was Andrew Sunno, who had also lived in the Unalakleet–St. Michael region and had stories from that area in his repertoire. Lucier's translator, Jessie Ralph, originally from Selawik, told one story. The following year, while at Sisualik, Kotzebue Sound, Lucier obtained more stories from a Noataker named Mark Mitchell and his Upper Kobuk–born wife, Jenny Mitchell. Jenny Mitchell told twenty-two of the twenty-five stories that Lucier recorded (Lucier 1958).

In 1953, while in Barrow conducting an ethnographic study, anthropologist Robert Spencer (1959) collected several stories. Among his informants were some Noatak and Kobuk people who were living in Barrow at the time. Due to the lack of data on Spencer's informants, it is not possible to pinpoint who told each story. Additional story collections were later compiled by anthropologists who conducted their ethnographic studies in the Arctic Northwest, for example Don Foote's *Eskimo Stories and Songs of the Upper Kobuk River* (1966). The twenty-four stories Foote recorded from Robert Nasruk Cleveland were later published as *Unipchaaɲich Imaġluktuġmiut: Stories of the Black River People* (Cleveland 1980). An extensive collection of 190 Noatak stories, collected in 1962 from Edna Hunnicutt and Paul Monroe, appears in Edwin Hall's *The Eskimo Storyteller: Folktales from Noatak, Alaska* (1975). Hall's collection, with ethnographic descriptions of Noatak village, the storytellers, and the Noatak storytelling tradition, is the most extensive folktale collection ever recorded from the region.

Additional collections made by Iñupiaq writers, educators, and Alaska educational and Native groups expanded the range of published Iñupiaq narratives. In *Eskimo Legends* (1959), Lela Oman of Kiana made a "precise translation" of ten stories told by her aunt, Susie Lockhart. *Tales of Eskimo Alaska* (Frost 1971), on the other hand, was the first endeavor of Alaska Methodist University to present Eskimo folktales, with illustrations, as children's literature for primary school children. Another effort was the six retold and elaborated stories from Selawik in *Tell Me Ahna* (1975) collected by Susan Towne DeBree, a Selawik schoolteacher between 1966 and 1968. For Point Hope, William Oquilluk's *People of Kauwerak* (1973), a collection of oral histories, legends, and stories, many of them told by Oquilluk's grandfather, is a recognized Native authority on storytelling. Among Iñupiaq folktale books produced under Tupou P. Pulu's directorship,

Unipchaallu Uqaaqtuallu (1979) was the first to be published as a joint project of two Native organizations (the Northwest Alaska Native Association, or NANA, and Mauneluk Association), the Northwest Arctic Borough School District, and the National Bilingual Education Development Center, Anchorage. It was also the first publication of Iñupiaq folktales collected at the NANA Elders' Conferences from 1976 to 1978.

More recent folktale collections, containing both Iñupiaq and English versions for each story, were initiated and produced by the Iñupiaq Bilingual/Bicultural Education Program of the Northwest Arctic Borough School District: *Qayaqtauġiŋñaqtuaq* (Lee et al. 1991), *Lore of the Iñupiat: The Elders Speak* (Mendenhall et al. 1989), and *Maniilaq, the Prophet* (Pulu and Ramoth-Sampson 1981). The stories have been used extensively in Iñupiaq language classes in the ten village schools of the Northwest Arctic Borough School District. Collaboration between a folklorist/anthropologist and Iñupiaq language specialists led to the production of *Folktales of the Riverine and Coastal Iñupiat* (Anderson and Sampson 2003) as a bilingual textbook for Iñupiaq teachers and students. The book was produced in conjunction with a workshop for Iñupiaq teachers to encourage them to teach Iñupiaq folktales both as language and as culture. These bilingual folktale collections represent a step forward in the understanding of Iñupiaq history and culture.

The Dall Sheep Dinner Guest is a collection of eighty-eight stories told by sixteen Iñupiaq storytellers. Forty-three of the stories were published in *Folktales of the Riverine and Coastal Iñupiat* (Anderson and Sampson 2003) in a different form, with the English version of the stories edited and presented as a close literal translation to facilitate the use of the book for Iñupiaq language study. In this edition, I have balanced literal translation with English syntax and tried to maintain the voice and storytelling style of individual storytellers as much as possible in translation. The collection as a whole holds historical significance as a record of time past and the stories told by the great-grandparental generation. Except for Minnie Gray, the storytellers are now deceased.

The field collection spans a period of twenty-one years, from 1966 to 1987, with stories recorded from storytellers from Selawik, Shungnak, Ambler, Noorvik, and Kotzebue. A number of stories are from and about Point Hope, as they were told to two storytellers who explicitly identified these particular stories as Point Hope stories. The first set of stories comes from my 1966 summer field season at Onion Portage on the Kobuk River as a member of the Brown University Archeological Expedition. During that summer I collected ethnographic data, oral narratives, and songs from Iñupiaq excavation crew members, their wives, and relatives who came to stay at the Onion Portage site. This set of stories includes those told by Robert Cleveland, Willie Goodwin, Sr., Maude Cleveland, and Minnie Gray. Later field research, which was carried out with Douglas D. Anderson at Onion Portage (1967, 1968), Kiana (1975), and Selawik (1968, 1969, 1971–1972, 1977, 1978, 1981, and 1987) expanded the narrative repertoire to include stories from the Selawik River. Since my primary research areas are the Kobuk and the Selawik, the data from Kotzebue is limited and only includes stories from Willie Goodwin, Sr., who was born and grew up in Selawik.

The legends and stories in this volume comprise all the folktales that I collected on the Kobuk and Selawik. I have incorporated two Upper Kobuk legends recorded by Douglas D. Anderson on videotape in 1996 when Wesley Woods from Shungnak came to visit the Pah River archeological excavation. Except for the stories of Willie Goodwin, Sr., and a few of Minnie Gray, which I taped in English, the rest of the stories were taped in Iñupiaq as opportunities for more complete recording of the stories materialized. The stories were translated into English from the tapes. Stories recorded at Onion Portage were told in the summer tents that the Iñupiaq archeology crew had set up, similar to their summer camps along the banks of the Kobuk. Except for a story told by Willie Goodwin, Sr., which was told one evening to the Brown University crew, other stories were told during the day with the storyteller's family members and friends listening. All Selawik stories were taped in the home storytelling setting, mostly during the day, with family members and friends present. Within each field setting, I made my interest in Iñupiaq stories and life histories known. After spending time in each place and by building personal rapport, I was able

FIGURE 2 ~ *View of Selawik, summer 1969.* PHOTO: DOUGLAS D. ANDERSON.

to eventually obtain the consent of storytellers to tape their stories. What I taped was what each person was willing to tell, at the time of their own choosing, when they were in the mood, or when a social occasion inspired the storytelling. To encourage the storyteller's flow of thoughts and memory recall, I neither asked questions nor interjected my own comments during the telling of stories.

In this volume, context for each storytelling event is provided in the form of a date and location. Several stories represent versions of the same story theme told by storytellers from different villages and at different times. The data on the temporal and spatial contexts of storytelling serve as records for facilitating future comparisons across time and space.

Traditionally, Iñupiaq stories are not titled. The names of the stories presented here are taken from the narrators' statements when they mentioned that the story is about a certain character or subject. When the narrator did not make such a statement, I cued in on how family members and the audience referred to each story. In other instances I followed their referencing method of using the name of the main character or the story's key event as the name of the story.

Iñupiaq Storytelling Events and Contexts

IÑUPIAQ AS A WRITTEN LANGUAGE DID NOT EXIST UNTIL 1946 OR 1947 when Ray Ahmaogak, a North Slope Iñupiat, and Eugene Nida, a linguist, developed modern Iñupiaq orthography, which is in use today in a revised form (Kaplan 1990:149; Krauss 1980:50). Before that time, Iñupiaq storytelling was a significant aspect of Iñupiaq expressive culture and a social event. These narratives were oral literature, what Bauman has called verbal art, a mode of verbal communication (Bauman 1989:2).

Approaching storytelling as a contextual performance (Bauman 1989; Georges 1969; Goldstein 1964:92) and as a mode of communication, one can view a storytelling event as "situated, with its form, meaning, and functions rooted in the culturally defined scenes or events—bounded segments of the flow of behavior and experience that constitute meaningful contexts for action, interpretation, and evaluation" (Bauman 1989:3).

Rather than fairytales told primarily for the entertainment of children, Iñupiaq stories, especially those that are long and have complex plots, were meant for adult audiences, although more often than not, children were present at storytelling events. An elderly Selawik woman described storytelling in the past as a sort of competition during the winter. For each different story that was told, the storyteller cut a notch in a wooden pole of his living quarters. At

FIGURE 3 ~ *View of Shungnak, early summer 1969.* PHOTO: DOUGLAS D. ANDERSON.

FIGURE 4 ~ *View of Ambler, Gladys Downey (left) and Shield Downey, Jr., winter 1969.*
PHOTO: DOUGLAS D. ANDERSON.

the end of the winter, the person who had the most notches was the champion storyteller (DeBree 1975:6). Elderly storytellers report that Iñupiaq storytelling events in the past could take place at home or in the *qargi* (community house) while men were working on their tools and crafts (see also Hall 1975:39). Working together in a shared space and sharing Native technological knowledge became concurrently a context for sharing stories and for story performance. The storyteller Robert Cleveland informed me that he learned most of his stories as a young boy in the *qargi*. Storytelling in the *qargi* was often a lengthy social event and a narrative performance for the whole community, as described in the story "Isiqiak."

Perhaps the most renowned story was the narration of the Qayaq cycle, *Qayaqtauġiŋñaqtuaq: Qayaq, the Magical Traveler* (Lee et al. 1991), which is said to go on for as long as a month, depending on how the telling of the legend was spaced over time. Nellie Russell, a storyteller in this collection, was a member of the audience when Panitchiaq (Tommy Skin) told a story: "The time would pass till midnight and the storytellers would still be telling stories in a manner of one person telling a story and the other person telling another one in response. That was the manner the stories were told in the old days."

Collecting stories and oral histories in Selawik, I witnessed numerous interactive narrative events when the audience participated in a similar "flow of behavior and experience" that led to a meaningful and conducive context for spontaneous narrative performance (Bauman 1989:3). Once I went to John

FIGURE 5 ~ *Flora Cleveland, Robert Cleveland, Wanni Anderson, and Minnie Gray at Onion Portage, 1968.* PHOTO: DOUGLAS D. ANDERSON.

Brown's home with Nora Norton, a skilled storyteller, and her daughter, Emma Norton. Knowing that both John Brown and Nora Norton were born in the Upper Kobuk, I first played the taped stories of the well-known Kobuk storyteller Robert Cleveland of Shungnak for them to hear and enjoy. Their responses to Robert Cleveland's stories were a flow of stories, first in response to those they had just heard and second in response to each other's narration. Storytelling as the intended narrative event grew into multiple, interconnected performances when John Brown followed his storytelling with singing the Kuutchiaqmiut song (the song of the people of Kuutchiaq where John Brown once lived). It was the very first Selawik song I had ever heard. The first song was followed by a second, the Kuuvaŋmiut Blanket Toss song. Nora Norton, caught in the flow of this interactive performance event, was so inspired that she also sang a song and then got up and began to dance, which John Brown joined. Both were enjoying themselves and laughing. "I haven't danced like this for a long, long time," Nora said.

In another storytelling event in 1972, Nora Norton and John Brown were joined by a third storyteller, Flora Cleveland. After listening to the legend "Kinnaq, the Kotzebue Wife" that Nora had told, Flora proceeded to tell her story, "The Goose Feather People." The legend about Kinnaq, an "old woman," stirred Flora's recollection about an "old man" in the goose feather story. Her story became contextually more meaningful when she interjected a tease of the third storyteller, John Brown, into her story. Three sets of social identities were present at that particular storytelling event. The identity shared by John Brown and Nora Norton was a Kuuvaŋmiut identity. Flora's tease extended the existing social tie to incorporate another, the mutual Kuutchiaq tie that Flora shared with John Brown because John had lived at Kuutchiaq, her birthplace. On another occasion in Selawik, as a member of the audience, I was brought into fuller connection with the group when Nora Norton told the legend "Niġlaaqtuuġmiut and Kuukpigmiut." Two summers earlier, in 1969, my husband and I had built a house in Selawik on the Niġlaaq River in preparation for the full year we planned on spending in Selawik. Our house was and still is the only house on the Niġlaaq. From then on Selawik people have referred to us as Niġlaaqmik. These storytelling sessions emerged as dynamic events, shaped by the unfolding of the storytellers' behaviors, underscored by the particular structure of their social relations and evolving interactions that took place between them and the audience (Goldstein 1964:92). To quote Robert Georges (1969:324):

The total message of any given storytelling event is generated and shaped by and exists because of a specific storyteller and specific story listeners whose interactions constitute a network of interrelationships that is unique to that particular storytelling situation.

To present Iñupiaq storytelling in its totality as a culturally situated narrative event, I have retained introductory remarks and commentaries of the storytellers in parentheses whenever they occur, whether at the beginning or in the middle of the story. Analytically framed as "metanarration" and "metacommunication," storyteller's remarks are "devices that index or comment on the narrative itself" (Bauman 1989:98) and a narrative shift out of the narrative time and narrative text into asides and commentaries of various types. I argue that the interjection of a lighthearted remark and a tease of a specific person in the audience, as delivered by Flora Cleveland in the storytelling event mentioned above, is her metanarration and a narrative shift that some of the Iñupiaq storytellers here skillfully used.

As analyzed above, each specific remark interwoven into the story can be accurately understood as such only through the actual presence at the storytelling event and when the circumstances of the storytelling event and components of the narrative context were considered as interpretive frames for meanings. Who were members of the audience? What were the relationships of the people in the audience? Why did a certain storyteller make a specific remark while telling his or her story? To the audience, what was the meaning of the hinted remark? For example, when Flora Cleveland told her story "The Goose Feather People," John Brown, Nora Norton, Emma Norton, and I were her audience. When Flora told about the main character of the story, saying, "There was a man living alone," she followed it with a remark, "How did he happen to be living alone by himself? He was probably a Kobuk River man." Flora was not, in that particular instance, making a statement of fact identifying the character "the man" in the story as a Kobuk man, as might be interpreted. Flora was teasing the widower John Brown, originally from the Kobuk, who was living alone. John Brown, Nora Norton, and Emma Norton immediately understood the intended frame of reference. They all chuckled at the tease. Another level of cultural meaning was embedded in the tease. Implied in this reference to John Brown is the Iñupiaq concept of identity, defined through a finely demarcated regional identity and linked to the person's place of birth, where he or she was raised, and self-identification, rather than to the person's current place of residence. During my years in Selawik I had heard John Brown constantly being referred to as a "Kuuvaŋmiu" (Kobuk man) despite the fact that he had lived in Selawik for over half a century, until his death. Similarly, Nora Norton, who had lived in Selawik most of her life, was always perceived and referred to as a "Kobuk woman."

Iñupiaq concepts of personal identities are defined linguistically, spatially, and ecologically. Linguistically, the identification as an Iñupiaq signifies that the person is an Iñupiaq speaker. A Kuuvaŋmiu or a Siiḷaviŋmiu identity, for example, points out that the person was born and has grown up on the Kobuk or Selawik River, respectively. An Iñupiaq is also a native son or daughter of a particular settlement or village, for example, a Kiana villager. Each of these identities is taken seriously and, after the regional Native organizations were formed around 1975, NANA became an additional political regional entity acknowledged by the Iñupiat.

The significance of text in context was exemplified in another storytelling situation in Selawik in 1972, when Leslie Burnett told the story "The Orphan Who Won the Ring." Toward the end of the story when he interjected, "I wonder what Kingaq would do? . . . He's tough," Leslie was not, at that particular instant, referring to any character in the story. No character in the story was named. He was teasing his son-in-law, Kignaq, who at the moment was sitting there working while listening to the story his father-in-law was telling. Kignaq smiled and, being shy, did not respond. While the contextual connotation of the remark was explicit to the three of us present (Leslie, Kignaq, and I), without Kignaq's response as part of the taped, recorded text, non-Selawik audience and readers have no visual audience context to help decode the meaning of this particular remark in the story.

Another type of interactional storyteller-audience communication conveyed during a storytelling event is the audience's verbal interjection of "*Aa*," meaning "Yes," or a listener occasionally voicing the same phrase concurrently with the storyteller. These responses aim to encourage the narrative flow and signal to the storyteller that the audience is totally engaged in the story as its events progressively unfold.

Giddings (1961:157) and Hall (1975:412), citing their storytellers, mention the strong emphasis the storytellers placed on telling their stories exactly as they were learned. Although certain storytellers in this collection made a statement such as "I'm telling the story as I had heard it" or "It is said that . . .," an act of traditionalizing and authenticating the story, a great deal of the time the retold story is not quite an exact, word-for-word duplication. The same storyteller can also tell the same story somewhat differently on different occasions, due to the changed context of the situation. Robert Cleveland mentioned before telling the story "The Woman with Long Hair" that he was telling a shortened version. His reason for so doing, he explained, was to ensure that he had enough time left to tell another story afterwards. Each particular context of the storytelling event therefore needs to be taken into account (Ben-Amos 1993; Kirshenblatt-Gimblett 1975; Malinowski 1935) as it is intricately interwoven with the final product, with the narrative as it is actually told on that particular storytelling event, at that particular moment, expression by expression, and sentence by sentence.

Iñupiaq Concept of Story Ownership

AS PART OF THE STORYTELLING DEVICES, SOME STORYTELLERS IN THIS collection identified, either at the beginning of the story or at the end of story, the persons from whom they had heard the stories, phrased either as having heard the story from a certain person or that the story is a certain person's story. Communicated in this speech act is the Iñupiaq concept of story ownership, that is, a particular story belongs to a particular person. Robert Cleveland began the story "The Woman with Long Hair" with a disclaimer that although he learned the story from Akatauraq, he did not know to whom the story originally belonged. "It might be a story of a Kobuk River person. It might be a story of someone who had moved to live in this area. I don't think it was learned from elsewhere." Another storyteller, Flora Cleveland of Selawik, began her story "The Young Man Who Married a Wife from Across the Sea" with a statement of story ownership, "This is Jack Pungalik's story." Nellie Russell informed her audience that she heard the stories "The Floating Food Platter" and "The Old Man Who Loved Blood Gravy" from the storyteller named Atligauraq, but the stories were actually the Native pastor John Qaniqsiraq Wright's. It is apparent in these storytelling events that whenever story ownership was known, it was respected and publicly acknowledged, as was the person from whom the storyteller had heard or learned the story.

The concept of story ownership is a long-held Iñupiaq cultural tradition. Giddings (1961:61) reports that in 1941 a Kobuk storyteller, Noonagak, was quite resistant to telling stories. Finally, when she agreed to tell one story, she said that the story "belonged to her." A year earlier, Nasruk (Robert Cleveland) had told Giddings the story "The Eyeshade People," which Nasruk said "belonged to his father and now only belonged to him" (Giddings 1961:181). The legally defined concept of the fair use of public documents recently clashed with the Iñupiaq definition of story ownership and of indigenous intellectual property rights (Schneider 2002:149) when the Maniilaq legend was taken from a website and reproduced without the permission of any of Maniilaq's descendents. A Maniilaq descendent considers the publication an infringement of his family's intellectual property. Among a southwest Alaska Tlingit group, the concept of clan ownership and intellectual property allows only clan leaders or designees the right to interpret place names and tell associated stories (Thornton 1999:42). In comparison, among the Iñupiat, folktales and legends are defined as individually owned and are to be honored and acknowledged. Sharing of stories can take place, but the site of communal sharing resides solely in the storytelling event. Ruthie Sampson and I, for example, have conveyed to descendents of storytellers of *Folktales of the Riverine and Coastal Iñupiat* (Anderson and Sampson 2003) that the book was produced as a school textbook, not for commercial sale. Royalties from the publication of this volume go to the Northwest Arctic Borough, a Native organization in which all Iñupiat are shareholders and which had provided a grant in support of the translation and transcription of the stories.

Gender Differences and Individual Storytelling Style

IN HER STUDY OF THE STORYTELLING TRADITION OF A PENNSYLVANIA family, Baldwin (1985:149–162) reports that gender differences existed both in the storytellers' spheres of interest and in their narrative styles. Gender differences also exist in Iñupiaq narrative culture. From the close literal translation of the original Iñupiaq texts, it is possible to discern even in the translated English version that male storytellers, such as Robert Cleveland, John Brown, and Leslie Burnett, followed the story line in a straightforward, motif-by-motif narrative technique. Female storytellers such as Nora Norton and Maude Cleveland, on the other hand, imbued their stories with more behavioral details and dwelt more on the feelings and emotions of their characters.

There are ten sets of stories in this collection that are versions; that is, ten stories that were told by different sets of storytellers. Compare, for example, Robert Cleveland's "The Ground Squirrel and the Raven" with his sister-in-law Maude Cleveland's version. Although the ground squirrel was always depicted as a woman, Maude painted a more feminine picture of the ground squirrel. While Robert's ground squirrel simply "darted home," Maude's ground squirrel was in the midst of picking berries when she heard the raven singing that he had blocked the entrance to her burrow. She "darted back home, spilling her berries along the way."

In the two versions of "The Raven and the Fox," one sees a different type of textual variation—the differences between two female storytellers, Nora Norton and Sarah Goode, living in the same village. Interestingly, the two versions of another story, "The Ptarmigan and the Crane," told by two women from two different villages, painted different scenarios and different characterizations of the two animal characters. While Minnie Gray's male crane was smitten with the ptarmigan widow, who rejected him for his big, ugly head, Nora Norton's crane was haughty. He belittled the ptarmigan widow's new spring head coloring, the supposed hood she was wearing and was so proud of. And the haughty crane was nicely matched in the final song of the lady spurned. The story "The Ground Squirrel and the Raven," on the other hand, allows a comparison between the versions as told by Robert Cleveland and his daughter, Minnie Gray. In Robert's variant, the raven was the character who danced to the ground squirrel's singing, whereas in his daughter's version, it was the reverse. Although Minnie acknowledged after hearing her father's taped story later in 2003 that she misremembered it, what happened exemplifies how textual variation develops. Good storytellers are very much aware of textual variations in a story. Robert Cleveland, upon hearing Beatrice Mouse tell "Wolf, Fox, and Raven Brothers," said that his was different before proceeding to tell his version.

Individual narrative style stands out most noticeably in the enigmatic storyteller Nora Norton. Often Nora would provide ethnographic explanations of traditional Iñupiaq houses, objects, or lifeways that featured in the story. Her narrations also provided insight into the interaction between an Iñupiaq narrator and her texts. Nora did not simply narrate the stories as she heard them. More than other storytellers, she engaged in metanarration, intermittently commenting upon the turn of the events, on specific storytelling devices, and voicing approval or disapproval of a certain character's behavior as the story progresses. In "The Goose Maiden," when the protagonist stole the clothing of one of the beautiful maidens swimming in a lake, Nora made a critical aside, "*Aanna!* I wonder what kind of man this guy was!" Voicing tongue-in-cheek, analytic comment, she critiqued a stylistic turn of events in the narratives. In several stories she told, character after character came upon a house after walking some distance. She quipped in "The Woman Caught on a Fishing Line," "The people of long ago seemed to come across a house whenever they needed it!" Just as frequently, she deftly inserted humorous remarks. In the Qayaq story, after several episodes of Qayaq's marriages to young girls in each new place he came to, Nora remarked, "Qayaq always stopped at the right place! He would always find a couple with a daughter as their only child!" These asides are presented in parentheses (…) to distinguish them from my editorial notes in brackets […] and the story proper.

In terms of vocalization, two female storytellers, Nora Norton and Beatrice Mouse, are more playful in their storytelling styles and injected more feeling into their voices while narrating than male storytellers. Of all the storytellers of "Wolf, Fox, and Raven Brothers," Beatrice Mouse made the closest imitation of the cries of the wolf, the fox, and the raven in her songs.

Likewise individualistic as a storyteller, Willie Goodwin, Sr., intermittently posed questions to his audience while telling "The Girl Who Had No Wish to Marry." His storytelling technique invites audience participation. Leslie Burnett likewise developed his own storytelling style. Now and then, he interjected English words and new English-Iñupiaq composite words, such as *ring-aq* (English word "ring" with Iñupiaq "*aq*" post base) into his storytelling, a new linguistic form spoken frequently also by the younger generation, claiming they were speaking Iñupiaq (R. Sampson, pers. comm. 2001). Andrew Skin, for his part, injected more life into his stories with his animated hand and finger movements, for example, mimicking an animal running. Like the King Island storytellers who often used the word "*tavra*" to indicate a shift in thought (Kaplan 1988), Iñupiaq storytellers in this collection used the word "*tara*" to accomplish similar transitions.

Alaskan historical and administrative contexts following the United States' purchase of Alaska from Russia have had significant impact on Alaska Native cultures and languages. Iñupiaq traditional narrative culture bears a noticeable imprint of these post-contact cultural changes. The Americanization of Alaska and a federal education policy under Sheldon Jackson, general agent for Alaska education, brought in American-style education. The English language was mandated as the only language spoken and studied in schools, in association with Christian missionary efforts of various denominations. Native students were punished if they did not obey (Kaplan 1984, 1990). The evangelical California Quaker Friends Church received a federal concession to teach in village schools and to proselytize in the Iñupiaq region of northwest Alaska, starting with Kotzebue, the most accessible site by ship in 1897, and later on in other villages. Despite the advent of other religious denominations into the area (with seven churches currently in Kotzebue), the Quaker Friends Church, with Iñupiaq pastors preaching in Iñupiaq, maintains the strongest hold among Iñupiaq parishioners in this part of Alaska (Roberts 1978).

Nowadays, in Selawik where I conducted most of my research, the Quaker Friends Church is also the predominant church. Selawik storytellers Leslie

Burnett and Nora Norton in this collection were devout Christians. The influence of religious teaching is apparent in the way these two storytellers at times attributed certain events in the story to God and evaluated the characters' behavior in Christian religious terms. The concepts of God's will, God the Creator, and God as the helper appear in several remarks of these storytellers. Observe the juxtaposition of shamanistic power with the power of the Creator in Leslie Burnett's "The Legend of Magic." These religious nuances are maintained in the narrative texts to indicate the interplay between the post-contact religiosity, perceptions, and textual interpretations of religious storytellers. These reinterpretations of traditional narratives can be interpreted as attempts of these storytellers to forge an interconnection between Iñupiaq traditional culture and the logic and meanings acquired from Christianity.

The vivacious storyteller Maude Cleveland, on the other hand, created playful asides from post-contact material culture and observable changes in Iñupiaq lifeways. For example, in the story "The Brother Who Rescued His Lost Sister," when Maude Cleveland came to the point when the hero, his wife, and his *suunaaq* (male friend of the same age) were setting off for his home village, she narrated, "They took off." Then she quipped, "They probably didn't drive a car." In the next sentence, she emphasized, "They left," then quipped, "They probably didn't leave in a sno-go."

Regional Characteristics

Vocal distinctions between Kobuk and Selawik story deliveries are audible in the actual storytelling event. To stress a statement, Kobuk storytellers made a long, drawn-out articulation of the final word of the statement as a narrative technique. Selawik people nowadays tend to speak with a mixed Selawik-Kobuk vocal speech pattern, due to the influx of a considerable number of Kobuk spouses, relatives, and emigrants into Selawik. Nevertheless, true Selawik utterances can be noted in the use of the high tone at the end of the sentence (R. Sampson, pers. comm. 2001). To Noataker Paul Monroe, Selawik terminal sound is "like that of a rock dropping in the water" (Hall 1975:40). Riverine Iñupiat can immediately discern coastal dialectic differences and coastal vocabularies in stories from coastal villages. For instance, the distinction in the use of the coastal term for mother, "*aakaan*," can be observed in Nora Norton's story, "The Mother Who Made Her Son Blind," also recorded from Noatak by Lucier (1958:96–98) and elsewhere narrated by Noatak storyteller Paul Monroe (Hall 1975:245–246). The same Iñupiaq word can carry different contextual meanings to coastal versus riverine audiences. For example, the word *akutchi* in the story "The Husband Who Took Seals to Another Woman," told by Selawik storyteller Nellie Russell, can be understood as "to make *akutuq*" (Eskimo creamed fat) by riverine listeners. But since the contextual setting of the story is coastal, with seal hunting as the husband's subsistence activity, the meaning of the verb should be coastal, meaning "frying the blubber." In the folktale workshop for Iñupiaq teachers in Kotzebue in 2003, participants from riverine and coastal villages found themselves in disagreement over the interpretation of this Iñupiaq dish. These linguistic markers and contextual meanings, in addition to the textual descriptions of coastal subsistence practices, help to identify the stories as being of coastal origin. Linguistically, the presence of many old Iñupiaq terms used by elderly storytellers such as Robert Cleveland, terms that are no longer used and understood by the younger generations, makes the Iñupiaq language version of the stories valuable textual records of Iñupiaq language development and change.

Narrative Structure

THE STORIES IN THIS COLLECTION VARY IN LENGTH. A LONG NARRATIVE, for example, "The Woman with Long Hair," covers a sequence of three time frames, each with its own series of episodes building up to the climactic event. The first time frame sets up the prologue: all the characters are introduced, the core problem is spelled out (how the *umialik*'s son won the girl he wanted as his wife), and they get married at the end. The second time frame starts with the young couple's married life in the house of the wife's grandmother, goes through their change of residence from the house of the wife's grandmother to the husband's family home and the new core problem (how to convince the wife to have a child), and ends with the birth of a son. The final time frame is the denouement: the disclosure of the wife's mysterious origin, the encounter with mysterious beings from "the other realm" and the core problem is solved. Structurally, each of the three time frames is self-contained, with its own climactic event and its own ending. The structure of these long stories contrasts with shorter stories where generally only one episode is present: the beginning scene, the central episode, and the ending, such as in the stories "The Floating Food Platter" and "The Goose Feather People."

Narrative Categories

NONE OF THE EARLY REPORTS OF IÑUPIAQ FOLKTALES, SUCH AS NELSON'S *The Eskimo About Bering Strait* (1899), Rasmussen's *The Alaskan Eskimos* (Ostermann 1952), and Curtis's *The Alaskan Eskimo* (1930), provides information on how the Iñupiat classified their stories. It was only through constant probing that I was able to infer the "emic" categories (Ben-Amos 1969; Pike 1964), the Native taxonomy of these differently structured narratives as they were recognized by Iñupiaq storytellers. Especially helpful was the information obtained from the two most prolific storytellers in this collection, Robert Cleveland and Nora Norton, and also from Lena Larkin, Willie Goodwin, Sr., and Nellie Russell. In his introductory remark to the two stories he was going to tell, Robert Cleveland mentioned that one story, "The Woman with Long Hair," is an *unipchaaq* (story, legend) *utuqqaq* (old), which he explained in English as an "old story," whereas "Isiqiak," another story about a person living along the channel of the Black Fish River, is "not so old" and that it is "easier to believe in" compared to the first, the old story. Robert's narrative categorization, based on the time dimension, posits two categories: old stories and not-so-old stories, that is, newer stories. And the newer story "Isiqiak" that Robert attributed to a B'ack River person is what folklorists refer to as a legend.

The storyteller Nora Norton provided an additional narrative category, "real incident" (*uqaaqtuaq*) and how and when this "real incident" category crosses over to become another narrative category. To elucidate the Native conceptual framework, Nora's exact words from her introductory remark to the legend "The False Alarm at Kobuk" are quoted here:

> The incident occurred to the Kobuk River people. When an incident occurred to a person when he was young, it becomes an *unipchaaq* when he is old.

What Nora referred to is how and when a real incident or a real happening occurring at a specific time, at a specific location, and to specific people becomes, as time passes, a legend, an *unipchaaq*. A real-life event will, through time, become a legend. "The False Alarm at Kobuk" is a good example of this narrative category shift. Nora Norton heard this narrative from her mother and two older sisters, who experienced the event themselves. To the three women, the narrative recounts a real incident, a life story, a true story, what actually happened to them and to other fellow villagers and how they experienced the event. But to the narrator, Nora Norton, who was not yet born when the incident occurred, the narrative took on the character of a legend.

Combining what Robert Cleveland and Nora Norton have told us, there appear to be, on one level of Iñupiaq narrative classification, three narrative categories: old story (*unipchaaq utuqqaq*), not-so-old story (legend or *unipchaaq*), and real incident (*uqaaqtuaq*).

Two narrators, on the other hand, used perceived reality, that is, whether the story is considered true or not true by the storyteller, as the determining factor in classifying stories. The elderly Lena Larkin called the story she was going to tell about her own life in the past a "true story" (*uqaaqtuaq iḷumutuuruaq*). Willie Goodwin, Sr., likewise called the story "The Raven at Kuugrauq River," which is an incident a friend of his witnessed, a "true story," whereas "The Man in the Lake," the story about the blackfish that entered the mouth of the mudshark, is "not a true story." What are culturally considered to be true stories are what folklorists and anthropologists call life stories (life histories, oral histories) and real incidents.

Lately, the length of the story, long or short, becomes another parameter for narrative categorization. Nora Norton began telling many of the stories by identifying them as being *unipchaaġuraq* (small, little story). Nellie Russell likewise referred to all of her stories by the English term "short stories."

Within the Iñupiaq cognitive system of narrative classification there exists then a multilayered system, signifying a sophisticated Iñupiaq conceptualization of multiple realities, designating (1) the time element (temporal level); (2) their perception of the narrative as real or not real (perceptual level); and (3) whether the narrative is long or short (length of the story, proportion level).

Except for the last story, "The Raven at Kuugruaq River," which belongs to the "real incidents" category, other stories in this collection are legends and old stories. Under the "old stories" category, longer stories are presented first, followed by short stories, thereby embedding within it the subcategory length of the story. Sets of stories that form a story complex, for example, the orphan story complex and the raven story complex, are grouped together. Subsumed under the "old stories" category are horror stories, such as "The Cannibal Child" and "The Arm." Although Native classification of what folklorists and Giddings (1961) call "animal stories" does not exist, this type of story, mostly single-episode short stories, are presented together as a final set to facilitate folkloric identification.

Legends

IÑUPIAQ LEGENDS (*UNIPCHAAT*) IN THIS COLLECTION ARE REPRESENTED
by the Qayaq cycle, "Qayaqtauġiŋñaqtuaq," and thirty-two other legends.
While the Qayaq cycle tells about a legendary hero, generally believed to be a
real person living at a time now long past, the temporal context of other legends is comparatively more recent. For example, the legendary Indian raids
on the Upper Kobuk took place probably in last decade of the nineteenth
century, but the fear and suspicion of the raids lingered on among Upper
Kobuk people until the early part of the twentieth century, as evidenced
by the legend "The False Alarm at Kobuk," which tells about the terror of
impending death experienced by Nora Norton's parents and other villagers.
The fear of unknown entities, of people from outer territories, labeled "the
iksiak," lingers still among the Iñupiat as periodic rumors of *iksiak*-spotting.
Suspicious events, construed as possibly *iksiak*-related, resurface now and
then in certain areas, including the Selawik and the Kobuk. The Iñupiaq cultural practice of having visitors report their arrival first at the village before
venturing out elsewhere carries practical rationalization, a safeguard against
anxieties and fears of unknown outsiders.

Other legends in the collection are identified with a particular region or
location where the narrated event occurred, for example, in Kotzebue, on the
Selawik River, etc. In some legends, locational identification is indicated as
the place where the legendary person is said to have lived, such as in "The
Two Coastal Brothers," where one brother was clearly identified as living in
Kotzebue, the other brother vaguely identified as living on the coast, but the
adventure took place on the Noatak. In "Alaaqanaq, the Man with a Little Drum,"
Alaaqanaq is said to be a Point Hope man who married a Kotzebue wife and
lived in Kotzebue.

Iñupiaq legends are at times characterized by a narrative device marking the
time frame in the past, but not as far back into the mythic time as in the "old
story" narrative category. These temporal markers are narrative descriptions
such as "the time in the past when there were no missionaries," "the time when
there were no white man's things," and "the time when there were no flashlights."
This is not to infer that the contact period is the only demarcation point for
legends. Nora Norton's analytical insight on when a real incident becomes a
legend, discussed earlier, is another Native cognitive framework for categoriz-
ing legends. These identified cognitive and temporal frames locate the legends
with the recent past.

Since the Upper Kobuk region is geographically close to the region of the Koyukon Indians, the relationship between the Kuuvaŋmiut and the Koyukuk River Koyukon Indians (Clark 1996:27) in the past has been a topic of interest to anthropologists (Burch 1998, Clark 1974) and Native Iñupiat alike. For the Iñupiat, it is part of *nunaaqqiurati iḷitqusriat* (what happened in the villages, group history). What was the nature of the Indian-Eskimo relationship as retained in cultural memories? Legends in this collection tell about the time in the historic past when their relationships were contentious and warlike, when fear, surprise raids, killings, and revenge feature as the themes of many narratives. A few legends, however, tell of friendships formed and romances and intermarriages between Kuuvaŋmiut and the Koyukon Indians. In "Aagruukaaluk's Revenge," told by Wesley Woods, the legendary character Aagruukaaluk was identified as a mixed-blood Koyukon Indian-Eskimo. Living along the Upper Kobuk were inhabitants who were said to be descendents of Eskimo and Indian intermarriages. The legend "The Last War with the Indians" tells about the prevalence of the Indian language in the area during that particular period of intensive Eskimo-Indian interaction and increased Indian settlement on the Upper Kobuk. Considering this prevalent theme of Eskimo-Indian hostilities, the range of events narrated in these legends suggests that, in the past, at times it was the Indians and at other times it was the Eskimos who initiated the offensive strike. Wesley Woods' version also gives an intriguing historical account of the time when Lower Kobuk people were said to have regional, territorial involvement over the Upper Kobuk and had a strategic policy of policing Indian emigration, most likely to maintain a strong Eskimo dominance over the whole river system. The last section of Woods' narrative brings us up-to-date on the contemporary trend in Eskimo-Indian interaction in which "burying the hatchet," cooperation, and coexistence are viewed as viable, mutual goals of both groups, inclusively and geopolitically defined as Native Alaskans. The fact that many old settlements on the Kobuk and the Selawik rivers were named in these legends also makes the legends valuable sources of information on historic settlements and the place names the Iñupiat had given to their landscape.

The Qayaq Cycle

"QAYAQTAUĠIŊÑAQTUAQ" AS A LEGEND BELONGS TO THE HERO-TALE tradition in which the principal character embarks on his adventures, told in a series of episodes, each one highlighting a different heroic feat and featuring a different cast of characters. The earliest and the most inclusive collection of the Qayaq cycle is Rasmussen's recording of Qajartuarungnertôq adventures with twenty-two episodes, collected in August 1924 from Nasuk of Kotzebue (Ostermann 1952:229–253). In 1927, Edward Curtis likewise recorded fifteen episodes of "The Kobuk Traveller" and two episodes of "Story of Uguknik" from the Noatak, with the first episode told like the first episode of the Qayaq cycle. A storyteller of *Qayaq, the Magical Traveler* (Lee et al. 1991) identified the Uganik story, the *Ukuunaaqtuaq*, as the story of Qayaq's maternal cousin. From the storytellers Kahkik and Pegriluk from the Upper Kobuk, Giddings obtained seven Qayaq episodes, which he reported in *Kobuk River People* (1961:94–98). The Qayaq cycle with twenty-one episodes in this collection, collected in 1977, was narrated by Nora Norton who identified her husband, Edward Norton, as the source of her repertoire. Nora frankly acknowledged that certain episodes or certain details within the episodes might be missing from her narration because she was at times absent when her husband was narrating the story. The fifth Qayaq collection, *Qayaqtauğiŋñaqtuaq: Qayaq, the Magical Traveler* (Lee et al. 1991), derived from the Elders Conference in Kotzebue. Following the conference, twenty-four episodes were recorded over seven years (1976–1983) from seven storytellers from Selawik and the Kobuk. Nora Norton was one of the storytellers at the conference. The present Qayaq cycle collection differs from the version presented in Lee et al. (1991) in that some of the episodes Nora told in this collection are not in Lee, Sampson, and Tennant, and vice versa. While the episodes on Qayaq's birth and Qayaq's departure from home have been presented as two separate episodes in Lee et al., Nora told them as sequential events within the beginning episode.

To folklorists, Qayaq would be identified as a culture hero in the sense that in his exploits he made the land safe from murderous beings and dangerous things and eventually brought about the present order of things, from introducing

FIGURE 6 ~ *Kahkik paddling a Kobuk River qayaq, 1947.* ORIGINALLY PUBLISHED IN *KOBUK RIVER PEOPLE* (GIDDINGS 1961:164).

natural childbirth to women to establishing the present mountain habitat of Dall's sheep. Iñupiaq elders see Qayaq as an adventurer with a typical Iñupiaq sense of humor (R. Sampson, pers. comm. 2001). While the journey was phrased in Rasmussen's Qajartuarungnertôq story as the hero's attempt to fulfill his parents' wish for revenge for his lost older brothers, in the present collection Qayaq's adventures were culturally framed by the storyteller Nora Norton as being typical of young men "at the age when young men sought adventures." Qayaq's home, where he started on his adventures, has been identified as the Selawik River in six sources: Rasmussen 1924 (in Ostermann 1952); Curtis 1930; Giddings 1961; Brown 1981a; Lee et al. 1991; and Nora Norton's 1977 version in this volume. His birthplace was identified as within the vicinity of Sauniqtuuq, around the area of Selawik Lake. His identity as a Siiḷaviŋmiu positions Qayaq as a Selawik Iñupiaq legendary figure, "one of us," as I heard many Selawik people proudly claim. Another related Qayaq cycle published as *The Longest Story Ever Told: Qayaq, the Magical Man* (Brown 1981a), with Auligi of Shaktoolik as a storyteller, also gave Selawik Lake as Qayaq's birthplace but identified his father as a mixed-blood Koyukon Indian and Eskimo who came to the Selawik River area and married a Selawik woman.

As an Iñupiaq legendary figure, Qayaq holds a prominent place alongside Maniiḷaq (Pulu and Ramoth-Sampson 1981), regionally regarded as a prophet. Maniiḷaq is said to have lived at the mouth of the Ambler River, a tributary of the Kobuk. The Qayaq cycle has widespread distribution in the Eskimo area. Many Iñupiat saw the similarities between their Qayaq story and the Koyukon story *K'etetaalkkaanee* (Attla 1990) in the multi-episode adventures of the hero and his unusual encounters along the way. Given the accounts of many storytellers that the narration of the Qayaq cycle could continue for days in the past, how much and how many episodes have been lost is not known.

Names of characters are generally not mentioned in Iñupiaq stories. The narratives in the legend category, including the Qayaq cycle, are exceptions because the persons named are legendary. To clearly identify them by name is to reinforce the credibility of the legends as historical facts. Variations in the name assigned to Qayaq exist among the Iñupiaq variants. His name in Rasmussen's collection, Qajartuarungnertôq, means "he who will always want to journey far in a kayak" (Ostermann 1952:230). Curtis (1930) refers to "the canoe traveler" in the story he named "The Kobuk Traveler." Giddings (1961) gives the hero's name as Kayaktaonektok. Lee et al. (1991) use his name as the title of the book *Qayaqtauġiŋñaqtuaq* and translate his name as "he who characteristically and leisurely travels by kayak." Emily Brown (1981a) approximates the spelling of his name as "Quyaqtuaguynaqtuuq." The spelling "Qayaqtuaġiŋñaqtuaq" is here used for Nora Norton's variant as the closest rendering of his name in the accepted Iñupiaq orthography, adopted by the Bilingual/Bicultural Education unit of the Northwest Arctic Borough School District.

Below I provide a comparison of the oldest existing version of Qayaq, the Rasmussen version recorded in Kotzebue in 1924 (Ostermann 1952:229–253), with Nora Norton's version. I have arbitrarily divided Rasmussen's story into episodes and named all the episodes to facilitate comparison between the two versions. The Iñupiaq words in Rasmussen's collection are spelled as in Rasmussen's report.

Rasmussen's "Qajartuarungnertôq, His Adventures and Experiences"		Nora Norton's "Qayaqtuaġiŋñaqtuaq"	
1	Qajar's birth	1	Qayaq's birth
2	The people carrying turf	2	Qayaq's ptarmigan wife
3	The man with bow and arrow	3	The porcupine man
4	The woodpecker man	4	The wolverine man
5	The wolverine man	5	The Dall sheep dinner guest
6	The lynx man dinner guest	6	The crazy man
7	The *kingnaq* (fool)	7	The gold man
8	The *sutapia* fool	8	The woodpecker man
9	Qajar's night owl wife	9	The boreal owl family
10	Qajar introduced natural childbirth	10	Qayaq introduced natural childbirth
11	The giant with two wives	11	The man who created fish
12	Animals building a canoe for Qajar	12	When Qayaq became a pike
13	Qajar met his uncle	13	The crushing cliffs
14	The woman with no womb	14	The man with a spear
15	The man who created salmon	15	The wolf man
16	The *inoqarnailaq* (cannibal) woman	16	The cannibals' sticky ball
17	The cannibal with sticky ball	17	Qayaq fought the rock ptarmigan
18	The crushing cliffs	18	Qayaq fought the fireballs
19	The Indian with a throwing board	19	When Qayaq became a peregrine falcon
20	When Qajar became a trout	20	When Qayaq got snared and cooked
21	Qajar fought a giant grouse	21	Qayaq returned home
22	Qajar returned home		

The two versions were collected fifty-five years apart. Despite variation in specific details in the story, amazing parallels exist between episodes. Both versions chronicle Qajar/Qayaq's trip from the Selawik River, through the Kobuk River, and then into the Indian Yukon River before returning home. In both versions Qajar/Qayaq introduced natural childbirth, encountered a man who created fish, the fool, the owl family, the wolverine man, the cannibals with a sticky ball, and the crushing cliffs. While Qajar fought the giant grouse, Qayaq's adversary was the rock ptarmigan. The *sutapia* fool and the *scu-ta-pa* gold man are also two versions of the same episode. At the end of the legend, Qajar became a trout, and Qayaq became a peregrine falcon.

Iñupiaq Cosmology

MANY IÑUPIAQ OLD STORIES AND LEGENDS WERE TEMPORALLY SET within what folklorists refer to as mythic time, that is, the time before things became what they are now and when fantastic, magical happenings are regular features of the stories. From these stories, it appears that in Iñupiaq cosmology there existed three parallel worlds: the sky world, the world where humans lived, and the animal world. These worlds were parallel in the sense that all living beings there lived more or less similar lives. The three worlds were held in balance through the relationships that humans formed across the worlds. In "The Sky People," and "Two Men from the Moon," the sky beings and the moon beings looked just like humans. They differed from earthlings in that they could fly without wings. The social organization of the sky world was conceptualized as a mirror image of the Iñupiaq world. Their leader was an *umialik*. They lived on caribou meat, mountain sheep meat, and seafood like humans and, as on earth, environmental changes could cause food scarcity.

Three stories in this collection portray sky people. In two stories (two versions of the same story), earthlings helped out the sky people in times of need, and in the third story a hunter in the sky world assisted a lost earth woman. In "The Shaman in the Moon," recorded by Nelson (1899), the shamans who had magical power to go to the sky world were mediators between the sky world and earth. The *umialik* on the moon would give moon animals to the shaman as presents to bring back to earth, where they later proliferated. The snowstorm on earth was said to be snow particles from the leaves of grass rustling in the wind on the moon. And the stars humans see were small shining lakes among the moon grass.

The world where humans live with sustaining animal and food resources was also conceptualized as being fraught with dangers. Embedded into the narratives is the Iñupiaq worldview of the "bad land," that is, the area or areas where strange things can happen, where one can get lost, encounter a dangerous being, and lose one's life. Witness, for example, the land of the cannibals in "The Head" and in the Qayaq cycle. Hinted at in "The Woman Caught on a Fishing Line" was another set of humanlike beings, the mermaids (see also "The Two Mermaids of the Kobuk" in Mendenhall et al. 1989:175–180) and little people (in "The Two Little Men" in Mendenhall et al. 1989:215–223).

Animals in the animal world, in the mythic time of Iñupiaq narratives, were endowed with magical powers. As a hunting culture, Iñupiaq taboos and ritualized practices connected to game animals, from whale hunting and bear hunting to salmon fishing, carry the worldviews that the Iñupiat hold toward their environment. Oral narratives can be another window through which Iñupiaq-animal relationships can be viewed.

In the narrative mythical world, Mudshark could create himself, taking his parts from different kinds of animals as well as from humans. In the story "How the Mudshark Created Himself," it was not until all these parts were assembled that the zoomorphic mudshark form took shape and he swam away as a mudshark. Wolf, Fox, and Raven were originally not in their current animal forms. In "Wolf, Fox, and Raven Brothers," they were human orphans who were left by themselves after their parents' death. It was through their effort to escape loneliness and to find food that each took the form of a different animal. Similarly, in "The Orphan in the Beaver House," beavers were described as having human form inside their house. It was only when they left their house that they took on animal forms. Even the tussock was alive in an anthropomorphic sense. It "shivered" when Raven stabbed it with his spear in "Raven Who Brought Back the Land."

Within this narrative collection, the transposition between the human world and the animal world occurred frequently. Anthropomorphosis, an animal temporarily taking on a human form, sometimes occurred. Zoomorphosis, the transformation from a human being into an animal, could also take place, as when Nakasruktuuq became a caribou in "Nakasruktuuq, the Sleepyhead," when geese turned into humans in "The Goose Maiden," and when Sauliksauliq and her children turned into grizzly bears in "Pisiksuġliq and Suġli Suġli." How the transformation was achieved appears in the story "Nakasruktuuq, the Sleepyhead." At the moment of transformation from caribou into a human being, the caribou took off his caribou hood, thus becoming a human being. Similarly, in Hall's

Noatak stories (1975), the sliding off of the animal-head skin was described as a way to "reveal the human face."

In this mythical universe, humans and animals lived parallel lives. Animals lived in houses, ate, slept, and talked, as in "The Orphan in the Beaver House"; sang songs in "Wolf, Fox, and Raven Brothers"; played games both in "The Orphan in the Beaver House" and in "Isiqiak"; and had family in "Wolf, Fox, and Raven" and "The Orphan in the Beaver House." Like humans, they had emotions, such as the kindness the beavers showed in "The Orphan in the Beaver House." They knew loneliness, as in "Wolf, Fox, and Raven Brothers." The aging wolf husband and wife in "The Lost Little Brother" also felt the need to be taken care of when they could no longer hunt in their old age. Animals also knew sacrifice, as did the beaver parents who sacrificed their own child for the survival of the orphan in "The Orphan in the Beaver House."

In Iñupiaq stories, humans and animals freely interacted with each other as friends, helpers, adoptive parents, adoptive children, and in many stories as adversaries. The loon helped the wronged son regain his eyesight in "The Mother Who Made Her Son Blind." In "Nakasruktuuq, the Sleepyhead," the caribou befriended Nakasruktuuq and taught him how to live a caribou life. In "The Orphan with Bear Helpers," the bear couple took care of the orphan, warned him about his future encounter with the manslayer, and came to his aid, killing the manslayer and other troublemakers in the village. But the caribou killed a young boy in "How the Caribou Lost Their Teeth." In other stories, humans also killed the animals, as in "The Orphan in the Beaver House." The human-animal boundary was not fixed and was constantly crossed and re-crossed. Anthropomorphosis and zoomorphosis that frequently occurred in the stories were taken as a matter of course by Iñupiaq narrators and listeners.

In a commentary to the story "The Girl Raised by the Grizzly Bear," Nora Norton, the narrator, provided an explanation of anthropomorphosis. "It is said that creatures can turn into humans because they live like humans." Then Nora proceeded to tell how in the story the female bear in the anthropomorphic form of a woman of the house not only lived like a human mother, preparing all the "delicious food" for the little girl she had abducted, but also raised the little girl fondly as her daughter, always addressing her by the kin term "daughter" while talking to her. Like a loving mother, she was concerned for the little girl's well-being and safety, dressing her warmly before allowing her to go outside the house in spring and warning her not to venture away from home. In "Isiqiak," Raven was a man named Tulugaq (raven). He played games with the people with whom he had been living, the anthropomorphic arctic terns. He attended their feast where human food was served, including berries, Iñupiaq potatoes, and other sorts of food gathered during the summer. He watched them play Iñupiaq games of skill. The feast was held in a "large house," but the description of its setting suggested that it was a *qargi*, an Iñupiaq community house. So the birds' world, anthropomorphized, also had been given Iñupiaq social structure by the storyteller, complete with the *qargi*, Iñupiaq games, and the Iñupiaq end-of-the-summer feast.

Following the convention of the Native American trickster narratives, when anthropomorphosis is a salient characteristic of animal characters such as Raven, Coyote, and Bear, they are personified in the following stories with the first letter of their names capitalized.

Iñupiaq Animal Stories

IÑUPIAQ WIT AND ABUNDANT SENSE OF HUMOR SHINE IN ANIMAL STORIES. Frequently short animal stories are told as children's stories. These stories tend to have simple story lines with animals as the main characters. The animals are portrayed fondly, sometimes comically, sometimes with their little tricks that they play on each other, as in "The Ground Squirrel and the Raven." Often Iñupiaq storytellers integrate their intimate knowledge of the animals' physical characteristics and habitat into the story, as in "The Ptarmigan and the Crane" and "The Ground Squirrel and the Raven." Through these stories, they teach children about the Iñupiaq animal world. Many animal stories have songs, which storytellers sing for their little listeners. Many times I have heard these songs sung by themselves without the stories to entertain children or as lullabies to lull little children to sleep.

As in Native American trickster tales, the Raven in the Iñupiaq narrative tradition has the dual role of culture hero and trickster. In Giddings's *Kobuk River People* (1961), one of his five raven stories is "Raven Brings Light" in which the man/bird Raven helps humans who, in earlier days, lived with no light. In this story collection, Raven performed another heroic act. In "Raven Who Brought Back the Land," when the land was inundated by the flood, the man/bird Raven managed to bring back the land for people to live on again. But in "The Raven and the Fox" and "The Raven and the Loon," Raven played tricks on other animals. As with the tricksters of other cultures, he was outsmarted and was soundly beaten by a small, female ground squirrel in "The Ground Squirrel and the Raven."

Another unique feature of Iñupiaq animal stories lies in the ways Iñupiaq storytellers put themselves in the heads and in the eyes of the animals of the Iñupiaq animal world. The caribou in "Nakasruktuuq, the Sleepyhead" told Nakasruktuuq that Nakasruktuuq was lucky, for he had an easier life as a human being compared to his life as a caribou. The orphan in "The Orphan in the Beaver House" told his uncle, who was roasting the rabbits, "I'm looking at you through the eyes of the rabbits." His statement so thoroughly perturbed his uncle that the uncle subsequently plotted the orphan's demise. Iñupiaq storytellers have in these instances deftly provided an inverted view, the view of the human world and human behavior as seen from the perspective of "the other," the animals. It is a sophisticated narrative device through which the narrator, for a moment, steps out and looks in, through a different lens.

Iñupiaq Narratives and Culture
The Interplay

A large group of people was making a living along the river. Living among them was a young girl who was secluded upon reaching puberty. Her seclusion period had not yet terminated.

from "The Brother Who Rescued His Lost Sister"

TELLING A STORY IS *UNIPCHAAQ* OR *UQAAQTUAQ* IN IÑUPIAQ LANGUAGE. Each Iñupiaq storyteller has his or her own way of commencing a story. However, many start with the sentence "There was . . . making a living," as in the sentences quoted above. "A Point Hope man was making a living" is the opening sentence of "The Wife Killer" story. "There was a family making a living" is the opening sentence of "The Girl Raised by a Grizzly Bear." Even when the storyteller Nellie Russell made a new story, "The Husband Who Took Seals to Another Woman," she began the story with "It is said that there were two people living along the coast." The fact that this opening statement was used by a number of Iñupiaq storytellers makes it a formulaic Iñupiaq storytelling device, parallel to the opening formula used by Western storytellers, "Once upon a time . . ." or "There was once. . . ." I have maintained this stylistic storytelling device literally in the English version to preserve and highlight the device.

The opening sentence "There was . . . making a living," a literal translation of the Iñupiaq word "*iñuuniaqtuq*," can be viewed analytically as a method of conveying from the very beginning, from the very first sentence of the story, the concept of Iñupiaq lifeways. Characters in Iñupiaq stories did not simply live, they had to "make a living" as real-life, flesh-and-blood Iñupiat do. Later in the story we are told of specific ways Iñupiaq characters make their living off the land, depending on the ecological setting that constitutes the story setting.

Stories that have riverine Iñupiaq characters say that their subsistence is based on hunting, fishing, and gathering berries. For instance, a riverine Iñupiat was fishing from his qayaq in "The Woman Caught on a Fishing Line" when he caught a woman's items of clothing and finally the woman herself. The hero in "The Young Man Who Married a Wife from Across the Sea" brought home caribou and bear meat he had hunted. During the summer he brought home molting ducks. These are riverine Iñupiaq subsistence activities. Stories that tell about coastal villages or coastal settlements, on the other hand, depict coastal landscapes and hunters of sea mammals. Some stories specify the type of animals hunted, as in "The Floating Food Platter," in which the husband hunted seals under the sea ice. The family of the hero in "The Brother Who Rescued His Lost Sister" was portrayed as living off both the sea and the land, hinting at the subsistence life-style of a coastal family with access to both subsistence resources or vice versa, that is, a riverine family with access to coastal food resources.

Most of the stories in this collection came from the repertoires of Siiḷaviŋmiut and Kuuvaŋmiut storytellers. As riverine Iñupiat living along the Selawik River and the Kobuk River, the storytellers' conceptualizations of adventures, heroic missions, or the search for a way home after getting lost or being taken away from home were all framed with a riverine environmental mindset, for example, the character "followed the river," "went upriver," "qayaq[ed] downriver." Directionals and locatives such as "lived up there" or "went down there" or "looked down the river" have been retained in the narratives to preserve such semantic devices associated with the Iñupiaq cognitive map of the environment and sense of place. In a few stories with coastal settings, such expressive devices can be seen, worded in terms of coastal landscape and coastal lifeways: for instance, in the story "The Floating Food Platter," in which the husband day after day "went down to the sea" to hunt for sea mammals. When storyteller Nellie Russell described the progression of events from day to day, she employed the same stock phrases to describe his daily routine of going down to the sea and to convey the notion that those activities were the daily rhythm, the daily subsistence activities of the coastal Iñupiaq husband.

Very much in evidence is the understanding that Iñupiaq subsistence life is closely linked to the mastery of skills and Native knowledge of how to survive in the arctic environment. In real life as well as in stories, when an Iñupiaq needs to travel, he does not simply take off without preparing carefully for the trip with the proper type of clothing for the season and a sufficient supply of "travel food," as referred to in "The Orphan in the Beaver House." Narrators such as Nora Norton and Leslie Burnett explicitly described these survival preparations.

For example, in "How the Caribou Lost Their Teeth," the old grandmother first searched for her missing grandson closer to her home. But when she failed to locate him and realized that her search would have to cover wider territory, she returned home to "get ready for leaving." I have maintained this stylistic expression, "getting ready for leaving" or "preparing for leaving," in the stories as a meaningful narrative marker of Iñupiaq survival strategy. A seasoned Iñupiaq, man or woman, knows full well that in the unforgiving arctic environment, even in the twenty-first century, failure to observe the practice can result in injuries, starvation, or death. A Selawik young man lost one arm to frostbite because he took off to another village without proper clothing and encountered a snowstorm along the way. Women embarking on a trip were described as making similar pre-trip preparations. In "The Young Man Who Married a Wife from Across the Sea," the wife who felt insulted by her father-in-law's negative comment about her son "prepared herself to leave" before leaving the house of her in-laws. Iñupiaq listeners immediately understand the contextual implication. To leave it out of the story is to tell the story incompetently.

House, Home, and *Qargi*

LINKING THEIR NARRATIVES COGNITIVELY TO IÑUPIAQ MATERIAL CULTURE, storytellers integrate, wherever appropriate, informative data on traditional types of dwellings and the living arrangements within them. In "The Brother Who Rescued His Lost Sister," when the hero arrived in the manslayer's village, a messenger was sent to the house where the hero was staying. They heard the message from the sky window, which conveys the image of a traditional house with the sky window on the roof. In "One Who Walked Against the Wind," another piece of information about an Iñupiaq house is conveyed, not as a direct description but in descriptive phrases. For instance, the messenger sent by the manslayer in this story "jumped up from the *qanisaq*," indicating a traditional house with a lowered entrance tunnel. A traditional Iñupiaq semi-subterranean house had double entries: entrance through the tunnel and entrance to the house proper. Here in the English rendering of the stories, the word "entryway" is used for the entryway into the outside (*paa*). From the entryway ran a tunnel, lower than the main part of the living area. The term "entrance" is used in the translation here to signify *taluksraq*, the entrance from the tunnel into the living area. In the past, the entrance had just a caribou skin or a bear skin hanging. I have retained Iñupiaq expressions to convey spatial meaning.

A combined understanding of Iñupiaq material culture and Iñupiaq language in all of its nuances is crucial for retrieving such cultural information embedded in the story texts. The data on temporary spring, summer, and fall living accommodations is given in "The Woman with Long Hair." The three young girls, playing house, erected a spring/summer tent made of caribou hide and then spread more caribou hides on the ground to sit on. Befitting his wealthy status, the *umialik* in "The Woman with Long Hair" was described as living in a big house with the flooring made of logs "as big as the trees."

Inside a house, a married son or daughter's family was said to be given a living space in the back part of the house, as mentioned in "The Woman with Long Hair" and "The Cannibal Child." Unmarried children slept in the front part of the house with parents or grandparents. Nora Norton called this traditional two-bedroom house style *akilligiilik* in "The Cannibal Child." The bedding arrangement separated the sleeping quarters from the living quarters. Work inside the house, including inside an *umialik*'s house, was carried out while sitting on the floor, as in "The Orphan Who Married an *Umialik*'s Daughter," where the *umialik* and his daughter were described as being seated on the floor working on something when the orphan's grandmother entered the house to ask for the hand of the *umialik*'s daughter. Often when the main character of a story entered a house, he or she walked in on a domestic scene of someone cooking, sewing, or attending to a household chore.

As is apparent in many stories, the *qargi* is the community's gathering place where villagers met to consult with each other, where men worked on their sleds, boats, and tools, and where community entertainment, singing, dancing, telling stories, and playing traditional games took place. When the *qargi* is the setting of the major event in the story, certain details on its architectural features and the seating arrangement are at times conveyed, such as in "Isiqiak," "The Orphan with the Doll," and "One Who Walked Against the Wind." In "Isiqiak," the *qargi* was described as having a skylight window. In "The Brother Who Rescued His Lost Sister," the floor of the *qargi* was said to be covered with tree branches. The raised seating inside the *qargi* was implied in the verbal descriptions of certain characters as sitting "up there" and of having to "step down" from their seats, as in "The Brother Who Rescued His Lost Sister." The spatial arrangement in the seating behavior carries hierarchical information. The most powerful man of the community/village, the *umialik* or the manslayer who controlled the villagers with his brute force, was described as seating himself farther inside, at the rear of the house. Visitors customarily seated themselves around the entrance. Although not explicitly verbalized, the visitor's seating behavior is a culturally understood polemic behavior in the minds of the Iñupiaq audience. It was a strategic, survival seating preference for outsiders, ensuring a quick exit should something untoward occur. As an outsider in the community/ village, one could never be too certain, and as many stories tell, a newcomer's life could be threatened.

Life Stages and Gender

AN IÑUPIAQ TRANSITION FROM CHILDHOOD TO ADULTHOOD IS CLOSELY linked to the mastery of the subsistence lifeways. There is a very close correlation between this cultural concept of human development and the way in which the growth of an Iñupiaq character is portrayed in the narratives. For men, the transition from being *nukatpiaġuk* (a boy) is at times announced through a culturally understood statement, such as "he became *nukatpiġaatchiaq* (almost a young man)," said to be around eighteen years old. Thence he became *naiviaqsiġaatchiaq* (a person of marriageable age), a person who "should live his life with a wife" as the *umialik* told his son in the story "The Woman with Long Hair." He became a *nukatpiaq* (a young man). He was "poised at the threshold of manhood" as expressed in "One Who Walked Against the Wind." Beyond these Iñupiaq terminologies for life stages, in many stories the storytellers gave descriptive, ethnographic details. The hero in "The Lost Little Brother" one day realized that he was no longer dependent on others. He was capable of doing things for himself. He could go hunting by himself. He had become a young man.

For male Iñupiat, proven hunting skill leading to self-sufficiency is pivotal. Among the Siiḷaviŋmiut in the past, a young man's "First Catch" was given to the parents of his prospective wife. Their acceptance of his gift was an indication that his proposal had been accepted. If no betrothal took place, the meat was cooked and then given to all villagers (Curtis 1930:227). Among the Kuuvaŋmiut a feast was given to friends of the young boy who successfully hunted his first animal or bird and for the entire village if he caught a fox. The young hunter also received the finest skin clothing from his parents (Curtis 1930:209). Even in contemporary Iñupiaq life, a young man's "First Catch" (*aŋuniatlasriruaq aŋuqqaaqman*) still symbolizes the attainment of manhood. Its meat is distributed, especially to village elders. During the Thanksgiving and Christmas feasts, if a young man makes his first catch, the meat is cooked as the stew to be served at the feast. In the story "The Woman with Long Hair," the hero, even though he was the only son of the richest man of the village, went hunting for game animals before he presented himself at the house of the girl he wished to marry. He did not return to his parents' home with his game animals, and the implication was that he presented the hunted animals to the girl's grandmother as a gift and as proof of his skill as a competent subsistence provider. In "The Orphan Who Married an *Umialik*'s Daughter" the orphan, as a young man, was portrayed as a skilled hunter. Although we are not told how he developed his skill, we are told that he "could catch all sorts of game animals: caribou, wolves, wolverines, and different kinds of animals." The *umialik*, his father-in-law, liked him so much that he invited his daughter and his son-in-law to live next door. The son-in-law continued to hunt and "made his father-in-law even richer."

For women, the transition from girlhood to womanhood is often articulated in the narratives as *iḷaqatnikkumiñaqsiruaq,* that is "approaching marriageable age." Another way of expressing this developmental stage is the use of the term *niviaqsiaq,* meaning a young lady. Another interesting old Iñupiaq descriptor emphasizing the peak of young womanhood is *niviaqisiaġruk,* literally meaning a young woman at the peak of her youth and beauty. This signals the transition to the next developmental stage, "being ready for marriage." In Robert Cleveland's story "The Woman with Long Hair," Robert used an old Iñupiaq expression, "*niviaqsiġaksraq,*" literally meaning "the one lying there ready and waiting," a disturbing connotation to contemporary Iñupiaq women and thus no longer in current usage. The descriptor commonly used nowadays is *naviaqsiġaatchiaq,* meaning a girl who is ready for marriage.

Women's physiological maturation as studied by physical anthropologists, the first menstruation, was marked in Iñupiaq culture in the past by a period of residential isolation and visual avoidance, as described to a certain extent in "The Brother Who Rescued His Lost Sister." The Iñupiaq descriptor for a young girl in this transitional period to womanhood is *agliñġaaq* (literally the first-time grown-up, or the secluded one). The secluded woman had a birch bark hat, which she put on as soon as someone approached the shelter her family had built for her to live in for the whole year. She was supposed to avoid looking directly at others. Another type of face screen was mentioned by Giddings in *Kobuk River People.* According to Pegliruk (Giddings 1961:20–21), the woman who was secluded wore a hood that hung down in front to the waist. Only her mother and little boys could visit her, said Pegliruk.

Curtis (1930:227) mentions that Selawik women's counterpart to the men's "First Catch" was the first berries picked or the first fish caught. The berries were given to elderly people. Women's gender roles in subsistence practices are presented in the narratives as being consonant with the men's roles and vice versa. Two Iñupiaq terms that encapsulate the ideology of Iñupiaq marriage are *iñuutri* and *iḷaqan* (Kobuk) or *tuvaaqan* (Noatak). "*Iñuutri*" refers to the person/ spouse who will take care of the other person/spouse. The terms "*iḷaqan*" and "*tuvaaqan*" carry the connotations of spouse, partner, or companion. Marriage is therefore conceptualized as a partnership, companionship, and commitment to take care of each other.

While men in the roles of father, husband, son-in-law, and adult sons worked hard as hunters to supply meat for the family, women as mothers, wives, daughter-in-law, and as adult daughters likewise worked hard in the culturally expected female subsistence roles. Whatever the man brought home from the hunt, the "woman in the house" was supposed to take over the cutting, drying, storage, cooking, and processing the skins for making clothing, tents, and bedding. This complementarity in the Iñupiaq husband and wife roles was most clearly articulated in "The Man Who Married a Wife from Across the Sea." The husband was such "a good provider" that his family was said to be "never in want of food." Even though they lived in a riverine area, the husband also obtained food from the coast. The family "didn't suffer from food scarcity" and "life was good for them," the storyteller said. His young wife, a good partner to her husband, was described as "a good worker. She worked fast and always worked with ease." Interestingly, in one story, "The Mother Who Made Her Son Blind" (versions also in Lucier 1958:96–98, "The Blind Boy and the Loon," and in Hall 1975:245–247, "The Blind Boy and the *Mulgi*"), the responsibility for processing food was described as at times overwhelming, especially for older women. The hero of the story loved hunting and was a good hunter. Since he had no wife, the woman who processed the game animals was his mother, who also picked berries during the summer. After a while his mother was so exhausted from processing the game animals her son had brought back from his hunts that she felt she needed a reprieve. She wished that her son would go blind so that he would hunt no more. And she had her wish! Her subsistence work was reduced to simply picking berries and preparing food for her blind son. Juxtaposed against the culturally expected women's behaviors were the waywardness and willfulness of the woman who met her tragic end, becoming old overnight and passing away in "The Head," told by Lois Cleveland.

Women were also depicted as hunters. While men were big game hunters, some women were small game hunters. In the legend "Kinnaq, the Kotzebue Wife," Kinnaq hunted rabbits and ptarmigans to feed herself and her small son while her husband was gone most of the winter.

Culturally prescribed women's roles appear even in animal characters. Anthropomorphic animals such as the mother beaver in "The Orphan in the Beaver House" and the female grizzly bear in "The Girl Raised by a Grizzly Bear" all cooked the family meals. The female grizzly bear was described as cooking "delicious food." She was tender and loving of her abducted human daughter.

An Iñupiaq wife's commitment to her marital life, as articulated in the narratives, went beyond fishing, gathering, and processing the game animals her husband had hunted and taking care of home and the children. She was expected to be loyal, patient, and understanding. Isiqiak disappeared for the whole year, but his two wives remained faithful to him and awaited his return, constantly looking over the river course to see if they might see their husband making his way back. So did the wife of Tomitchiałuk in "Tomitchiałuk and His Brothers." The wife in "The Floating Food Platter" and in "The Man Who Ate Mysterious Food" maintained her wifely responsibilities while worrying about her husband and continuing to cook for him, despite his rejection.

Iñupiaq marital relationships were further supposed to be bonded by trust, with honesty between husband and wife as depicted in "Pisiksuġliq and Suġli Suġli" and "The Two Loving Brothers." A possessive husband, a husband who constantly bullied his wife, was said to live a married life "not the right way," as voiced by the storyteller of the family tragedy "The Wife with a Jealous Husband."

Iñupiaq daughters were generally represented as being responsible. In "The Woman with Long Hair," the two daughters of the *umialik*, the rich man of the village, "were never hesitant whenever they were asked by their parents to do something." Obedient they might be, but they did not lack spirit. They were capable of making their own decisions when the situation called for it. In fact the two sisters, not the parents, were the successful marriage go-betweens for their brother who wanted to marry the woman with long hair. In a number of stories, such as "The Orphan with No Clothes" and "The Orphan Who Won the Ring," the heroines were described as having no wish to marry, a culturally distinct character type, referred to in Iñupiaq as *uiluaqtaq*, the one who does not want to marry. But when the right man, the hero, came along, they married, as expected of daughters. An early reference to this character type can be found in Rasmussen's collection in the story "The Raven Who Married the Arrogant Girl Who Refused Men" (Ostermann 1952:157–159).

The reality that Iñupiaq subsistence living critically depends upon the hunting skills of men and the hard work of men and women was emphasized in many stories. To further accentuate the point, a number of stories point out adverse consequences when the picture was reversed. The main character in the story

"Nakasruktuuq, the Sleepyhead" got his bad name "Nakasruktuuq" from his exasperated father-in-law because he was too lazy, sleeping late all the time instead of rising early and working. Feeling hurt, Nakasruktuuq began to feel worthless himself. Negative subsistence behaviors were juxtaposed against positive, desirable behaviors that contributed toward a productive, viable Iñupiaq household and ultimately the family's survival.

Narrative Construct of Iñupiaq Society

THE NEED FOR SURVIVAL IN THE HARSH ARCTIC ENVIRONMENT HAS LED to development of key aspects of Iñupiaq social organization that nurture communal life: cooperation, cohesion, and hospitality. Critically examining how storytellers wove these facets of social organization into the story texts and how they articulated them as the Native viewpoints, I have noted that the behaviors were represented in one story as ritualized and in other stories as of serious community concern. Travelers arriving in the community after a long trip are always accorded the hospitality of food and lodging, as narrated in "The Brother Who Rescued His Lost Sister," where the two husbands in search of their lost wives and a brother-in-law were given food and lodging in the very first house they saw. In numerous stories, as soon as a newcomer arrived at a new place, he or she was fed, as is still the hospitality pattern among present-day Iñupiat. In the story "One Who Walked Against the Wind," this hospitality was presented as being further institutionalized by the village tradition of competing prospective hosts racing toward the newcomer. Whoever was the first to reach the newcomer had the honor to entertain the guest at his home. With such a prescribed code of conduct, the murderous intent of the manslayers in both stories about them was obviously a breach of Iñupiaq social order. That this disruptive, antisocial behavior has been depicted in many stories, with different casts of characters behaving in diverse situations, serves to underscore the Iñupiaq ideal of group cohesion. No excuse could be made for the transgression, not even one's own brothers, as in the story "The Lost Little Brother." The hero of "One Who Walked Against the Wind" perceived his killing of the manslayer as getting rid of the terrorist who had been killing visitors and fellow villagers. "The tyrant is dead," he proclaimed after he killed the manslayer. To the villagers, he is a hero.

The Iñupiaq traditional form of settlement, as reported ethnographically by Giddings (1961:123), was organized around a single-family unit, which can be an extended family unit, called in Iñupiaq iḷagiikpaurat. This pre-contact settlement pattern, spread out along river or coastal sites, has been documented archeologically for the Selawik (Anderson and Anderson 1977). In narratives, it is mirrored in a number of stories, for instance, in the Selawik legend "Qayaqtauġiŋñaqtuaq" and the Upper Kobuk legend "The Old Woman of Quliruq." The setting of other stories, on the other hand, is a community or village. On the definition of "village," mentioned in stories and oral accounts, Giddings (1961:148) states that it refers to "neighborhoods" of families with dwellings spread out over the banks of the river. Generally the substantial size of the village is not overtly stated in the stories but implied by the presence of the *qargi*, the community house, as in "The Orphan Who Married an *Umialik*'s Daughter" and "One Who Walked Against the Wind." Within the village, the person on top of the power hierarchy is the *qaukłiq* (the top man, manager) who can be the *aŋaayyuqaq* (chief) or the *ataniq* (headman, boss, ruler of the village). An *umialik* (rich man) could become the *aŋaayyuqaq*, the chief of the community, as John Brown described an *umialik* who was also the *aŋaayyuqaq* of the island village in the story "The Orphan with the Doll."

Within a village, there might be more than one acknowledged *umialik*. In the story "The Orphan Who Married an *Umialik*'s Daughter" there were two *umialik* living in the village. Life at the top of the social hierarchy was depicted in a number of stories, especially in the story "The Orphan Who Married an *Umialik*'s Daughter." Here we are given a glimpse of the economic factor that accounts for the making and unmaking of an *umialik*. An *umialik* and his family lived their subsistence life like the other villagers except that they were more successful at accumulating subsistence wealth. Hints of the *umialik*'s material wealth were given in descriptors of his house, for example, a "big house," a "house with flooring of logs as big as the trees" in the story "The Woman with Long Hair," and a "two-story house" in "The False Alarm at Kobuk." The daughter of another *umialik* in "The Orphan Who Wanted to Marry an *Umialik*'s Daughter" was said to have clothing "all fluffy with wolf and wolverine trimmings."

Umialik status was presented as changeable within a person's lifetime, depending on how well he could maintain his wealth, his subsistence supplies. In "The Orphan Who Married an *Umialik*'s Daughter," the *umialik* with a skilled hunter as a son-in-law prospered. Another *umialik* who had spurned the orphan's request for his daughter's hand, in contrast, suffered a decline of his family's fortunes. When he could no longer hunt in his advanced age, he no longer had the rich supplies to sustain his *umialik* status. At this point in the story, Nora Norton, the storyteller, succinctly called him "the former *umialik*." In "The Young Man Who Married a Wife from Across the Sea," Nora Norton provided further insight into the *umialik* concept when she talked about the family of the young man's wife. She gave a concise definition of a rich family. When the family "acquired surplus food supplies, they were considered rich." Nora Norton had an insider's knowledge of Iñupiaq *umialik*-ship; her father, trader Riley Jim Suġunuuquu Wood of Long Beach, Upper Kobuk, was referred to as an *umialik* and chief during his lifetime.

The figure of the shaman, a person much feared because his shamanistic powers can incur serious consequences in other people's lives, appears in the legends "The Duel Between the Point Hope Shaman and the Barrow Shaman" and "Siaksruktaq." In Willie Goodwin, Sr.'s, story "The Girl Who Had No Wish to Marry," the figure of shaman, generally equated with malevolent forces and power, was given the role of a helpful character who cooperated with village elders and tried his best to help a choosy young woman find a husband.

The lack of predictability and certainty from year to year due to variability in subsistence resources and cycles led to critical emphasis on kin networks and relationships. A relative is supposed to help another relative in dire need. The brother of the widow with young children supplied his sister with needed food in "The Widow and the Stingy Sister-in-law." He left his wife after he discovered her uncharitable behavior toward his widowed sister and her children. A daughter whose marriage went astray could count on being able to go home and be taken care of by her birth family, as in "The Young Man Who Married a Wife from Across the Sea."

Iñupiaq kinship pattern recognizes both cross-cousins and parallel cousins. Iñupiaq terms exist to distinguish three types: *illuq* (cross-cousin), *aġraqatigiik* (maternal parallel cousin), and *aġnaqan* (paternal parallel cousin). Iñupiaq cross-cousins have a joking relationship. They can behave toward each other without restraint and without evoking bad feelings. Loud talk, public derogation, teasing, and laughter are behavioral characteristics of cross-cousin relationships (Burch 1975:188). The two storytellers of "Wolf, Fox, and Raven Brothers" clearly identified Fox and Raven as cross-cousins, thereby implying contextually why Fox played tricks on Raven.

To cope with the harsh reality of arctic life and unforeseen contingencies, the Iñupiat have evolved an elaborate system of economic and social networks. These institutionalized non-kin relationships, marked by Iñupiaq terms (Anderson et al. 1998:64–66), specify expected behaviors of the people involved. Textual data on Iñupiaq institutionalized economic and social networks are embedded in a number of stories. For instance, in "The Brother Who Rescued His Lost Sister," a type of male partnership appears in the persons of the hero and the new friend his own age whom he met in the village where his sister had been taken. They became fast friends and teamed up in a football match against the team of the villain and beat them. They became *suunaaq*, male friends of the same age. The hero's friend accompanied him to the hero's village, helped him build his house, and the hero found a wife for him. The orphan in "The Orphan with the Doll" considered the *umialik*'s son, who had kindly given him clothing and helped to organize the trip to the village across the sea, his *suunaaq*. The orphan would not trade his magic doll for all the riches the *umialik* had to offer, but instead asked for the daughter of the *umialik* to be a wife—not his wife, but the wife of his friend. A type of women's institutionalized network appears in "The Woman with Long Hair," where a daughter of the *umialik* and their intended sister-in-law were referred to as being *uumaa*, the Iñupiaq term for female friends of the same age. And having grown up together as childhood friends, they were comfortable with each other. The two sisters were able eventually to persuade the woman with long hair to accept their brother.

Iñupiaq Heroes and Heroic Acts

MANY NARRATIVES IN THIS COLLECTION LEND THEMSELVES TO THE exploration of the Iñupiaq concept of a hero and what are culturally defined as heroic, admirable acts.

A folktale hero is generally depicted as a person who is courageous, strong, skillful, and good—a man who can defend himself against a stronger adversary, overcome hardships and obstacles, and lend assistance to others in trouble. Many Iñupiaq heroes are all of these. Frequently they were also represented as good sons, good brothers, good husbands, and good friends. Set within the Iñupiaq subsistence-economy framework, some stories define the Iñupiaq concept of self-reliance beyond practical subsistence skills to include the mastery of other skills. The heroes of "The Orphan with No Clothes" and "The Fast Runner" were fleet-footed, a physical skill required also in the *kivgaq*, the traditional messenger (Giddings 1961:25). Both of the heroes in "One Who Walked Against the Wind" and "The Brother Who Rescued His Lost Sister" were, on the other hand, valorized not only as brave but also as resourceful. Without a teacher and through their own resolve, each cultivated physical strength and agility, one by constantly walking against the wind and the other by gradually uprooting bigger and bigger trees. This self-imposed, disciplined training eventually enabled the heroes to kill the villains.

In other narratives, humility, not self-aggrandizement, was represented as an admirable Iñupiaq value. For example, in "The Woman with Long Hair," told by Robert Cleveland, the grandmother approached by the *umialik*'s wife for the hand of her granddaughter did not demonstrate delight at this wonderful marriage prospect. Neither did she praise her granddaughter. Instead she responded that her granddaughter "might not be a good wife!" The hero, the only son of the *umialik* of the village, was just as self-effacing when he stated his choice of a wife. "The granddaughter of the old woman is my choice, if she would have me." Humility as upheld in contemporary practice can be seen in the person of the storyteller Nora Norton, who kept apologizing that she did not know many stories, when in fact she had a large repertoire of stories.

If humility is an admirable cultural value, then what of the orphan who wanted to marry the daughter of an *umialik* in "The Orphan Who Married an Umialik's Daughter"? Was he not deluded, oblivious of his impoverished status?

That the orphan's ambition could be interpreted as such was articulated by the orphan's grandmother, who frankly reminded him not to forget his place: as the prospective husband of the *umialik*'s daughter, she said, "you're not a suitable person!" One of the two *umialik* he approached was, in fact, insulted by the impertinence of the orphan's marriage proposal. In another story, "The Orphan with the Doll," the orphan likewise lived in abject poverty. He had no home, no clothes, lived on the charity of other villagers, and ate whatever food was given to him in the *qargi*.

How are we to reconcile these contradictions, especially when many of the heroes in Iñupiaq stories are orphans? In this collection there are seven orphan stories that form the orphan story complex. Textually, there are orphans who possess magical skills or have magical helpers, and there are orphans who, against all odds, succeed on their own. For the latter group, perhaps, the *umialik* who gave his daughter in marriage to the orphan provided the best answer. "Life is unpredictable. An orphan might one day become someone to be reckoned with." His answer was grounded in Iñupiaq worldview. The orphans in these stories had all succeeded, becoming rich or extraordinarily skilled and accepted in the community because of their own boldness and determination to prove themselves. The tone of these orphan stories makes a great deal of sense in Iñupiaq culture. Witness the *umialik* who became poor and became the "former *umialik*," as the storyteller called him, when he was too old to hunt and had neither a son nor a son-in-law to hunt for the family. The "orphan" is an Iñupiaq narrative character type just as "the woman who does not want to marry" (*uiluaaqtaq*) and "the fool" (*kinnaq*) (see also Pulu 1979:87–92) are two other colorful character types.

A recurring theme in the narratives is the theme of killing. The young man in "The Orphan in the Beaver House," following the instructions of the head of the beaver family he was living with, killed a little beaver. He was instructed that he should not take off to find his way home without taking along some travel food. So the young man killed the little beaver, an owl, and a bear, all food items. While the killing was justified as a survival strategy, the act of sacrifice by the beavers was admired. It was a heroic act. The beaver who gave his child "had extended himself beyond others, including me," the storyteller John Brown said.

Except for the killing by the cannibal, the manslayer, the bad shaman, and raiders, killing is not due to blood lust. In two stories, the heroes faced with the killing task were represented as being torn by doubts and by the gravity of the decision. Anger and resentment at being subjected to loneliness and separation from his family were replaced by the feeling of remorse after the lost brother killed the wolf couple in "The Lost Little Brother." He was painfully aware that the wolf couple had kept him clothed and fed. As atonement for the killing, he gave them a burial. Later on, he was again in emotional turmoil when he learned the devastating fact that his two older brothers had become homicidal and violated the code of village hospitality by killing every newcomer to the village. The lost little brother, now a strong young man, had to come to grips with the fact that it was his responsibility to take care of his crazed brothers, since others could not. He "felt bad for his two brothers," the storyteller Nora Norton told us. In fact, he deliberately positioned himself to be killed by his brothers. The reluctant killing was a socially responsible act and brought about societal order to his home village. "This village no longer has terrorists," he announced. This interpretive textual reading is further supported by the legend "Satluk, the Man Who Could Not Be Killed," culturally regarded as a true story. In the legend, the Kuuvaŋmiut are said to have sent out a team of warriors to hunt down and kill Satluk, who had been making trouble for other villagers.

Killing can also be read as a social metaphor. A case in point is the son in "The Mother Who Made Her Son Blind," who dropped his mother into the sea after he discovered that she, his own mother, was the perpetrator of his blindness (for the Noatak version, see Hall 1975:245–247). Here, if we take the killing act on a literal level, the son's response appears to be extremely harsh. On the metaphorical level, however, the act serves as a teaching device, reminding listeners of the behavioral norms expected of Iñupiaq mothers. Where life critically depended on subsistence success, the mother should have been thankful that she had a hard-working son, a good hunter who filled their storage caches with food and other necessary supplies. Although the mother had to work hard as her son's food processor since he had no wife, and she felt overworked, she should not have entertained a negative wish for her son's blindness. In contrast to the two unhinged brothers in "The Lost Little Brother," she was neither remorseful nor compassionate. She continued to be deceitful and to mistreat her son even after he suffered the blindness she had caused. The portrayal of the mother's character addresses the flaws in the human character, an issue that appears also in other stories such as "The Wife with a Jealous Husband," "The Widow and the Stingy Sister-in-law," and in the legend "The Wife Killer." Although the son ended up killing his mother, he did so with a heavy heart. The narrator tells us he "felt great anguish." The fragile web of family relationship crosscuts these stories. The story reminds listeners not to forget social codes that keep the family and community together and identifies painful consequences if these codes are violated. The moral underpinning of the story is underscored by the narrator's aside. When the narrator came to the part where the mother had the negative thought about her son, the storyteller commented, "She shouldn't have thought like that."

Contemporary Contexts of Storytelling

THROUGH TIME, AS THE SOCIOCULTURAL STRUCTURE OF IÑUPIAQ CULTURE altered and diversified, new contexts for storytelling appeared and new meanings and new interpretations of the narrative texts have been offered. The storyteller Nellie Russell said that she heard her story "The Floating Food Platter" from John Wright. Wright was an Iñupiaq traveling Quaker preacher who traveled from village to village in the 1950s to proselytize, probably taking along with him also food to trade (R. Sampson, pers. comm. 2001). Apparently Wright used stories, framed as Iñupiaq stories, to proselytize. His story "The Floating Food Platter" bears similarities in a number of motifs to the story "The Fisherman," which Curtis collected from a Noatak storyteller in 1927 (Curtis 1930:200–201). The "Floating Food Platter" could have been a reworking of "The Fisherman" into a Christian morality tale. In Leslie Burnett's version of the same story, "The Man Who Ate Mysterious Food," Burnett said that he heard the story in a Wednesday service of the Selawik Friends Church (California Quaker Friends Church). The story was told in that particular instance as a parable of "a man who yielded to sin." Apparently the story has through the years obtained its foothold in the region as an appropriate morality tale.

On the regional level, storytelling has been adapted to new venues in Alaska's Northwest Arctic region, now strategically linked to introduced elements. Introduced mass media in the form of a regional radio station—an affiliate of the Associated Alaska Public Broadcasting Stations (AAPBS), the Associate Public Broadcasting Commission (APBC), and Alaska Public Radio Network (APRN)—has become a new context for storytelling. A popular program among elderly Iñupiat is the Kotzebue radio station's "Eskimo Stories" hour, when tape-recorded Iñupiaq stories are played. Those who hear the stories retell them to others who miss the hour. For the younger generation, estranged from the traditional culture, television programs hold more appeal. Integrating Iñupiaq folktales into the Iñupiaq language-learning program of the Northwest Arctic Borough School District, initiated and fought for by the Iñupiaq leaders, has become a strategy for remembering and revitalizing Iñupiaq language and culture. The step taken is an emerging grass-roots ethnic movement, away from the melting-pot, cultural-assimilation ideology that has been so long a policy of the federal government for Alaska Natives. It represents an Iñupiaq reconceptualization of Native cultural identity and self-determination. A recent folktale collection, *Folktales of the Riverine and Coastal Iñupiat* (Anderson and Sampson 2003), incorporates an applied educational goal, an attempt to develop regional, culturally familiar folkloric materials to increase analytical and creative writing skills in Iñupiaq school students.

At the small-group interactional level, storytelling these days takes place in a variety of interpersonal contexts. Within the context of the home, some parents tell stories to children before or after dinner or before bedtime. The visit and overnight stay of a guest, especially an elder who knows stories, is an occasion for a storytelling event. Outside of the home, spontaneous storytelling can take place when hunters or gatherers take a lunch break, sit around a campfire, or when firefighters relax and swap stories before going to bed. A rainy day at summer camp can bring people together in a tent and someone will tell stories to entertain and while away the time. Before the advent of telephone service, taped stories interspersed with other messages, such as Happy New Year wishes, were sent as presents to friends and relatives in other villages. The application of modern technology to storytelling, for example, the tape-and-mail stories, has been an effective method of story transmission and sharing beyond the family that received the tape. A recent reframing of Iñupiaq storytelling is the wake-like storytelling event at funeral gatherings to help lessen the grief of mourners. A few storytellers, such as Nora Norton, are known to have traveled to and participated in funerals in different villages in that particular capacity. In another setting, the archeological excavation at Onion Portage on the Kobuk in 1969 offered Willie Goodwin, Sr., a context for his storytelling performance. One evening, Willie and a number of Iñupiaq crew and their families joined the Brown University crew who were cataloguing artifacts they had unearthed during the day. After chatting and joking for a while, Willie proceeded to entertain the group with his stories, told in English for the benefit of all present. On another occasion, on an archeological survey of the Noatak in 1968 with Douglas D. Anderson and me, Willie, along with his wife Mary, told more stories over a campfire dinner by a lake. New contexts continue to be created.

Elderly storytellers that I worked with were well aware of the roles of tape recording and printed media in documenting the past for the future. The storyteller Robert Cleveland considered the taping of his stories a medium through which they will be preserved for future generations. With typical Iñupiaq humor, he told Willie Goodwin, Sr., a member of his audience, in one storytelling event, "I'm recording my stories in the tapes for my grandchildren before I pass away."

Telling a story is implicitly a transformative, communicative event. The narrative voices of the storytellers in this collection tell who they are as people, what is important to them, and what it means to be Iñupiaq. Each of the storytellers, in his or her own way, has contributed to the current narrative forms and continuity of Iñupiaq narrative culture through the act of storytelling and, on occasion, creating new stories. Specific stories in this collection may stir the recollections of Western counterparts. The parallel in the central theme of "The Goose Maiden" and "The Swan Maiden" is recognizable. "Isiqiak" can be viewed as the Iñupiaq "Rip van Winkle" in the character of the protagonist who fell asleep and woke up to a different time and to a different world. But as the narrator Robert Cleveland testified, "Isiqiak" is an old Iñupiaq story. One can also argue that "The Woman Caught on a Fishing Line" is the Iñupiaq mermaid story. However, "The House of Three Brothers" and "The Husband Who Took Seals to Another Woman" are not old, traditional stories. Nora Norton's story "The House of Three Brothers" is, by her own account, a recasting of "Goldilocks and the Three Bears," thereby adding an Iñupiaq version to those already in print (London 2003:41). Nellie Russell told me that she remade "The Husband Who Took Seals to Another Woman" from a story she had read in her teenage daughter's comic book. Both new stories became part of the current Iñupiaq storytelling performances. Nellie later told "The Husband Who Took Seals to Another Woman" on the Kotzebue radio station's "Eskimo Stories" hour, in essence extending the first small group, home storytelling context to a larger, northwest Alaska audience. Both stories were enjoyed by the Iñupiaq audience, and both narrators took pride in the compliments they received. The latest creative performance of Iñupiaq narratives was the dramatic performance of Nunachiam Sissauni (Buckland) high school students based on the stories they had written for their creative writing class (D. A. Mitchell, pers. comm. 2004). The latest in the cross fertilization of this folktale collection is the Cook Inlet Tribal Council's adaptation of one of Willie Goodwin's stories, "The Two Brothers," into a visually beautiful and engaging video game, "Never Alone." New stories are still being created, narrated, and performed with fascinating Iñupiaq cultural twists and nuances. What we see are the dynamics and the richness of Iñupiaq expressive culture, not as a vestige of the past, but as a milieu and voices of the present. It is intertwined with the essence of Iñupiaq culture as a whole and who the northwest Native Alaskans are as Iñupiat.

Note

ALTHOUGH SOME ESKIMO GROUPS EAST OF ALASKA CONSIDERED THEIR folktales to be history (Rasmussen 1931:363), there is no record in earlier ethnographies of Iñupiaq storytellers as to whether they considered all stories they told to be true. Recognized storytellers in this collection, however, stated their perception explicitly in some stories. I cannot ascertain from the data available from the region whether the "true" or "not true" categories were introduced from the outside, for example by missionaries, and therefore represent non-Iñupiaq perceptions of Iñupiaq oral tradition and belief system.

References

Anderson, Douglas D.
  n.d.   The Proto- and Early History of Northwest Alaska. Manuscript in preparation.

Anderson, Douglas D., and Wanni W. Anderson
  1977   Prehistoric and Early Historic Human Settlements and Resource Use Areas in the Selawik
          Drainage, Alaska. Final Report (Part 1) to the National Park Service, Washington, D.C.

Anderson, Douglas D., Wanni W. Anderson, Richard Nelson, Ray Bane, and Nita Sheldon Tawarak
  1998   Kuuvaŋmiut Subsistence: Alaskan Eskimo Life in the Twentieth Century. Washington,
          D.C.: National Park Service.

Anderson, Wanni W.
  1974/75 Song Duel of the Kobuk River Eskimo. Folk 16 & 17:73–81.

Anderson, Wanni W., and Ruthie Tatqaviñ Sampson
  2003   Folktales of the Riverine and Coastal Iñupiat. Kotzebue: Northwest Arctic Borough and
          the National Endowment for the Humanities.

Attla, Catherine
  1990   K'etetaalkkaanee: The One Who Paddled Among the People and the Animals. Nenana, AK:
          Yukon Koyukuk School District; Fairbanks: Alaska Native Language Center.

Baldwin, Karen
  1985   "Wolf?" A Word on Women's Roles in Storytelling. In Women's Folklore, Women's Culture,
          pp. 149–162. Rosen A. Jordan and Susan J. Kalcik, eds. Philadelphia: University of Penn-
          sylvania Press.

Bauman, Richard
  1989   Story, Performance and Event: Contextual Studies of Oral Narratives. Cambridge: Cam-
          bridge University Press.

Ben-Amos, Dan
  1969   Analytical Categories and Ethnic Genres. Genre 2(3):275–301.
  1993   "Context" in Context. Western Folklore 52:209–226.

Brown, Ticasuk (Emily Ivanoff)
  1981a   The Longest Story Ever Told: Qayaq, the Magical Man. Anchorage: Alaska Pacific Univer-
          sity Press.
  1981b   The Roots of Ticasuk: An Eskimo Woman's Family Story. Anchorage: Alaska Northwest
          Publishing Company.

Burch, Jr., Ernest S.
  1975   Eskimo Kinsmen: Changing Family Relationships in Northwest Alaska. Monograph 59,
          American Ethnological Society. St. Paul: West Publishing Company.
  1988   The End of the Trail: The Work of the Fifth Thule Expedition in Alaska. Special Edition
          "L'Oeuvre of Knud Rasmussen." Etudes/Inuit/Studies 12(1&2):81–100.
  1998   The Iñupiaq Eskimo Nations of Northwest Alaska. Fairbanks: University of Alaska Press.

Clark, Annette McFadyen
　　1974　*Koyukuk River Culture.* Canadian Ethnology Service, Mercury Series 18. Ottawa: National Museums of Canada.
　　1996　*Who Lived in This House?: A Study of Koyukon River Semisubterranean Houses.* Archeological Survey of Canada, Mercury Series 153. Ottawa: Canadian Museum of Civilization.

Cleveland, Robert Nasruk
　　1980　*Unipchaaŋich Imaġluktuġmiut: Stories of the Black River People.* Anchorage: National Bilingual Materials Development Center, University of Alaska.

Curtis, Edward S.
　　1930　*The Alaskan Eskimo.* Norwood, MA: Plimpton Press.

DeBree, Susan Towne
　　1975　*Tell Me Ahna: Alaska Eskimo Folktales.* No place of publication. Manuscript on file at Rasmuson Library, University of Alaska Fairbanks.

Fejes, Claire
　　1966　*People of the Noatak.* New York: Alfred A. Knopf.

Foote, Don Charles
　　1966　Eskimo Stories and Songs of the Upper Kobuk River. Research Report No. 3, Human Geographical Studies in Northwestern Arctic Alaska: The Point Hope and Upper Kobuk Projects, 1965. Montreal: McGill University.

Frost, O. W.
　　1971　*Tales of Eskimo Alaska.* Anchorage: Alaska Methodist University Press.

Georges, Robert
　　1969　Toward an Understanding of Storytelling Events. *Journal of American Folklore* 82:331–328.

Giddings, J. L.
　　1961　*Kobuk River People.* College, AK: Department of Anthropology and Geography, University of Alaska. Studies of Northern Peoples, No. 1.

Goldstein, Kenneth S.
　　1964　*A Guide for Field Workers in Folklore.* Hatboro, PA: American Folklore Society.

Hall, Jr., Edwin S.
　　1975　*The Eskimo Storyteller: Folktales from Noatak, Alaska.* Knoxville: University of Tennessee Press. Reprinted by the University of Alaska Press, Fairbanks.

Kaplan, Lawrence D.
　　1984　*Iñupiaq and the School: A Handbook for Teachers.* Juneau: Bilingual/Bicultural Education Programs, Alaska Department of Education.
　　1990　The Language of the Alaskan Inuit. In *Arctic Languages: An Awakening,* pp. 130–158. Dirmid R. F. Collis, ed. Paris: United Nations Educational, Scientific and Cultural Organization (UNESCO).

Kaplan, Lawrence D., and Margaret Yocom, eds.
　　1988　*Ugiuvangmiut Quliapyuit / King Island Tales: Eskimo History and Legends from Bering Strait.* Fairbanks: Alaska Native Language Center and University of Alaska Press.

Kirshenblatt-Gimblett, Barbara
　　1975　A Parable in Context: A Social Interactional Analysis of Storytelling Performance. In *Folklore: Performance and Communication,* pp. 105–130. Dan Ben-Amos and Kenneth Goldstein, eds. The Hague: Mouton.

Krauss, Michael E.
　　1980　*Alaska Native Languages: Past, Present, and Future.* Alaska Native Center Research Paper No. 4. Fairbanks: Alaska Native Language Center.

Lee, Linda, Ruthie Sampson, and Ed Tennant, eds.
　　1991　*Qayaqtauġiŋñaqtuaq: Qayaq, the Magical Traveler.* Kotzebue: Northwest Arctic Borough School District.

London, Sara
    2003   Still Eating That Porridge. *The New York Times Book Review* 108(46):43.

Lucier, Charles
    1954   Buckland Eskimo Myths. *Anthropological Papers of the University of Alaska* 2(2):215–233.
    1958   Noatagmiut Eskimo Myths. *Anthropological Papers of the University of Alaska* 6(2):89–117.

Malinowski, Bronislaw
    1935   *Coral Gardens and Their Magic.* New York: American Book Company.

Mendenhall, Hannah, Ruthie Sampson, and Ed Tennant, eds.
    1989   *Lore of the Iñupiat: The Elders Speak,* vol. 1. Kotzebue: Northwest Arctic School District.

Nelson, Edward William
    1899   *The Eskimo About Bering Strait.* 18th Annual Report of the Bureau of American Ethnology, 1896–1897. Washington, DC: Government Printing Office.

Oman, Lela Kiana
    1959   *Eskimo Legends.* Nome: Nome Publishing Company.

Oquilluk, William A.
    1973   *People of Kauwerak: Legends of the Northern Eskimo.* Anchorage: Caxton Printers.

Ostermann, H.
    1952   *The Alaskan Eskimos: As Described in the Posthumous Notes of Dr. Knud Rasmussen. Report of the Fifth Thule Expedition, 1921–24,* vol. 10, no. 3. Copenhagen: Gyldendalske Boghandel, Nordisk Forlag.

Pike, Kenneth L.
    1964   Towards a Theory of the Structure of Human Behavior. In *Language in Culture & Society.* Dell H. Hymes ed., pp. 54–62. New York: Harper & Row.

Pulu, Tupou L., ed.
    1979   *Unipchaallu Uqaaqtuallu: Legends and Stories.* Anchorage: National Bilingual Materials Development Center.

Pulu, Tupou L., and Ruth Ramoth-Sampson, eds.
    1980   *Unipchaallu Uqaaqtuallu: Legends and Stories II.* NANA, Mauneluk, Northwest Arctic Borough School District and Anchorage: National Bilingual Education Development Center, University of Alaska.
    1981   *Maniilaq, the Prophet.* Anchorage: National Bilingual Education Development Center, University of Alaska.

Rasmussen, Knud
    1931   *The Netsilik Eskimos: Social Life and Spiritual Culture.* Copenhagen: Gyldendalske Boghandel, Nordisk Forlag.

Roberts, Arthur
    1978   *Tomorrow Is Growing: Stories of the Quakers in Alaska.* Newberg, OR: Barclay Press.

Schneider, William
    2002   *...So They Understand: Cultural Issues in Oral History.* Logan: Utah State University Press.

Spencer, Robert F.
    1959   *The North Alaskan Eskimo: A Study in Ecology and Society.* Washington, DC: Smithsonian Institution.

Thornton, Thomas F.
    1999   What's in a Name? Indigenous Place Names in Southeast Alaska. *Arctic Research of the United States* 13:40–48.

Iñupiaq Exclamations

The following exclamations have been retained in the stories and legends to maintain Iñupiaq linguistic flavor:

aa—"Yes" (can be used interchangeably with *ii*) and to give permission, as in "You may."
aa aa—"No, no!"
aanna—Exclamation expressing pain, sorrow, or disappointment; similar to "Oh no!" or "Oh dear!"
aarigaa—Exclamation expressing happiness or contentment; similar to "good" or "wonderful."
arii—Exclamation expressing pain or dissatisfaction.
ii—"Yes. Okay."
iikii—Exclamation of disgust, similar to "Ugh!"
ki—"Let's ... " or "Let's go." When the word is dragged out "*Ki-i-i*," it is a comment similar to "I told you so."
yaiy—Exclamation of satisfaction or to express how lucky a person is.

Iñupiaq Terms

agliñguaq—Girl in seclusion at puberty.
akutuq—Creamed fat; a food item.
aŋaayyuqaq—Village chief; title of high prestige held by few men.
ataniq—Head of the village.
iksiak—Strangers; people from other territories.
kivgaq—A messenger.
nuniaq—To sing endearments.
qargi—Community house where stories were often told.
saulik—Sod-covered house.
suunaaq—Male friend of the same age.
umialik—A rich man.
uuma—Female friend of the same age.

Legends

Unipchaat

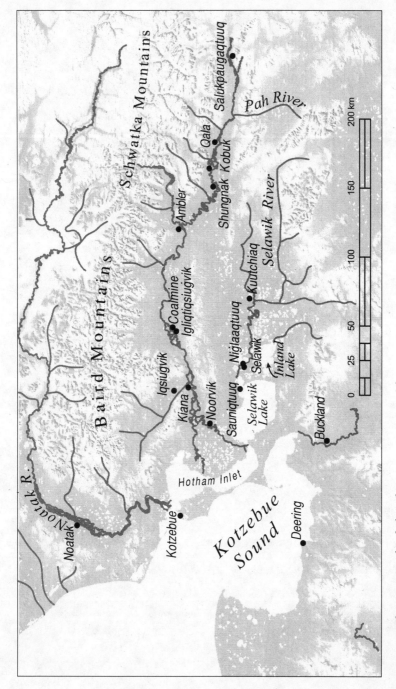

FIGURE 7 ~ *Places mentioned in the legends.*

The Qayaq Cycle
Qayaqtuaġiŋñaqtuaq

Nora Paniikaaluk Norton

FIGURE 8 ~ *Nora Norton, Selawik, 1968.*
PHOTO: WANNI W. ANDERSON.

"Qayaqtuaġiŋñaqtuaq" is one of two famous Iñupiaq legends. This version, told by Nora Paniikaaluk Norton, was passed on to her by her husband, Edward Norton, who was born at Point Hope and had lived also in Candle. The birthplace of the hero, Qayaq, around Sauniqtuuq, on the Selawik River, positions Qayaq as a Selawik Iñupiaq hero.

The storyteller Nora Norton, born in 1910, was one of three daughters of Minnie Paniagruk (Reed) Wood and Riley Jim Sugunnuuquu Wood, a trader and umialik of Long Beach (present-day Kobuk). Nora resettled with her parents in Selawik during the 1920s after her father was commissioned to build the First Baptist Church in the village and the family grew to like the area. Nora's husband, Edward Norton, worked as a reindeer herder in Buckland for the Laplanders from the Loman Company before becoming a freighter and storekeeper for the Ferguson's Store, an early trading post on the Selawik River.

Nora loved to tell stories and had a large repertoire of Upper Kobuk stories that she learned from her father and coastal stories that she learned from her husband. Nora had four children. She passed away in 1987.

RECORDED IN SELAWIK, JULY 1 AND JULY 21, 1977

I'M GOING TO TELL THE STORY OF QAYAQ, BEGINNING WITH THE FIRST part of the story, the birth of Qayaq. I might not have all the details of the story and some episodes may be rather short. This can't be helped, I'm afraid, because when my husband was telling the story, sometimes I wasn't there to hear it.

Qayaq's Birth

DOWNRIVER, ABOVE SAUNIQTUUQ, HUNTERS MAY STILL SEE AN OLD frame of a house. My husband had seen it. That particular site was Qayaq's homeplace, the place from where Qayaq began his journey.

There at Sauniqtuuq Qayaq's parents made a living. They had children and their children were all sons. These sons, older brothers of Qayaq, went hunting, but not a single one of them returned home. The sons, growing into young manhood, didn't come back because they all wanted to explore the world and experience adventures. So the couple lost almost all of their sons. The remaining son, Qayaq, was probably the youngest.

When Qayaq was born, his father brooded, "When this one becomes a young man, he too will probably go hunting. And he too probably won't want to return home."

Even when Qayaq was still a small child, his father launched attacks on him.

One day, coming back home from the hunt, his father climbed up to the skylight of the house and threw his spear down at the child. The child Qayaq, however, managed to dodge his father's spear.

When Qayaq was old enough to play outside, his father resorted to a different tactic. He set traps to try to catch him. Still the child Qayaq, while playing, managed to dodge every single one of the traps. (Qayaq's father shouldn't have done this to his son!)

As time passed Qayaq, like any normal child, soon grew up. He became a young man.

Qayaq's mother made Qayaq a vest. Often the young Qayaq would ask his mother, "Mom, what particular kind of food would you like to eat?"

When Qayaq asked his mother the question, it was most likely sometime during the summer. Qayaq's mother replied, "Wouldn't it be wonderful to have a meal of beluga."

Qayaq didn't hesitate. Immediately he took off to hunt. He was gone for a while and when he returned home, he brought back a beluga! His mother immediately processed it. She made beluga oil and stored the leftover beluga meat for eating later on.

But Qayaq was at the age when young men sought adventures. When he kept on insisting about leaving home, his mother began to make him a new parka. It had all kinds of animal hides on it. She sewed these hides together. Qayaq could hardly wait to depart when the parka was finished. It was at that time of the year when long days began to arrive. Qayaq's mother also made him a new pair of mukluks for his travel.

Qayaq's father tried his best to discourage Qayaq from leaving. But when he found that it was to no avail, he was much saddened. "If you go away, you too will never return home! All of your older brothers took off and never returned home! You'll disappear just like all of your brothers!"

But Qayaq couldn't be stopped. He too wanted to have his adventures.

His mother prepared whatever was needed for the trip. She prepared *akutuq*, the Iñupiaq creamed fat, putting all kinds of ingredients into it. (When other storytellers told the story, they'd list the ingredients. But the way my husband told it, he didn't list the ingredients.)

The day after his mother finished making the creamed fat, Qayaq departed. His mother packed for him all sorts of food, including dried fish and different kinds of meat. Qayaq was well prepared for his trip. He filled the small sled he could drag behind him with these provisions, then took leave of his parents. He left the Sauniqtuuq area and began his journey, walking along the foothill of the mountains.

Qayaq's Ptarmigan Wife

QAYAQ HAD BEEN TRAVELING ALL DAY.

The sun was setting on the horizon when Qayaq reached the top of a long mountain range. When he looked down, he saw down below a large group of people. That was the time when Qayaq encountered his first group of people. He had never seen nor met other people before. His parents were the only people he knew. The people Qayaq saw appeared to be having a lot of fun. He could hear them shouting and laughing.

When Qayaq finally arrived in the area, he stopped at the house of a couple living at the end of the village. They were the very first people Qayaq met. The couple had a daughter. Qayaq became their guest and married their daughter.

Qayaq was a welcomed guest in the family. They gave him wonderful food to eat. They gave him dried fish and dried fish roe. He was given all sorts of food including fish oil. Happily Qayaq ate all the food that was served.

When nighttime came, they all went to bed. Qayaq fell into a deep slumber because he had been traveling all day and dragging his sled. In the middle of the night, however, Qayaq was startled out of his sleep. He found that around him it had turned freezingly cold. And there was nothing around but the stars high above. Qayaq was so cold that he was shivering.

Qayaq got up quickly. He looked around but all he was able to see was the tail feathers of a ptarmigan. He had stopped to live with a flock of ptarmigans. The ptarmigans had turned into humans for him.

Qayaq proceeded to warm himself. After eating a small meal, he took off, dragging his sled behind him.

The Porcupine Man

QAYAQ TRAVELED ALL DAY.

Toward the end of the day he saw a man. The man was moving slowly while he worked. When something occurred to impede his work, he would quickly turn his back on it. He carried many, many weapons with him.

That man was a porcupine. (A porcupine has weapons. It has quills which can pierce into things. Those quills are dangerous.) When Qayaq met this person, he must have stayed with him for some time.

I don't know if Qayaq shared a meal with this person or not. When Qayaq met him, he noticed that the person was eating.

The Wolverine Man

QAYAQ LEFT THE PLACE WHERE HE MET THE PORCUPINE MAN AND continued on his journey. That was at the time of the year when the days were long. He had his snowshoes on and was dragging his small sled. Along the way, he met another person.

Earlier, before meeting this man, Qayaq had come across a beaver's igloo. The igloo had traces of being broken into. He also spotted a tooth, a wolverine's tooth, lying next to the igloo.

When Qayaq met this man, they had lunch together. Qayaq was quite hungry by then, so he was happy to share his lunch with the man he just met. While eating, Qayaq casually mentioned, "Over there at the beaver's igloo where someone has broken in, I found this wolverine's tooth."

The man asked, "What's a wolverine?" (Wolverine didn't know his name!)

Qayaq stayed with him for a while. When they parted, Qayaq continued on with his journey. (Gosh, where did Qayaq spend the night?)

The Dall Sheep Dinner Guest

QAYAQ STAYED OVERNIGHT AT DIFFERENT PLACES AS HE TRAVELED. AS he traveled on, he came across another person. Qayaq did not meet all of these people in one day.

The person he met this time was a young man. The man had on a beautiful parka made of sheep skin, with nice trimmings. The young man also wore a nice pair of mukluks.

"*Aarigaa*! Finally I've someone I can talk to. Finally I've someone I can share my food with. Food is delicious when it's shared with another person," said Qayaq.

Qayaq began preparing his campsite. He gathered some tree branches and laid them out at the spot where the two of them could sit together. He built a fire, took out his supply of food, and prepared his meal. Qayaq sat cross-legged. The young man sat his own way.

As it happened, one side of Qayaq's mukluks had a hole in it. The soft-bottom mukluks he had been wearing had got wet and the sewing thread was broken. So Qayaq's big toe was showing through the hole of that mukluk. Perhaps Qayaq did that deliberately. With his big toe exposed, Qayaq wiggled his toe every once in a while. He noticed that the man who was eating the meal with him stared at his foot, wide-eyed. Sitting across from Qayaq, the man began to eat fast. He grew more and more nervous as Qayaq continued to wiggle his big toe. After a while, the young man couldn't take it any longer. He asked Qayaq, "What does your big toe eat?

Qayaq replied, "My big toe brings me shame. He wants to eat you!"

In a flash the young man jumped up and grabbed his shoes.

"Hold on to it! Hold on to it!" he cried. He put on his shoes, ran up the hill, then headed toward the mountain.

"Hold on to it! Hold on to it!" he kept shouting.

Whenever the young man looked back, Qayaq would grab his foot and hop around. He did that on purpose.

"I'm holding on to it," Qayaq shouted back.

The young man soon disappeared out of sight, still yelling, "Hold on to it! Hold on to it!"

That person was a Dall sheep. There used to be Dall sheep living on the lowland, but Qayaq had scared the Dall sheep so badly that it climbed up to the top of a mountain. That's why the Dall sheep nowadays dwell only on the mountaintops.

The Crazy Man

QAYAQ LEFT THE AREA AND TRAVELED ON.

On the way he met again another person. By this time he was so famished that he was ready to share his meal with any person he met. He didn't travel both during the day and during the night. He did stop to sleep along the way. (I'm telling the story as I heard it.)

So the two men started to eat. Qayaq gave the person a small portion of his creamed fat. The man loved Qayaq's creamed fat. "Your creamed fat is so good. I'm going to eat all of it—including you!"

Qayaq jumped up and fled.

The man chased after him. They went around in circles. They probably ran through willows and other trees. After a while, Qayaq began to perspire from the exertion. (He shouldn't have let the other man eat part of his creamed fat because that food made the other man stronger.)

The two ran in circles. Qayaq then had an idea. He pulled off his parka and stuffed tree branches into it. He had earlier noticed that the man had set a snare. As he was running, he was pushing the snare aside with his arm. The man really wanted to eat Qayaq.

Qayaq dropped his stuffed parka into the snare, then climbed up a tree. When the man arrived at the snare, he was happy.

"It isn't hard at all to catch you!"

The man wanted to eat his catch. He flipped the parka over, grabbed his knife, and then cut into the parka. Inside the parka there were only tree branches! He stared at the thing he thought he had snared—there were only tree branches stuffed inside a parka!

Up in the tree, Qayaq called down, "You are crazy! Why don't you just cut your own throat and fall into the fire."

The man built the fire as Qayaq suggested. When the fire was blazing, he cut his own throat and fell into the fire.

(That man was certainly crazy! If he weren't, he wouldn't have done so.)

The Gold Man

WHEN QAYAQ TRAVELED AGAIN, HE PROBABLY VENTURED QUITE CLOSE to the place called Alaaniq. When he finally reached Alaaniq, night was just closing in.

Qayaq arrived at a steep bank. After checking to see if he could possibly climb down the bank, he backtracked and decided that it was safer for him to climb down from the spot that was not as steep. After he climbed down, he stopped for the night at a place, below the steep bank he had contemplated climbing down earlier. He made his camp. He spread tree branches on the ground as his sleeping pad, then made a shelter. He also made a fire.

As Qayaq was preparing for his camping, he heard someone coming. Qayaq could hear that the person was dragging a small sled. (When someone is walking with his snowshoes on, you can tell.) Qayaq definitely could tell that the person had snowshoes on. Listening, he realized that the man was following his first set of footprints. This particular part of the incident probably occurred after it turned dark.

The man called out to Qayaq, "Where did you come down the bank?"

Qayaq called out his reply, "From there! I came down that way."

Qayaq lied to the person because he actually came down a different path. He didn't come down the steep path.

The man started to come down.

"Scu-ta-pa, scu-ta-pa! Scu-ta-pa, scu-ta-pa! Scu-ta-pa, scu-ta-pa!"

Then came loud clanging noises! Apparently the man had crashed as he was trying to come down the steep bank!

When Qayaq woke up the next morning, he saw the man who had crashed during the night. The man was all red in color. His snowshoes, his sled, and all of his belongings were also red. It was probably gold.

That happened at Alaaniq.

(The gold probably will be discovered there later on. I've heard that the shamans of Selawik had buried some gold underneath the ground in the Selawik area. They did so because they knew that the land of their descendents would be taken by white men. That's why they had buried the gold in the ground. The person Qayaq met, I don't know what it is, but he probably was the Gold Man. Gold is red in color.)

The Woodpecker Man

QAYAQ SPENT THE NIGHT THERE, THEN SET OFF AGAIN. HE TRAVELED FOR some time, then stopped for the night. He built a shelter and put down tree branches as his sleeping pad.

Qayaq was preparing to spend a few days at that location when a man stopped by. The man was small, quick, and agile. He moved fast while doing his chores. Qayaq invited the man to spend the night there. Together the two spent the evening sitting by the fire.

As they were sitting by the fire after their meal, the man grabbed his small knife. He lunged at Qayaq. Qayaq grabbed him and singed him in the fire. It wasn't until then that Qayaq discovered that the person was a woodpecker. That's why the tail feathers of a woodpecker look like they were singed. (I haven't seen a woodpecker myself. When you live at a place where there are groves of trees, you can hear woodpeckers pecking on the tree trunks.)

The woodpecker turned into a man that day. He thought that he could knife Qayaq and kill him. But Qayaq wasn't easy to kill.

The Boreal Owl Family

FROM THERE, I DON'T KNOW EXACTLY WHERE QAYAQ WENT NEXT. HE did however go on to the Kobuk River and traveled for a while along the Kobuk. After that period, Qayaq came upon the Qillich, the people without anus.

(I forgot. Qayaq had earlier stopped at another group of people before he came to the Qillich. I don't like to be forgetful like this when I'm telling a story. I'm thinking hard, trying to recall. And here I'm not telling the story the way it should be told!)

So Qayaq came upon a group of people. Living among them was a couple with a daughter. Qayaq married her and lived there with them for a while. The people at that place would cook tiny, tiny portions of food. When a rabbit was caught, they would cook the rabbit's shoulder blades.

One day Qayaq felt famished, for he wasn't used to eating tiny portions of food like these people. So he went out to hunt and looked for rabbits. He caught enough rabbits to feed the whole family. He hung the rabbits he got on his belt and returned home. Qayaq was throwing his catches, the rabbits, into the house when he heard his wife's father cry out, "Watch out! Don't get hit! Don't get hurt!"

Qayaq entered the house, skinned enough rabbits so that each person in the family could have a whole rabbit for the meal. He threw the rabbits' entrails that he removed to the back of the house. When he did this, the grandmother unfortunately got hit and smothered by the entrails. She was accidentally killed.

Qayaq roasted the skinned rabbits on the fire. When the food was cooked, he invited the family to eat. Qayaq started to eat his rabbit, but the others in the family didn't. Each grabbed a rabbit, took it outside the house, and ate it outside.

Qayaq lived with the family for a while. One day he heard his father-in-law talking to his daughter, "Daughter, things are different from day to day. Today isn't the same as the day before. This man, this husband of yours, isn't good to have around in time of scarcity. He eats far too much!"

I think the group is the boreal owl family. Qayaq lived there for a while. When he ate rabbits that day, he ate and ate until he felt sated.

Qayaq Introduced Natural Childbirth

WHEN QAYAQ LEFT THIS LAST LOCATION, HE HAD TO TRAVEL FOR SEVERAL days before he reached the Qillich, the people without anuses.

Qayaq married a couple's daughter and made a living there with the group.

It wasn't long before Qayaq's wife got pregnant. Her parents appeared to be in distress. They thought they had to open their daughter's abdomen in order to take the baby out and their daughter would certainly die. They didn't want their daughter to die. Qayaq had been wondering why his father-in-law and his mother-in-law had been crying since they knew about their daughter's pregnancy. Both thought that they had to open their daughter's abdomen to take the baby out and that their daughter would consequently die.

Qayaq told his in-laws that he would help his wife have a natural childbirth. His wife's parents didn't believe him. But when his wife's delivery time came, Qayaq helped his wife with the delivery. They didn't have to open her abdomen and the young woman had her child naturally. Had Qayaq arrived at this place earlier, many young women wouldn't have lost their lives.

As Qayaq continued to live with his wife, he also discovered that the people he was living with sucked on their food. They sucked on animal fat and all kinds of good food. At first Qayaq followed their practice.

One day, Qayaq felt famished. He felt that he couldn't survive sucking on the meat like they did. So he went hunting and caught an animal. (I wonder what he caught. Maybe a bear!) Qayaq brought his catch home and cooked the meat. The people he lived with didn't cook their food at all; they simply sucked it. Qayaq cooked a big meal and ate and ate.

The father-in-law, watching Qayaq eating, said, "Our son-in-law has solid food in his stomach. He won't live!" He thought so because Qayaq ate solid food and he thought it would not empty out later on. He saw Qayaq ate real food.

They all went to bed after the meal. Qayaq went to sleep. When Qayaq woke up, daylight was breaking. He felt the urge to excrete. He had had a huge meal the day before. He had eaten the meat as well as the fat of the animal he had hunted.

Qayaq got up, went outside, and walked up a small hill. He turned his back to the people, sat down, and had a big bowel movement. He made a big pile of excrement! Qayaq hadn't eaten like this for a long time! All of the people stepped out of their houses to watch what Qayaq was doing. After Qayaq did this, he walked back down the trail.

As Qayaq was on his way down, a man was on his way up, along the same the trail. The man wanted to see Qayaq's excrement. The people there didn't know what excrement looked like. When the man reached the excrement pile, he stared at it for a while, poked at it with his index finger, and then licked it! Afterwards he went back down the trail.

All day long people went up and down that trail. As they licked the excrement on their fingers, they developed anuses. After a while there was nothing left of Qayaq's excrement. That group of people finally had anuses. (*Arii*! I wonder what kind of people they were.) From then on, they had their anuses and they were able to eat solid food. Also young women no longer needed to have their abdomen cut open. They were able to give natural childbirth. Qayaq had assisted this group of people.

The Man Who Created Fish

THIS PART OF THE STORY BEGINS FROM THE TIME QAYAQTUAĠIŊÑAQTUAQ was at the Yukon River.

Qayaq built for himself a qayaq for traveling on the Yukon River. When his qayaq was completed, he began his journey.

Qayaq was paddling downriver when he came upon a man. The man was chopping wood. He was chopping wood, working laboriously. He threw the wood chips into the river and the chips turned into fish. He worked laboriously at his job. The trees he was chopping were spruce trees, cottonwood trees, and other kinds of trees.

Qayaq got closer to the man and arrived just in front of him. The person was working so hard that he wasn't paying attention to anything else. As Qayaq was beaching his qayaq, he thought to himself, "This man certainly has big ears!"

The man on the shore spoke, "Even though I have big ears, I am making fish for other people."

That man knew what others were thinking. He could read Qayaq's thoughts.

(If a person is able to read other people's thoughts, it would be rather awkward, wouldn't it?)

When Qayaq Became a Pike

FROM THERE, QAYAQ TOOK OFF DOWN THE RIVER AND CAME UPON another man. The man was spearing fish at the mouth of a slough. (The Kuuvaŋmiut, the Kobuk River people, called this way of fishing "kapuuqkaaq.") Qayaq watched him for a while. The man was totally absorbed in what he was doing, paying no attention to other things around him.

Qayaq retraced his steps up the river, beached his qayaq, then walked to the slough. When he arrived there, he took off his clothes and swam away—as a pike. He swam down the slough. As he was swimming down, the fisherman saw him. He saw a big pike coming down the slough. He threw his spear at the pike and speared it. But when the spear hit the pike, the point of the spear broke and the pike took off with the spearpoint. The man who was fishing sadly bemoaned the loss of his spearpoint. He looked and looked for it in the water. He thought that somehow the pike might have dropped his spearpoint at the bottom of the slough.

Qayaq in the meantime went back to where he left his gear and put his clothing back on. He had the spearpoint with him. He launched his qayaq again and traveled a short distance until he reached the fisherman. When he came abreast of the fisherman, he asked, "What happened?" Qayaq asked the fisherman what he was doing.

The fisherman answered, "A big pike broke my spearpoint and made off with it." He was truly upset by the loss.

After watching the fisherman search for his spearpoint for a while, Qayaq showed him the spearpoint that he made off with earlier.

"I found this spearpoint," Qayaq told him.

Retrieving the spearpoint, the fisherman commented, "This looks exactly like my spearpoint." He recognized his spearpoint.

Qayaq didn't tell the fisherman that he was the party responsible. He didn't say, "I was the person who did it."

After resting there for a while, Qayaq set off again.

The Crushing Cliffs

QAYAQ PADDLED DOWN THE RIVER.

While moving along downriver, he came upon a location where the riverbanks were so steep that one couldn't climb up. The river turned narrower too. Qayaq realized that he was in great peril. That morning he had taken a small bite of his creamed fat because he was feeling uneasy. He was advised to do so by his mother while she was preparing his traveling gear. She had advised him that whenever he felt uneasy, he should eat a little of the creamed fat. (His creamed fat didn't get spoiled even though he didn't keep it in a freezer. It was probably prepared in a certain way so that the creamed fat didn't turn rancid.)

The land he came to was about to crush Qayaq! Two large boulders were moving, banging and crashing into each other!

The two boulders had killed many people who tried to pass through this passage.

Seeing the crashing boulders, Qayaq began to sing a song. He sang his song and safely made his way through. From then on, the land ceased crashing and trying to crush people.

Qayaq didn't simply travel. He got rid of many bad things in the land. (God probably made him travel in this manner. There were all kinds of things that you couldn't do, or places where you could get killed.)

The Man with a Spear

AFTER QAYAQ HAD PASSED THROUGH THE CLIFFS AND WAS TRAVELING downriver he came upon a man coming in the opposite direction, traveling up the river.

When Qayaq approached close enough, he heard that man talking to himself. "Finally, someone has the nerve to travel in his qayaq into this area!"

The man called out to Qayaq, "Yoho! You there! Do you think you'll stay alive? You've been qayaqing downriver alive, but now you will die!"

But Qayaq wasn't afraid.

They paddled closer to each other. When the distance was right for throwing a spear, the other man seized his spear and threw it at Qayaq. He aimed to hit Qayaq's right arm, but Qayaq wouldn't be hit. He couldn't be hit, for he was no longer a baby. While he was still a baby, his father said, "This boy will grow up and won't return home." When Qayaq's father returned home from his day's hunting, he used to look down the skylight and throw his spear down at the child Qayaq. But the child Qayaq had been able to move before his father's spear hit him.

Qayaq was no longer a child. He shifted his position to avoid being hit by the spear. He backpaddled his qayaq and seized the spear thrown at him. He then threw it back at the man who was challenging him. He hit the man in the right arm. The spear tore off his arm and the severed arm flew behind him.

The man who was hit backpaddled with his left arm. He retrieved his severed right arm from the spear and threw the spear at Qayaq again. But again he couldn't touch Qayaq. Qayaq couldn't be hit. The man continued to paddle with his left arm.

Imitating the man, Qayaq seized the spear and threw it back at the man. He hit the man on the left arm. The spear flew away with the man's severed arm. This time the man bit on his paddle. He paddled back to his spear. He then bit on the spear and aimed his spear to decapitate Qayaq. Qayaq, however, couldn't be decapitated.

Qayaq again moved to be out of harm's way. He bit on his paddle the same way the other man did and retrieved the spear thrown at him. He bit the spear the same way the other man did. When Qayaq decapitated the man, the latter keeled over and Qayaq finished him off.

This person had been killing people he met in the area for a long time.

The Wolf Man

WHEN QAYAQ TOOK OFF FROM THERE, HE CONTINUED TRAVELING downriver.

On this leg of the journey, Qayaq saw a house—probably a sod house. Qayaq beached his qayaq and went up to check the house. Inside he saw many weapons. He waited. He waited around because the house appeared to have someone living in it.

Sure enough, Qayaq soon heard footsteps coming toward the house. Qayaq grabbed a spear and waited. The instant the person made his appearance at the entrance, Qayaq speared him. The man grunted. He was hurt. He retreated and took off from the river.

After waiting around for a while, Qayaq followed the man's footprints. The fleeing man walked a long way before disappearing among a large group of people.

Qayaq spotted a small house, sitting some distance away to the side of the village. He walked to the house. Night was setting in and it was getting dark. (Probably he reached there at dusk). Qayaq entered the house. Inside he saw two old women sitting across from each other. They were hunched over in their bedding. (They were probably talking to each other.) Two pitiful old women!

Qayaq came into their house and, in a flash, killed one old woman. He threw the dead body behind the house. He then killed the other old woman and removed her clothing. He hid the second body and put on the clothing of the dead woman. He was able to fit into her clothes. (If Qayaq was physically a big person, I wonder how he was able to fit into the dead woman's clothes?)

Qayaq went to the poor woman's bedding. (The bedding was probably strewn with clothing or animal skins.) He hunkered down and waited.

Soon, he heard a man entering the house. Qayaq had probably heard the two women talk before they were killed. When Qayaq talked to the man, he made his own voice sound just like the voice of one of the women he had killed. The man informed Qayaq that the community's hunter who had returned home wounded from his hunting trip was dying from the wound. Qayaq listened. He then told the man to assemble all the people in the community at the meeting place. He instructed the man to make sure everyone was present and to place the wounded man in the center of the place. He also instructed the man to dim the lamps. "I'll try to cure him," he said.

The man went to tell others what Qayaq had instructed. After a short wait, Qayaq picked up a cane and walked to the place where the people had assembled. As he entered the place, he grunted, acting like an old woman. Once inside the gathering place, Qayaq complained that it was still too bright. A man went to dim the light some more. Qayaq then went to the man with the wound and asked, "Where is the pain?"

The man pointed to the spot. "Right here! The pain is excruciating!"

Qayaq examined the wounded man and found the point of a spear. When he located it, he also felt around the hurt spot. Quickly, he pulled out the spear-point, then escaped, running. He ran as fast as he could, hearing noises coming after him.

"Rascal! Don't think you'll live if we catch you!" the people yelled as they gave chase. "So, it was you who speared our only hunter! Don't think you'll live!"

When they were about to catch up with Qayaq, he lifted the sod and covered himself with it. He became part of the ground and disappeared. (That's the way the story was told of people who lived a long time ago.)

When this large group of people chasing after Qayaq reached the spot where Qayaq disappeared, they combed the ground for Qayaq.

The pursuing group was quite perplexed about Qayaq's whereabouts. "Right here. I think he disappeared here," someone said, almost stepping on Qayaq.

After searching for a while, they said, "You, Arctic Fox. You always boast that you know everything. Find this man. If you can locate him, then you can truly say that you know everything. You said you know everything. Hurry, get going and find him!"

Arctic Fox didn't hesitate. He began to search for Qayaq, sniffing as he went. When Arctic Fox finally spotted Qayaq, the latter implored him, "Oh no! You've found me. Please don't tell the group that you've found me. I'll give you anything you want to eat after these people leave. Whatever you don't have, I will get for you."

Arctic Fox did as he was asked. He pretended to continue looking even though he had already found Qayaq. The people began to speak badly of him.

"You're good-for-nothing, Arctic Fox! You are nothing! You boasted that you know everything. You said you can find just about anything. Why haven't you found this man yet?"

"I wanted to find him all right. But unfortunately I didn't find him!" Arctic Fox answered.

After looking some more for a while, the group stopped clamoring and returned home. They weren't able save their hunter. When they left him, he probably died. The hunter was a wolf. Qayaq had speared him. The wolf became a man and did things like a human being.

When the clamoring stopped, Qayaq remained in his hiding place a while longer. When he came out of his hiding, Arctic Fox was waiting for him. The departing group no longer welcomed Arctic Fox into their homes because he was incapable of finding things.

Qayaq asked Arctic Fox what he wanted to eat. Arctic Fox replied, "I want to have seal meat and seal fat."

"*Ii* [yes], I'll go and get a seal for you," said Qayaq.

Qayaq launched his qayaq and took off. He was gone for a while and returned with a big seal in his qayaq. He gave the seal to Arctic Fox. "I'll get food for you again sometime."

After he said this to Arctic Fox, Qayaq took off, leaving Arctic Fox behind. Arctic Fox continued to live there somehow after Qayaq left. But the rest of the people no longer liked him because he failed to find Qayaq for them.

The Cannibals' Sticky Ball

QAYAQ TOOK OFF FROM THERE AND TRAVELED ON DOWNRIVER.

After traveling a long distance, he came upon a ball hanging in the air by a tether. The wind was pushing the ball in all directions. Qayaq got out of his qayaq and walked toward the ball. Playfully he slapped the ball with his hand. His hand got stuck! He put his other hand on the ball to try to pull the stuck hand free, but it didn't work. Now both of his hands got stuck! So he decided to shove his leg at the ball to again try to free himself. His foot got stuck too! He had only one foot left that was not stuck. He thought he could still try to free himself with the remaining foot. Again he shoved at the ball. Now he was really stuck! He was left hanging on the ball! He wanted to pull free, but it was impossible. Luckily for Qayaq, he didn't get his head stuck to the ball too. There he stayed and froze. He looked exactly like something that had been frozen onto the ball. While hanging in that position, Qayaq heard footsteps coming toward him. He saw coming toward him a man pulling a small sled.

"Thank you," the person intoned. "I finally caught something for my children! Thank you, my trap has caught me a game animal!"

Qayaq couldn't be pinched. He was frozen. The man was very happy. He thought Qayaq was dead because Qayaq had closed his eyes and appeared to be frozen solid. He removed Qayaq from the trap and lashed him onto his sled. He then reset his trap, the ball, again.

The man took off from the river pulling the sled with Qayaq in tow. After a while, the man reached a path cut through the willows. He pulled Qayaq along the path. While busily pulling the sled, the man didn't see what Qayaq was doing. Qayaq had been holding onto willow branches by the side of the path as he went along and had been able to make the sled stop and go as he pleased. The man didn't realize what was happening and just kept on walking. As he arrived closer to home, he could hear his children telling each other joyfully, "Our daddy has caught some game! Our daddy has caught some game!"

The children were happy with their father's catch. They walked behind their father's sled. The father was still working hard, pulling his sled. After a while, Qayaq opened one eye just a little to take a look at one of the children. The child whom he looked at screamed, "*Aa aa* [Oh no], Daddy! He opened an eye! He opened his eye a long, long time."

The father said, "Son, he's just having his last look at the world!"

The father was working hard to bring his game home. As the father was pulling Qayaq along, Qayaq opened his eye just a little again. "*Aa aa*! He opened his eye again," his son said.

The father didn't investigate what happened because he was too anxious to bring his catch home. When he reached his house, his wife came out. Husband and wife grabbed Qayaq and carried him indoors. They probably placed him at the place where they usually placed their game animals to thaw. A frozen body couldn't be pinched and it would take a long time to thaw.

The children, hungry, began to beg their parents for food. They were told they would have their food when the game animal thawed out.

Evening came. The children got all tired out and went to sleep.

Qayaq knew what was happening even though he was frozen. The husband and wife couple told each other, "This game will probably thaw out while we sleep. We'll just have to wait and have it for breakfast." They both felt very sorry for their children, having to go to bed hungry.

While sitting there, the wife all of a sudden remembered, "Oh! I usually place my *ulu* [Iñupiaq knife] under its head." (*Arii*! What if she cut Qayaq's throat?)

The wife seized her huge *ulu*, the one she used to cut up people and things. These people were cannibals! She grabbed Qayaq's head and slid her *ulu* under his head. Qayaq let her do that and pretended as if nothing had happened. The couple then went to bed and fell asleep.

Qayaq lay still until the whole family fell into a deep sleep. The father began to snore loudly and the mother was sound asleep.

Quickly Qayaq got up, seized the *ulu*, and, beginning with the father, cut their throats, decapitating them. Those people were cannibals. After that, Qayaq left the house. He barely made it. The bottom of his parka was all ruined, but he was able to escape. He left running.

Qayaq almost got trapped inside this house. Had he stayed longer, he would have been trapped. Maybe Qayaq couldn't be harmed by anything. In this episode, Qayaq barely escaped. He left the area. When he reached his qayaq, he continued to paddle downriver.

Qayaq Fought the Rock Ptarmigan

Traveling downriver, Qayaq came upon a large group of people.

At the village, at the place where he finally stopped, there was a couple with a daughter. Qayaq married the daughter. They made a living there and lived there as husband and wife for a certain period of time.

One morning, Qayaq noticed that his father-in-law was sitting with his back turned, his head bowed. Apparently he was unhappy with something. Qayaq generally liked to sleep late, but once he was up and working, he would accomplish what he was supposed to do to perfection. After acting unhappy for some time, Qayaq's father-in-law spoke. "Son-in-law here isn't out hunting! Why isn't he out hunting, trying to get some game? He sleeps so late every morning. When hard times come, daughter, he won't be much help."

He told his daughter, "Up on the hill there's a big ptarmigan with a body hard as a rock."

Hearing his father-in-law's comment, Qayaq got out of bed. He told the family that he would go hunting the next morning. The day went by as usual and when it turned dark, they all went to bed.

Early the next morning, Qayaq asked his father-in-law for directions to go hunting the ptarmigan his father-in-law was talking about. The father-in-law told Qayaq that there was indeed a rock ptarmigan to be hunted and gave Qayaq directions on how to get there. The father-in-law told Qayaq that if Qayaq went where he pointed, he would ultimately reach a ridge. On top of the ridge, if he looked down, he would see the rock ptarmigan.

Qayaq knew the rock ptarmigan couldn't be caught by a lone man. He tried to sneak up on the ptarmigan, but he wasn't successful. The ptarmigan was too vigilant. When the situation became impossible, Qayaq tried turning himself into other kinds of animals. He became a mink, then a mouse, and then other kinds of animals. He became a bird and tried all sorts of tactics, but still couldn't get close enough to the ptarmigan. That ptarmigan wasn't an ordinary rock ptarmigan! It was a huge ptarmigan! It was what his father-in-law had used to kill people!

Qayaq had already tried all other tactics. Finally he tried becoming a piece of down on the ptarmigan. (When you pluck a ptarmigan, you'll see single-down strands on its thighs.) Qayaq became one of those single-down strands. He made a wish. "I wish for a small wind to blow me toward the rock ptarmigan." He had already tried all other tactics.

A small breeze came as Qayaq wished and blew him toward the rock ptarmigan. It was fast asleep and didn't wake up. Qayaq was therefore able to get close to the ptarmigan and throw his spear at the ptarmigan's anus. The spear hit its mark and the rock ptarmigan fluttered in pain. Qayaq was caught in its thrashing and had a difficult time trying to stay alive. (All of you know what happens when a ptarmigan gets caught in a snare. If you try to catch it while it's still full of vigor, it will flutter its wings wildly. This happened to Qayaq.) He had a difficult time, but he was trying his best to survive.

It wasn't until the evening that Qayaq was able to kill the rock ptarmigan, finally.

Qayaq took a rest after the kill and wiped off his sweat. He had put in a lot of effort killing the bird, and he had succeeded. Looking around, Qayaq saw all sorts of skeletons. That bird was what his father-in-law had used to kill people.

When Qayaq finally decided to walk home, it was beginning to get dark. His father-in-law had assembled all the people in the village in the community house because he was sure that Qayaq wouldn't be able to make it home. The people were holding a celebration, having a dance celebrating the destruction of their in-law.

In the meantime Qayaq arrived closer to the village. He noticed that of all the houses in the village, his house was the only one with a light on. When he entered his house, he saw his wife there, crying, mourning for him. Qayaq asked his wife where her parents were and was told that they were at the dance. They were so certain that Qayaq wouldn't make it back. Qayaq told his wife that he would go over to attend the dance. His wife tried to stop him, but Qayaq told her that he had to. His wife didn't go with him because she had been crying so much that her face was swollen. Her parents felt no pity for her.

When Qayaq arrived closer to the *qargi*, the community house, he could hear people singing about him. They sang, "Our in-law didn't return home," then whooped with joy.

Qayaq entered the *qargi* and right away began to dance. A woman came to the middle of the dance floor and danced with him. The woman was probably happy to see Qayaq still alive. Qayaq had intended to dance alone because he wanted to watch the singers. But he didn't tell the woman not to dance with him. When the song was about to end, Qayaq danced backward and left through the door. He went back to his wife.

After a long absence at the dance, the father-in-law returned home. He didn't apologize when he saw Qayaq. He didn't say, "I'm sorry I sent you to danger."

For a while Qayaq continued his life with his wife as if nothing untoward had happened. His father-in-law didn't try to do away with him again after that failed attempt to kill him with the rock ptarmigan. When the father-in-law was hungry for something, Qayaq would go out to hunt for it. When nothing was needed, he just stayed home. Only when something was needed for food did he again go hunting.

Qayaq Fought the Fireballs

AFTER LIVING FOR A WHILE IN THAT VILLAGE, QAYAQ BEGAN TRAVELING again. He traveled for a long time.

One day he came upon a large group of people. At the house where he stopped, the couple had a daughter. (Qayaq always stopped at the right place! He would always find a couple with a daughter as their only child!)

Qayaq lived with the family. They lived on the coast. After a long time of living with them, the father-in-law turned unfriendly.

One morning, the father-in-law said, "This son-in-law doesn't go out hunting. From here out into the ocean, beyond different kinds of game, you can find *uunut*." (I don't know what *uunut* are, probably some kind of ducks. The sea has all kinds of flying ducks. One type of these ducks was probably called *uunut*.)

When the father-in-law said that there were *uunut* out there in the ocean to be hunted, Qayaq took his father-in-law's qayaq and spears and paddled out into the sea. He passed all sorts of game, but he wanted to catch those his father-in-law wanted. He arrived at the spot and started to hunt that game animal until his qayaq was filled with the catch before heading back home.

The land where Qayaq was paddling back to was a long, long way away. As Qayaq started to glimpse a thin outline of the land ahead, he felt a strong wind swooshing toward him. He also saw two fireballs moving in his direction.

When the fireballs flew closer, Qayaq removed one of his sleeves. He ordered the fireballs to go back to where they came from. Then, he blew into his sleeve. The two fireballs moved back to where they came from and the wind also died down. It turned calm again and Qayaq continued home.

Qayaq returned home after he was able to blow the wind back. His father-in-law was the person who had sent those fireballs to destroy Qayaq. When the fireballs came back, they landed on the father-in-law. He tried to seize the fireballs but he failed and they burned his face. His hands were also burned. The old man didn't die, but he was in great agony.

Qayaq reached the shore safely. Everyone was worried. His wife went to the landing where Qayaq was getting out of his qayaq. She told Qayaq that two fire-balls burned her father's face and hand. Qayaq didn't say, "I did that to him."

When he entered the house, he found his father-in-law in great pain. Qayaq informed his father-in-law that he had *uunut* for him. The father-in-law was in so much pain that he ignored everybody. He lay with his back turned and was moaning. He was in agony. His bad deed came back to him. (That's how it is in the Gospel. That's how it was preached. When someone talked badly about someone else, what he said comes back to him. It's hard to take. But that's the way it is in God's Gospel.)

When Qayaq Became a Peregrine Falcon

AFTER LIVING THERE FOR A WHILE AND AFTER WHAT HAPPENED TO HIS father-in-law, Qayaq took off again.

On this part of the trip, Qayaq came upon a large group of people. There was a large cliff near their village. Qayaq stopped at the place where the couple had a daughter. He stopped there and married the daughter. He lived there for a long time, making his living.

One day, Qayaq's father-in-law said that many young men would go to the cliff to *asraaqaq*. (I do not know what *asraaqaq* is.) Qayaq's father-in-law said that the men who were going the next day should have a lot of fun together. He wanted Qayaq to join them too. No other information was given to Qayaq.

The next morning when the men left, Qayaq left also. That morning Qayaq's wife was sad.

The young men reached a large tree, hanging over a cliff. They sat on the heavy end of the tree. The father-in-law sent a man to walk to the end of the tree trunk, suspended over the cliff. Each man took his turn walking to the end of the tree, then walked back. After everyone else had attempted the feat, it was Qayaq's turn. Qayaq's father-in-law told Qayaq to try as the others.

Qayaq didn't hesitate. He walked to the end of the tree trunk. As Qayaq turned around to walk back, the men all jumped off the trunk. Both Qayaq and the tree fell down the cliff.

Qayaq turned into a peregrine falcon.

He flew home below the rim of the cliff. He heard the men shouting, rejoicing that he fell down the cliff. When the tree fell, so did Qayaq. But before he hit the ground, Qayaq became a peregrine falcon. Qayaq himself didn't know that he did this. When he reached home he found his wife sitting beside the bed. Qayaq lay down.

At the cliff, the father-in-law told the young men to compete at a foot race. Whoever was the first to reach his daughter would get his daughter as his wife, he told them.

The young men assembled, ready to start the race. They sprinted off when the father-in-law told them to go. They ran swiftly. Three men were in the lead, running swiftly behind each other. They raced closer and closer to the finishing point. The racer who was in front was so certain that he would eventually be the person to marry the daughter since no one was able to pass him.

When he reached the finishing point, the house, he went inside. Sweat was pouring down his face. What he saw inside the house was Qayaq, sleeping beside his wife!

The man who came in second similarly entered the house. Then the third. (Why did the men who came in second and third come into the house? They were not the first?)

They were all very disappointed, seeing Qayaq there. The three went out to tell the girl's father that Qayaq was not dead as he thought. Qayaq was, in fact, lying beside his wife. The father-in-law was not at all happy.

When Qayaq Got Snared and Cooked

AFTER SOME TIME, QAYAQ TOOK OFF TRAVELING AGAIN.

Qayaq took off flying for he had turned into a peregrine falcon. As he was flying along a coast, he came upon a village. One of the houses at one end of the village had a tall post. The peregrine falcon was about to land on the post when he found himself caught in a snare. He had not spotted the snare. He struggled to free himself but it turned out to be an impossible task. Qayaq knew what was going to happen to him next!

When the man of the house came out, he was quite happy to see a falcon caught in his snare and suffocated. He lowered down the falcon. Qayaq was aware of what was happening. The man took the falcon into the house and told his daughter to work on the bird so that they could have it for their meal right away. The young woman wasted no time. She put a piece of ground cloth under the falcon and began plucking its feathers.

During the plucking, Qayaq was thinking to himself, "I hope this young woman doesn't burn my feathers afterwards. I hope that she would drop my feathers at the spot where no one has stepped upon."

The daughter cut up the peregrine falcon and put the cut pieces into a pot to cook. When the pieces were all cooked, she and her parents ate them piping hot. They ate the peregrine falcon. Those days they probably ate peregrine falcons.

After the meal, the father told his daughter, "Daughter, gather all the bones and feathers and throw them at the spot where no one has stepped."

The daughter collected what her father told her to collect and left the house. She walked some distance from the village until she reached a spot where no one had stepped upon. There she dropped her family's food trash. She even shook her parka vigorously to remove the falcon's feathers that might cling to it.

Qayaq turned into a human being. When the young woman walked home, Qayaq walked with her. He walked into the house with the young woman even though earlier they had eaten him when he was a peregrine falcon. Her parents welcomed him because he was a young man. Qayaq married the daughter, the woman who had cooked him. They lived together for some time.

Qayaq Returned Home

TIME PASSED.

Qayaq felt homesick. He began thinking about his home from where he began his journey. He wondered how his parents were doing. He remembered that his uncle was sometimes with him while he was traveling. Most of the time, his uncle stayed home. But his uncle had turned into a lynx and left.

Because Qayaq was so homesick, he took off from this last place where he got married.

He turned into a peregrine falcon again and flew back to Sauniqtuuq where he had begun his journey.

He came back. But alas, the only thing he saw was an old frame of a house! The people living in it were all gone! Both of his parents were dead.

Qayaq was the youngest of the family. His older brothers had all left home and had not returned. Qayaq himself would have returned home earlier, but his adventures had taken him all over to different places. He had encountered and killed all kinds of strange things. But when he finally returned home, there remained only this old frame of their home.

Qayaq mourned and cried. He mourned for his parents. He then turned into a peregrine falcon again and flew away. He remains a peregrine falcon. The peregrine falcon is Qayaq. That's what people say.

The Sky People

Nora Paniikaaluk Norton

~~~~~~

In Iñupiaq cosmology there are three parallel worlds: the sky world, earth, and the animal world. "The Sky People" legend gives us a glimpse into the sky world and an incident when the earth people met the sky people. Point Hope people, as described in the legend, are known for their hospitality. Perhaps influenced by her husband's Point Hope hospitality, Nora's house was always a convivial place where many Norton relatives and friends ate together and socialized. "Food tastes good, taken with company," Nora says in this story. Nora's second daughter, Emma Norton, continues the family tradition of hospitality.

RECORDED IN SELAWIK, DECEMBER 27, 1971

~~~~~~

I'M GOING TO TELL A SHORT STORY, A TRUE STORY. THE EVENTS HAPPENED a long time ago.

There was a group of people living at a point of land in the village of Point Hope. A couple living in that village very much enjoyed having people come to their home and shared their meals with them. They liked to treat others to their food. They weren't tightfisted with what they had. The husband was a good hunter. They were never short of food in winter.

One year during winter the wife noticed that something wasn't quite right with the food they stored in the caches. She knew well what she had in her caches. Most likely there were sea mammals, whale meat, and other kinds of food. Those were the types of food the Tikiġagmiut, the people of Point Hope, lived on.

A new moon passed. The food in the caches still looked different. The wife grumbled to her husband, "I can't understand it. Our food in the caches looks different. I really can see that it is different."

Her husband didn't respond. Like his wife, he liked to treat others to the food they had. They were very much alike. They weren't tightfisted.

They continued to pass their winter. People came to visit them and they continued to treat their guests to their food. People ate with them and liked visiting with them.

One day, as evening approached and they were about to have something to eat, some guests arrived. After some conversation, the husband told his wife to procure some food. "Let's have dinner. We've guests to dine with us. Food tastes good, taken with company."

His wife didn't hesitate. She immediately went out to the caches to get the food. (The incident occurred before flashlights were available. Instead the coastal people had wood pieces soaked in seal oil overnight. These wood pieces would be lighted in the evening to provide some light.)

The wife took one of these torches, lit it, then went out to the caches. She was about to enter a cache when she saw something out of the corner of her eye. She wondered what it was. She scrutinized the floor of the cache but saw nothing unusual. She knew she had a glimpse of something. "Perhaps I imagined it," she thought.

But when she looked up at the ceiling of the cache, she spotted two men. They were somehow stuck there. The two men weren't ordinary people. They weren't people from earth. They were people from the sky. The wife found out then that when the new moon arrived, these men would come down from the other world to look for food. They had been taking food from this coastal couple. The wife rubbed the torch around her cache. She rubbed every spot she was able to reach. When that was all done, she returned to the house and informed others about the incident. She told them she had just caught two men in a cache.

"I think they're from elsewhere. They definitely aren't from this area."

She also told them that she had rubbed the torch all around the cache to prevent the two men from escaping. "You should all go to the cache and take a look," she said.

The people in the house got up and rushed out to take a look inside the cache. There they saw two men, stuck to the ceiling. They had a talk with them. They assured the two men that they wouldn't be harmed. They simply wanted to ask them questions, like where they were from. They also wanted to invite them inside the house.

After some coaxing, the two men descended from the ceiling and were brought into the house. They were told that the woman of the house would give them food to eat. They were given food. When people asked about their place of origin, the two men answered that they had come down from the sky. They said there were people living high above the earth, higher up in the sky. The villagers asked many more questions and requested them to tell more. The two men said that whenever they were about to run out of food in the sky, they would come down to earth to procure the needed food. Upon hearing this, the couple informed the two men that they would be happy to give them food. They would fill their rucksacks and give them as much food as they could possibly carry. They assured the two men that they wouldn't try to harm them in any way. (Point Hope people generally didn't talk like this. But this particular couple was really nice to the two men.)

The wife took the two men to her caches and put together food for them. She filled up their rucksacks with food. When that was done, she told them they could journey home. "Do go wherever you plan on going."

The two men prepared to leave. They were both well dressed. They had belts on top of their parkas and their boots were well tied. They had on clothing that wasn't meant for warm weather. When both were finally ready to depart, the villagers told them, "We won't harm you. We simply want to see what you'll do to go back."

Outdoors the two men strapped on their rucksacks, filled with food. Then they positioned themselves, one in front of the other.

(I don't know why I didn't attempt to learn the song these two men sang the way my husband did when he told this story. I should have learned it so that I'd be able to tell the story well later on as I'm trying to do now. There were so many things to learn, but I didn't learn all. I didn't try hard enough. My husband used to talk a lot about the ways people lived in the past. He would talk about the lifeways of several groups of people. The song he sang was a really nice song. It said something about floating up into the sky.)

The two men floated up into the sky. They moved toward the east where the day begins. They continued to float up and up until they disappeared from sight. Both disappeared, singing while floating up higher and higher.

The people of Point Hope didn't see the sky people again. They might have continued to come down to take more food had the villagers not discovered them. It was good that the couple had plenty of food to give.

I learned this story from my husband. His name is Edward Norton. He was born in Point Hope.

Two Men from the Moon

John Pakuraq Brown

~~~~~~

"Two Men from the Moon" is another version of "The Sky People." The two versions were told on the same day in a storytelling session at John Brown's house over the Christmas–New Year's week in 1971. The telling of the two versions exemplifies how, in a multiple-storyteller session, a storyteller can stimulate or provide a memory recall for another storyteller. Nora Norton and John Brown were good friends—both Upper Kobuk–born Selawik residents.

Storyteller John Brown was born around Shungnak in 1888. His wife, Mary Iriqłuk Brown, was also from the Upper Kobuk. Both came to live in the Selawik River area in the 1930s when John was about forty years old, first settling at Kuutchiaq, an old settlement that is now deserted. At the time when I first met him in Selawik in 1968 John was eighty years old and a widower, living by himself in a traditional log cabin he had built himself on the island in the middle of Selawik village, known as Akuliġan (meaning middle). By then, his children had all passed away. His only surviving relative in Selawik at the time was Annie Sun. John was known in Selawik as a skilled carpenter.

RECORDED IN SELAWIK, DECEMBER 27, 1971

~~~~~~

FIGURE 9 ~ *John Brown's log cabin overlooking the Selawik River, summer 1969.* PHOTO: DOUGLAS D. ANDERSON.

It was winter.

A group of people discovered that somehow someone had consistently entered their caches and stolen their food. They had no idea whom they should blame for the theft.

A man, puzzling over the identity of the food thief, decided one evening to stay outside to keep watch. The moon was just beginning to show in the sky that night. He asked another man to also keep a close watch over other food caches. Both men intended to find out who had been stealing their food. They looked at the moon while keeping watch. The rest of the men in the village, following their example, took turns at the night watch.

During the middle of the night when things grew quiet, the two men heard a noise. It sounded like people talking, but they hadn't the slightest idea where the voices came from. They had no idea whose voices they could be since everyone in the village was already asleep. They heard voices of people talking and laughing. The voices didn't come from close by.

When they looked up into the sky, they saw two men floating down. When the two men approached closer to the ground, they grew more cautious, whispering to each other. Once in a while they would stop to listen. They had backpacks strapped to their backs. They floated down toward a cache, then landed near the cache. Cautiously they looked right and left to see if someone might be around. They didn't see the two watchmen.

For a long time the two men floating down from the sky listened for telltale noises. Finally, hearing none, one man opened the door of the cache and entered. The other man staked a watch outside and later entered the cache. As soon as both men disappeared inside, the two watchmen quickly ran out from where they were hiding in the shed. They positioned themselves in front of the door of the cache and woke up the people in the nearest house. The people of that house, awakened by the watchmen, helped them wake up the rest of the villagers.

While the two men from the sky were still inside the cache, the villagers gathered around the cache. After a consultation they decided that the two watchmen should be the ones to enter the cache to look for the two men.

The two watchmen went into the cache. They looked and looked for the men they had seen but saw no one. They came out and informed the people that they found no one in the cache. The people waiting outside said that they themselves saw no one leaving the cache. The two watchmen mentioned that the two men they saw had backpacks. To double-check, other men entered the cache again but, like the two watchmen, after searching and searching, found no one. Then, one watchman happened to look up at the ceiling. There they were—the two men they were looking for—up there against the ceiling.

The people talked to the two men. They told the two men that they were delighted to have visitors. They told the two men not to be fearful of them. One of the watchmen stretched out an arm to touch one of the men at the ceiling. At the touch, the man fell onto the floor.

The villagers let the two men come down from the ceiling. Both of them were very young. The two watchmen told them not to be too sad about what happened because the villagers would give them all sorts of things. The villagers then invited them to their *qargi*. The two men accepted the invitation and the villagers all went to the *qargi* with them.

Inside the *qargi*, the two visitors received a warm welcome. The villagers held dances for them the whole night. The visitors informed the villagers that they had come down from the moon. Animals that lived in the mountains like the caribou and the mountain sheep also lived in the land they came from. But they had no seafood at the moment, they said. There was no longer open water on the moon, only ice. When the people on the moon ran out of food, their chief sent the two of them down to Point Hope. The two men, obeying the chief's order, had set off from the moon and come down to Point Hope. They told Point Hope people that their chief's name was Uqaqtoqaiyaq. They said they always obeyed their chief's order.

Upon hearing the two visitors' sad story, the villagers brought in sea products, such as seal oil, seal skins, seal-skin ropes, and others to give to the visitors. And just before sunrise, they all sang a song they had been practicing. At the end of the song, the two men from the moon prepared to depart. They informed Point Hope people in the *qargi* that if they wanted to, they could watch them take off for the moon.

With the backpacks strapped to their backs, they began to move, round and round, ascending higher and higher with each round. Finally they floated out through the window. The people all rushed out of the *qargi* to continue watching. The two men continued to ascend and their ascent was faster and faster the higher they floated. The wind was pushing them, giving them more speed. They went back to the moon, to their chief.

The Duel Between the Point Hope Shaman and the Barrow Shaman

Nora Paniikaaluk Norton

~~~~~~

Shamans and shamanism in the past are topics that Iñupiat are reluctant to discuss, except among trusted friends and family members. This legend, with song messages sent back and forth between two shamans who were adversaries, provides the only existing record on how shamans in the past settled their differences through the verbal art of the song duel. In the storytelling session, Nora Norton sang all the songs that were recorded with the legend. For more information about the song duel as an Iñupiaq conflict-resolution method, see Anderson 1974/1975.

RECORDED IN SELAWIK, MAY 7, 1972

~~~~~~

THIS STORY IS ABOUT A POINT HOPE PERSON AND A BARROW PERSON— two shamans. (Some time ago, not at present, the shamans had their power from the Devil. When they obeyed the Devil, they abided with him. This story is not from ancient times.)

Two shamans were related; they were cousins. They used to send verbal messages to each other through songs. This story tells about these two cousins who through the song duel tried to outdo each other. The Barrow cousin didn't win all the time because the Point Hope cousin's power was stronger.

One time the Point Hope cousin sent the following message to his opponent:

You want to have a fish hook?
So, you do want a fish hook!
I've pulled out my tooth and I'm sending it to you.
You can use my tooth as a fish hook.
Why don't you make it into a hook?
Then you'd have a hook for fishing.

"Sending a message to the other party" was what people called what the two shamans did. The two persons sending messages to each other didn't have to be shamans. "Sending a message to the other party" was also the term applied to two persons arguing and sending verbal messages to each other.

The Barrow cousin did his utmost to hurt his opponent, but he didn't succeed. When the Point Hope cousin sent his message back to his Barrow cousin, he hit hard. He sent a tooth!

On another occasion when the two cousins were again at odds, the Barrow cousin wanted to kill his Point Hope opponent. He used shamanism, invisible magical power. The Barrow cousin had turned himself into something with wings in order to try to harm his Point Hope cousin. When the Point Hope cousin who also had shamanistic power saw something coming at him, he responded with a counterattack. The Barrow cousin dropped his wings and retreated.

Later the Barrow cousin again initiated the attack. Both sides were sending their messages via a messenger. A man named Inavina was the messenger. These events occurred a short time ago. The messenger traveled back and forth between the two villages. He memorized and learned the precise messages the two were sending with him.

At another time when the Barrow cousin was on the attack, the Point Hope cousin was at the time sleeping. When he woke up, he found himself afloat on an ice floe in the ocean. That was the shamanistic feat of his cousin. Using his power, the Point Hope shaman returned to shore. He was not drowned as his cousin intended. So he won again in this fight.

After this incident, the Barrow cousin sent a message asking his Point Hope cousin for forgiveness and promising that he would no longer send songs and messages. The Point Hope cousin was delighted that they'd fight no more. He stopped worrying and continued to live his life.

But one day he received a message again from his Barrow cousin. The Barrow cousin made songs and messages that hit hard at the Point Hope cousin, trying to destroy him.

Hearing the message, the Point Hope cousin was unhappy for a long time. He said, "I thought he had already forgiven me. I've already accepted his apology." After brooding over his cousin's behavior for a while, he sent his message back with the message to Barrow:

Receiving your apology, I had accepted it.
I didn't expect any more messages from you.
After promising that no more messages would be sent,
You sent one again.

Then the Point Hope cousin made another song. (I didn't learn his whole song when my husband sang it. I can only sing the parts I remember. I'm not a smooth singer.) This is the reply song the Point Hope cousin sent back with the messenger:

Barrow Man, I've already told you.
I don't have dogs,
Therefore I can't go over to see you.
If I had gone, the load I carry would have to be heavy.

(There are many parts to the song. I remember some parts and I lost other parts.)

It was spring when the messenger arrived back at Barrow. The Barrow whaling crews were out on the ice trying to get some whales. The messenger, probably the man named Inavina, was a whaling crew member. The Barrow cousin, also out there on the ice with other crew members, asked the messenger, "You don't happen to be carrying anything with you, do you?"

He pretended that he hadn't heard the song message because what he had received from Point Hope hit him hard—too hard for him to accept.

I forgot to give you another part of the song. The last part of the song goes like this:

I thought you stopped sending messages.
Good Bye! Good Bye!

The Barrow cousin persisted, asking the messenger the same question over and over. Since he kept insisting, the messenger delivered the message again.

When the Barrow cousin heard the song, he hung his head. He sat in that position for a while, saying nothing, then he rolled up his sleeping bag and began packing. He headed back for land, toward Barrow village. Walking away, he was in anguish. His Point Hope cousin had sent him a message that inflicted great pain. He could no longer remain on the ice with the rest of the whaling crews.

The Wife Killer

Nora Paniikaaluk Norton

*Many Iñupiaq stories address the issue of family relationship, provid-
ing Iñupiaq cultural norms on social relations. The questions raised in
this legend are: What makes a good family? What should be the ideal
behaviors of husband and wife? In this legend, said to be from Point
Hope, the wives and their families behaved properly as prescribed by
Iñupiaq cultural norms, but the husband violated the rule, deceived
his family, and murdered his wives. Although the "wicked" husband
was killed at the end of the story, the brothers-in-law who killed him
were ambivalent about the revenge. Not a callous act, the killing
was tinged with regret—in the words of the storyteller "they felt bad
because murder was what that man did to their sister."*

RECORDED IN SELAWIK, AUGUST 8, 1968

I'M GOING TO TELL A STORY ABOUT A POINT HOPE PERSON.

A Point Hope man was making a living. When the caribou was ready to be
harvested during the summer, he would go hunting with his wife. He would
be gone all summer with his wife as his companion. He would use the caribou
hides for bedding.

The man returned to the village during the fall. He was crying and grieving
as he was approaching home. The boat he returned in was filled with dried meat
and hides that his wife had worked on all summer. The man told others that he
had lost his wife. Once back in the village, he stopped at the houses of his wife's
relatives. They welcomed him because they still considered him their relative.

The man didn't live long without a wife. He remarried. Since he was a good
hunter, the women didn't shy away from him.

So he married again. And when the caribou were ready to be harvested
during the summer, he took off again with his wife. He took off with his new
wife in the boat and boated away from Point Hope. He returned home during
fall, again with no wife.

He married again, a daughter of a couple. This new wife had two brothers. When the time came for the man to leave, as usual he left with his wife. When they arrived at the location where the husband usually did his hunting, he didn't stay around with his wife. Most of the time he would be out hunting the caribou. The husband was acquiring his bedding and his food in preparation for the coming winter. He was a good hunter. He had his wife work all through the summer. She dried the meat and the hides.

The wife worked all summer, wasting nothing. She did whatever her husband told her to do. When it was time to return home, back to Point Hope, the husband told his wife to ready for the trip back. She was told to tie up all the meat and hides into bundles. The wife did as she was told. She got everything ready for their trip back to the village.

They spent their last night at the camp. Early the next morning the husband told his wife that it was time to leave. He told his wife to load the boat. The young woman did as she was told. All the food and hides were loaded onto the boat. All that was left to do was for the two of them to step into the boat. When the boat was ready, the husband invited his wife to walk up the hill with him. "We'll leave right after taking our stroll on the hill."

His wife hesitated, saying, "There's nothing up there. There's nothing to be picked."

The husband however insisted on taking her up the hill. After more persuasion, the wife eventually gave in and walked up the hill with him.

"What are we doing on the hill?" she asked.

"Nothing really," her husband replied.

While walking up the hill, the woman noticed something on top of the hill. When they reached the top, she saw a big, gaping pit. She could hear humming sounds coming up from the pit. The husband told his wife to take a look. "This is your place!" he told her.

"Oh no, no!" The wife had no wish to be in such a place.

The husband had put all kinds of meat into the pit and all through the summer the rotten meat had produced maggots. The husband had been using this place to kill his wives. Year after year, he had been killing them. Point Hope people, however, didn't know that was what he had been doing.

The woman insisted that she didn't want to stay in such a place. She wanted to return home. She started to run but her husband chased after her, trying to seize her. For a long time, the two of them ran around the pit. The wife, perspiring heavily, began to feel as if she was going to faint. The husband was perspiring too from the chase, but he was a man and had plenty of energy. The poor woman grew weaker and weaker as she tried her best to flee from her husband. Finally he seized her and dragged her to the pit.

The wife tried to stop her husband. "If I had known you'd do this to me, I wouldn't have followed you. Is that why you always returned home without your wife? Is this how you did away with your wives? I want to go home," she tried to tell him.

But the wicked man wouldn't listen. He only wanted to drop her into the pit.

The wife got weaker and weaker, trying hard to hold on to her husband. Her hands grew weak. The husband fought, wanting to push her into the pit. There was no ledge for her to try to climb up. Unable to hold on any longer, her hands finally let go, and she dropped into the pit. The husband had been using this pit to kill women.

The husband was definitely demented. He took off and returned to Point Hope. As he was arriving, he could be heard crying. He was grieving. The villagers had no knowledge of what he had done. He told them that he had lost his wife and that she had got sick and passed away. The parents of the young woman took her husband into their home. The family tried to keep the memory of their daughter and sister alive through her husband. They believed that their daughter had really gotten sick and passed away. They didn't know the truth.

Thus the family continued to live together until fall arrived. The sea froze. During fall, the mother began to make new clothing for her sons and also for her son-in-law. She made them from the hides her dead daughter had prepared.

One night while spending the evening together inside the house, the mother was as usual busily making the clothing. After a while the rest of the family, her husband, her sons, and her son-in-law, felt drowsy and retired to bed. The mother, however, continued with her sewing.

All of a sudden her ears picked up a sound. At first she couldn't tell what the sound was. She continued to listen. Soon the sound came closer and she could hear it plainly. She began to recognize it as that of her dead daughter. The sound was that of a woman crying and calling out for her mother.

"Mother, my husband who is living with you dropped me into a pit of maggots! I can't come back to be with you. I'm not allowed to return home. I wasn't sick and died. My husband who is living with you dropped me into a pit of maggots. Other women before me were all dropped into that pit too!"

She was sobbing as she was telling her mother the story. The rest of the family woke up and understood what she was telling. She told them she had to go back and that she came only because she wanted to give them the facts. She wanted her parents to know how she was treated.

The husband continued to lie. He insisted that he could never think of doing what she said. "She really got sick and died," he kept repeating to his wife's family.

But the family had already heard the words of his victim.

The two brothers jumped up and seized their brother-in-law. The brothers killed their sister's murderer on the spot. Afterwards, they felt bad because murder was what that man did to their sister.

The Wife with a Jealous Husband

Nora Paniikaaluk Norton

~~~~~~

This is another story about a dysfunctional family. Here a husband's insane jealousy and mistreatment of his wife caused her anguish and finally drove her to commit suicide. The remark made by the storyteller at the end of the story tells about the stand she took on the issue.

RECORDED IN SELAWIK, SEPTEMBER 9, 1968

~~~~~~

AFTER LISTENING TO THE STORIES, I'M GOING TO ADD ANOTHER STORY. I'm telling stories about Point Hope because my husband was born there. Regretfully I hadn't learned all the stories he had told when he was still alive.

The people of Point Hope have game animals they catch during the spring-time—the bowhead whales. During that time of the year, Point Hope men would be out on the ice hunting the whales. In the past, after the whale hunting was done and the whaling season was over with, several boats would leave Point Hope for Kotzebue. Before the white people came and people didn't have yet the means of transportation we have nowadays, Point Hope people would sail in and when there was no wind, they would pull the boat. Those were their methods of traveling those days.

So there were several boats heading toward Kotzebue. Among them were a man and his young wife. They hadn't been married long because they had only one child. The man was very possessive of his wife because he was a jealous person. After the marriage, he bullied her relentlessly. He didn't live with his wife the right way. He was constantly jealous of other men.

The boats heading for Kotzebue reached a location where it was hard to travel any further, so they all stopped and camped near some bluffs. While they were camping, the jealous man bullied his wife again. When they woke up the next morning, again he railed at her because he was jealous of the other men in the camp.

The woman was so afraid of her husband that eventually she lost her mind.

She started to nurse her child (it was the period before we had baby bottles) who was at an age when he could sit up somewhat. That morning she had no breakfast because she was so afraid of her husband. She thought she should leave him. After nursing her child, she placed some clothes around the child, left him sitting where he was, then she went out. Her husband thought she went outside to relieve herself.

The wife took off toward the bluffs. After waiting for a while for her to come back in, the husband went out to check. He saw her climbing up a bluff at a fast pace. He ran after his wife, shouting, "I won't do it again! I won't do it again!"

The husband called her and tried to talk her into coming back. But she would not be caught. She was running fast up a bluff. The young man went after her, trying to catch up with his wife. As he was about to seize her, she turned to face him and smiled.

"I won't do it anymore. I promise I won't do it anymore. I won't bully you. Let's just go home to our child," the husband pleaded.

But his wife was already a broken woman because she had been living continuously in fear. (She shouldn't have endured this. She should have just left her husband to teach him a lesson!) She started to sing and dance. She looked at her husband, then danced backward—toward the edge of the bluff. She fell down the bluff; her body smashed against the rocks. The poor woman's body was smashed!

Other Point Hope people also woke up when they heard a man crying for help. They ran to where they heard him, but it was already too late. The woman had already destroyed herself, leaving her child behind. (I wonder how guilty the husband felt. He had treated her in the manner that drove her to destroy herself.)

The Two Coastal Brothers

Willie Panik Goodwin, Sr.

FIGURE 10 ~ *Willie Goodwin, Sr., Onion Portage, 1968.* PHOTO: DOUGLAS D. ANDERSON.

Willie Panik Goodwin, Sr., was the oldest son of Charlie Ayagiaq Goodwin and Freida Anniviaq Goodwin. Willie spent part of his early years along the Selawik River with his parents and grandparents. Later his parents moved to Candle, Noatak, and finally to Kotzebue. Willie spent the latter part of life in his home on Silliq Point in Kotzebue. An Iñupiaq crew member on the Brown University Archeological Expedition at Onion Portage for two consecutive summers, 1966 and 1967, Willie is fondly remembered as a warm, outgoing person with ready wit, laughter, and humor, who was never short of jokes and stories to tell.

Willie was married to Mary Qaulluq Goodwin, a skilled fisherwoman and a lively and well-known figure among visitors to Kotzebue as the official hostess of the Arctic Tours for a few years. The Goodwins had six children. Willie Goodwin, Jr., was a member of the Northwest Arctic Native Association (NANA) and is currently with the National Park Service in Kotzebue. Another son, Elmer, an Iñupiaq bilingual teacher in the Kotzebue Middle High School, carries on his father's storytelling tradition. He teaches Iñupiaq stories in his classes.

RECORDED AT ONION PORTAGE IN ENGLISH, JULY 3, 1966

OLD PEOPLE USED TO TALK ABOUT THIS STORY. IT'S NOT A TRUE STORY. It's about a hundred years old.

There were two brothers: one brother was living somewhere on the coast and the other brother was living in the Kotzebue area.

At another village, Noatak village, Noatakers had been telling a story about a canyon. They said that in the canyon there was a big lake and in the lake there was a gigantic mouse. Everyone and everything that came into that lake would get swallowed by that gigantic mouse. The mouse even came out of the lake into the big river. Any big boat that came through the main river, to the Noatak, was also swallowed. He was indeed a gigantic mouse!

The two brothers were brave men. Whenever they had to cross the sea from Deering to Kotzebue, they would use only willow as their boat paddles. They were both stout and strong. No matter what happened, they would take care of it and accomplish their task.

The two brothers one day decided to go up the Noatak to the lake. One brother was a good swimmer and the other brother a good fighter in Iñupiaq games and a good hunter. When the two brothers arrived at the lake, one brother told the other, "Go into the water. The mouse has his place somewhere in this lake. He sits, watching the lake." He wanted his brother, the good swimmer, to swim in first, then he would sneak in, right behind his brother.

The plan was that when the mouse saw the good swimmer brother, that brother was supposed to go first into the water and swim across the lake. Both brothers would be swimming, but the other brother, the good fighter, would fight the mouse from behind.

So the two brothers got closer to the mouse, one brother going in front and the other fighting the mouse. During the fight, the mouse slipped into the water and the good fighter brother grabbed it by its tail. You could still see the place where the bank broke off when the mouse slipped off the bank of the lake. He damaged the bank there quite a bit.

That's the way Noatakers used to tell this story. The two brothers did get the gigantic mouse.

Alaaqanaq, the Man with a Little Drum

Nora Paniikaaluk Norton

~~~~~~

The historic context of this legend is some time before the contact period when conflicts, wars, and raids occurred off and on in different settlements. Alaaqanaq, with the little drum that he used as his shield, is a colorful Kotzebue hero. An issue raised in this legend is, in warfare, where does a person's loyalty lie, in the land of his birth or in the land where he is residing? Alaaqanaq, born at Point Hope, married a Kotzebue wife and was living in Kotzebue when the Point Hope raiders attacked. He decided to throw in his lot with the Kotzebue people and helped them defeat the invaders.

RECORDED IN SELAWIK, MAY 7, 1972

~~~~~~

I'M HESITANT TO TELL THIS STORY. I'VE FORGOTTEN PARTS OF THE STORY and can remember only certain parts.

Qikiqtaġruŋmiut, the people of Kotzebue, had attackers from Point Hope coming over to wage war with them. This happened one summer when a boat crossed over from Point Hope to Sisualik. Actually many people came in the boat, but they hid themselves well in order not to be spotted by the Qikiqtaġruŋmiut, the Kotzebue people. Only two men were visible, paddling their boat into Kotzebue.

The people of Sisualik saw the two paddlers. They became suspicious because the boat was riding too low. The hidden men were lying at the bottom of the boat. Only the front paddler and the one manning the rudder were visible. When the boat reached the shore, the raiding party climbed out of the boat and quickly hid in areas that provided them good hiding.

The Kotzebue lookouts quickly sounded the warnings. On the Kotzebue side, only the lookouts were visible. The rest of them took to hiding in the hideouts they had built. With the arrival of the raiders, a battle soon broke out because the raiders came there for that purpose.

A Point Hope man named Alaaqanaq was living in Kotzebue at the time. The probable reason for his residence there was that he had married a Kotzebue wife. He was on the Kotzebue people's side. Alaaqanaq had a small drum in his hand as he was fighting alongside the Kotzebue people. Many Kotzebue people who had exposed themselves to Point Hope people were killed. For a while at the beginning of the battle Alaaqanaq with a small drum hid inside a hideout. Later on he went out, shouting at Point Hope raiders, "Fellow villagers, shoot me! Shoot me!"

Alaaqanaq waved his small drum while challenging Point Hope people. When an arrow came straight at him, he batted it aside with his drum. After a while, the people from Point Hope ran out of arrows. At that point many Kotzebue men still remained hidden. They collected the arrows that had been shot at them. When they figured that the Point Hope raiders had run short of arrows, they came out of their hiding place and killed almost all of the Point Hope men, except two men. Despite the fact that the raiders were his relatives, Alaaqanaq did what he did because he was on the side of the Kotzebue people.

The two surviving Point Hope men, realizing that they were the only two left, quickly made a getaway. As they were fleeing, Kotzebue men gave chase. But the two fleeing men were fast runners.

The Kotzebue men who tried to overtake them shouted, "We won't harm you! We won't harm you! We only want you to carry our message!"

The two fleeing men let the Kotzebue men catch up with them. The two men were then told to return to where they came from and to tell others in their village that they were the only two survivors. After giving the two Point Hope men this message to carry back, the Kotzebue men asked if they needed anything for the trip back. The two probably had no food with them. They were brought back into Kotzebue and were given assurance that they wouldn't be harmed. The two men were probably frightened nevertheless. The Kotzebue people gave them some food, then told them to go back and deliver their message.

(The area above Sisualik, according to my husband, had many shoulder bones and leg bones. He had lived there at that particular location as a child. He said that the bones are the bones of the dead from the battle.)

Many Kotzebue people got killed, but many more Point Hope people died.

Alaaqanaq had won the battle for them. Alaaqanaq couldn't be shot with the arrows. Point Hope people weren't able to have a shot at him and instead got themselves killed. Alaaqanaq hadn't shot a single arrow. He just waved his drum and batted the arrows aside, caroling "Come on! Come on! Shoot at Alaaqanaq."

The Fast Runner

Leslie Tusraġviuraq Burnett

Storyteller Leslie Tusraġviuraq Burnett was born in 1911, a son of
Mike Qanaiyaaqłuk Burnett and Emma Nasraqpiiñaq Cleveland Burnett. Married to Clara (Ballot) Burnett, Leslie had only one daughter,
Mary Mitchell. Leslie led an active subsistence life and was known
during his lifetime as an excellent storyteller. He was an active member
of the Friends Church. For years he had been recording songs that
were sung at annual quarterly meetings of the Friends Church. Leslie
passed away in 1985.

Compare this Iñupiaq version of "The Fast Runner" with the Inuit
version as presented in the famous Zacharias Kunuk film, Atanarjuat,
the Fast Runner (2002). In this Iñupiaq version, the reason the protagonist set out on his quest was to find his sister's murderers. In the
community where he located the murderers, he found a wife who was
also a fast runner.

Recorded in Selawik, February 11, 1972

This story was told to me by James Wells. I'll try to tell it.

There was a family making their living at Iqsiuġvik. Iqsiuġvik is downriver
from Noorvik. It is a creek with a lake by it. A young man from this family one
day went hunting with his younger sister. They went toward the Noatak River.
Since it was windy and cold, he let his sister stay behind in a sheltered area
while he pushed on. He caught his caribou by running after them on foot and
knocking them out with a kind of club he had. After catching several caribou,
he went back to check on his sister whom he had sheltered by the small willows
growing on mountains. But someone had killed her! The young man buried his
sister there, then returned home to their parents.

The young man stayed home for a while. Brooding over what happened to
his little sister, he decided to leave to search for her murderers. He went by his
sister's grave, then continued overland toward the Noatak River. At the Noatak,

he proceeded upriver. Whenever he saw a hill, he would climb up to look around, then would continue on up the river.

Finally he arrived at the house of an old couple who were living by themselves on the Noatak River. He stopped and they invited him to spend the night in their house. The husband told his wife to bring in the food he wanted the young man to have. They themselves ate nothing. They fed the young man all the food they had.

The young man spent the night there, but he had a fitful sleep. He kept thinking about the old couple who had kindly given him the only food they had. Deep into the night he was still lying awake.

Early the next morning he set off to look for caribou to hunt. When he found a herd, he hunted down a number of them and brought them back to the old couple. They were very happy. They appreciated his help for they themselves had no hunter living with them. The young man then told the old man that he was there looking for some men. He told them about his sister who was murdered during the fall while he was hunting caribou.

(I don't like to talk about Noatak people like this. But this story is from a long time ago. I'm not telling this story to make some people feel bad. It's a true story.)

The old man told him, "During the fall I saw three men going by our house up the river. They wore goggles." (James Wells didn't say that they wore glasses. He said they wore goggles. Those were probably made of wood.)

Upon hearing from the old man about three men walking by his place and heading upriver, the young man exclaimed, "*Aarigaa!*" They were the men he was looking for. Finally he was given the information he sought.

The young man hunted more caribou for the old couple, then took off again. He left the old man very happy because he himself was too old to hunt. The young man had given him and his wife food to live on.

Along the way the young man would often climb up small hills to have a look, then followed the river upstream. He spotted no human footprints. He slept anywhere he could. Further up the river, he began to see people's footprints occasionally. He would, once in a while, climb up a hill to have a look, still going up the river. It was winter and it was cold. When he stopped for the night, he didn't use a tent. He would sleep out in the open, probably making a snow cave to spend the night in. As he walked further up the river the footprints he had been following grew more numerous.

One day the young man heard noises of people going about their everyday chores. He could hear dogs and it was getting dark. When he arrived closer to where the sounds came from, instead of walking out in the open, he went through the willow brush so that he wouldn't be seen. There was still some daylight. At a house located somewhat away from the main part of the village he stopped. Inside he found an older couple who informed him that at that moment their son (or sons) was at the *qargi* having fun. The old couple were good hosts and when their son (perhaps two sons) returned home, the son also treated his guest well. He told his guest that they ought to go to the *qargi* together.

The next night the son took his guest to the *qargi* where Noatak people were enjoying themselves. At first the young man didn't join in their games of skills and games of strength. But when the game of high kick got going, he couldn't contain himself. He was able to kick the ball higher than any other men. Two men in the *qargi*, seeing his agility, remembered having seen someone just as agile. He heard the two young men's comment and managed to find out where both came from.

The young man lived with his host family for a while. One day his host told him about a young woman in the village who was a fast runner. Whenever the villagers gathered to play *aqsrautraq* (Eskimo football), this young woman would run shoulder to shoulder with the player who had the ball. The young guest had already seen this young girl. The host told his guest that a young man like him shouldn't live alone without a wife.

"If you want a wife, I'll go and ask for a girl's hand for you."

"*Aarigaa*!" the young man responded. "If you don't mind doing so for me, please ask her."

The young man didn't anticipate that his host would be able to find him a wife. But he remembered the fast runner who could run so well, just like his little sister.

The host returned with a young woman. To his surprise, she was the one he had been thinking about—the fast runner! He took her to be his wife.

I think that the old couple probably had two sons because they hunted caribou together. The two would go hunting and come back with the caribou someone else had hunted down. (When hunters get caribou, they would share their catch. That's what the sons brought home.)

After living there for a while, the young man decided to go hunting with other young men of the village. He wanted to find out how and where they did their hunting, so he went with them. This was after he married the young woman.

So the young man went hunting with other young men. He did everything without having to be told what to do. He knew that his host family would be given their share of the meat. The young man didn't use any weapon to hunt.

He caught the caribou bare-handed. He didn't have to work hard like others to try to get the caribou. But other young men in the hunting group acted belligerently toward the visitor because the latter had married the young woman they themselves desired to marry. They went after the young man, but he was able to escape unharmed and returned home without a fight. He told his wife who saw him running back home that he was just doing his running training.

When the village young men went hunting again, he went along. He was neither afraid of them nor did he tell anyone about their previous attempt to waylay him. He warned his wife not to follow him, should he return running by their house.

Then it happened again. When other young men tried to ambush him, he this time let them shoot at him with their arrows, but he kept himself from being shot. He caught two arrows, shot at him, by catching them in mid-air. When the pursuers came close, he shot back at them with their own arrows. Only one pursuer was left alive to tell other villagers what had happened and what these young men of the village had done.

After having successfully defended himself, the young man turned and ran.

His wife, although told not to follow, was waiting for him outside the house. She saw him coming around the bend of the river and then race along the long stretch of the river. It didn't take him long to cover the distance. Many Noatak people were around at the time. He ran toward the group, then shot a man with an arrow. After that he looked for the other man and shot him too. These were the two men who commented in the *qargi* that he moved just like the person they had killed. Then without looking back, he ran swiftly past the village. No one could keep up with him.

After some distance, the young man still running felt something touching his heels. It turned out to be his wife. She was running after him and was about to catch up with him. She ran as fast as she used to when they were playing football together. But he hadn't wanted her to come along. Had he not told her not to follow? Side by side and all through the evening, husband and wife ran down the Noatak River. The young man scolded his wife for following, but she didn't give up. Together they ran on downriver, passing a bend in the river and stopping for the night only after they were sure no one was pursuing.

The young man who was spared his life told other villagers that the young visitor wasn't the instigator of the fight. It was the other young Noatak men who went after him, tried to kill him, and got killed instead.

Next morning, the young man and his wife continued to run. Just as they were about to run out of food, they arrived at the house of the old couple with whom he had spent some nights on his trip over. The couple fed them. After the meal, they moved on running until they reached the mouth of the Kobuk River, across from Tikiġayuġruaq, Pipe Spit.

The young man returned home. But his parents had already passed away. He had however brought home a woman who was very much like his sister.

Siaksruktaq

John Patkuraq Brown

~~~~~~

Storyteller John Brown was a well-respected elder living on the island in the middle of Selawik. He lived by himself in a log cabin overlooking Selawik River. On many occasions his house was a gathering place for storytelling. Always kind and enthusiastic, John told many old stories and sang a number of songs for me to record.

Siaksruktaq, the protagonist of this story, is a handicapped man, lamed in one leg since childhood, but he could take care of himself. He had a reputation in Kotzebue and in other places he visited as a formidable opponent of braggarts and pompous people.

RECORDED IN SELAWIK, SEPTEMBER 6, 1968

~~~~~~

THERE WAS A MAN IN KOTZEBUE NAMED SIAKSRUKTAQ. WHEN HE WAS A child, the woman who carried him on her back had hurt his leg and that damaged leg didn't develop properly. It stayed like the leg of a child while the other leg grew normally into a man's leg when he became a man.

When this child became a man, he developed a bad reputation. He was known as a dangerous man. Whenever a man acted big, he would fight that person. He had no love for pompous people.

One time a man acted big. Siaksruktaq seized his ears, intending to tear them off. But his fingers slipped and he ended up tearing out that man's eyeballs. When Siaksruktaq was through with the fighting, the other man's eyeballs were hanging down from their sockets. Everyone was afraid of Siaksruktaq. He had no love for pompous people.

Eventually Siaksruktaq married. After his marriage, he'd travel to other villages and behaved similarly in those villages. Sometimes when he heard of a pompous man, he would take that man's wife and keep her. He allowed her to return home only when her husband stopped shooting his mouth off.

When there were no insolent men left in Kotzebue, Siaksruktaq went to Point Hope. When Siaksruktaq walked, he hopped and loped like a dog. Usually he traveled with a dog team. When Siaksruktaq went to Point Hope, the villagers there wanted badly to smoke tobacco. Siaksruktaq shared his tobacco that he had brought along with them. However, one Point Hope man acted big, so when Siaksruktaq offered his tobacco pipe to others, he deliberately bypassed him. The man wasn't pleased. He turned against Siaksruktaq and he wasn't afraid of Siaksruktaq.

When Siaksruktaq finally wanted to depart from Point Hope, this man wouldn't allow him to leave. Siaksruktaq told his family to proceed to the boat first. His family scrambled for the boat and when they were ready to push off into the ocean, Siaksruktaq had his last puff of tobacco. Then he walked away from the Point Hope man, heading for his family. He hopped and loped and when he reached a cliff, leaped onto the boat, landing right on its bow. Flipping onto his hands, he walked on his hands on the rims of the boat. Once he was safely seated, he glared back at his opponent who was glaring balefully at him from the cliff above.

Siaksruktaq returned to Kotzebue during the summer. That whole summer he was uncommunicative and stayed mostly inside the house. He had two wives. When fall arrived, he asked his wives to make waterproof mukluks for him. When he asked them to make clothing for him, he didn't share his travel plan with them. When the new clothing was finished, Siaksruktaq put it on.

The next morning Siaksruktaq walked to the beach, stepped onto a big piece of ice floe, and sat in the middle of it. He left Kotzebue that morning on an ice floe. He floated out into the ocean, taking along no food and with only a knife. He had on the waterproof clothing that his wives made. Siaksruktaq floated out into the ocean. When it turned dark, he couldn't tell where he was heading. Whenever he was hungry, he'd catch something from the sea. He had only seafood to eat.

When Siaksruktaq finally reached land, he tried to catch some sleep. But there were so many polar bears around the area that he wasn't able to sleep soundly. He felt so drowsy that he ended up collecting some dry wood, leaning the branches against each other. Then he slept inside that wood shelter. When he woke up the next morning, he walked the whole day. To his surprise, he found that he ended right back at the same location where he started from in the morning. He was on an island. So Siaksruktaq built a house to live in and killed a polar bear for food.

For two years Siaksruktaq lived on this island. He had no one to talk to. One day after killing a polar bear, he took its cub. He tamed the cub and trained it like training a dog. On the third year, Siaksruktaq began to need to have someone to talk to. Back home in Kotzebue, everyone thought he was dead. Both of his wives remarried. They both thought their husband was dead.

On the third year during spring, Siaksruktaq got ready to leave the island. He made a sled to be pulled by his dog/bear. He made a strap from the polar bear skin and sled runners with the whale bones. When he was finished, he put an extra pair of runners inside the sled. He left the island, traveling in the direction of the sunrise. He camped along the way. Always he traveled in the direction of the sunrise. When the runners of his sled wore out, Siaksruktaq replaced them with the new pair he had taken along. His second pair of runners wore out just when he was reaching land.

Siaksruktaq took a rest on the land he came to. After the rest, he started walking, following the beach line. He walked and walked until he finally came to a place with people. He had made it—to a village. As it turned out, it was the village of Point Hope. Siaksruktaq talked and talked and talked once he found people.

A few days or perhaps weeks later, the people in Kotzebue also heard that Siaksruktaq showed up at Point Hope.

When fall arrived, Siaksruktaq left Point Hope for Kotzebue. There was no ice yet on the water, but Siaksruktaq traveled in the water with his dog/bear swimming. Kotzebue people saw him arriving. He arrived back in Kotzebue on the fourth year of his departure. When he went home, he found that his wives were already remarried. Their new husbands wanted Siaksruktaq to have his wives back, and so Siaksruktaq did.

When Siaksruktaq made it home, he was nice to everyone from then on until his death.

Piñaqtuq Who Had No Wish to Marry

Andrew Nuqaqsrauraq Skin

~~~~~~

> *Storyteller Andrew Nuqaqsrauraq Skin, born in 1914, was a son of Tommy Panitchiaq Skin of Kobuk and Emma Atluk (Goode) Skin of Selawik. He lived at Kuutchiaq when he was a young boy. During his youth, he was one of Selawik's reindeer herders. He helped to establish the Tribal Doctor Program in the NANA area. Andrew's wife was Vera Mitchell Skin, the chief cook of the Selawik School for years until her retirement. They had twelve children. Their oldest son, Louis, is one of the three Iñupiaq bilingual teachers in the Selawik School. Andrew and his wife have both passed away.*
>
> *Andrew told two stories. "Piñaqtuq Who Had No Wish to Marry" is a character type that present-day Iñupiaq women find provocative.*
>
> RECORDED IN SELAWIK, 1972

~~~~~~

AT POINT HOPE, A RICH COUPLE MADE THEIR LIVING. THEY HAD A beautiful daughter. Her parents let her have everything she wanted because they were rich. They were the richest family in Point Hope.

Many men wanted to marry this rich man's daughter, but she wanted none of them. She was known as Piñaqtuq. Her name means "a girl much pestered by men." She was so tired of the men pestering her that she created a task for the men to accomplish. She had someone make her a slippery post, put her ring on top of the post, then set up the post. She made it known that she'd marry whoever managed to get the ring that was on top of the post, no matter how ugly he was. Many men made their attempts, climbing up the post, but none could reach the top.

There was a poor man living in Point Hope. He too decided to try climbing the post. He was so poor that the caribou parka he was wearing had worn down to the skin. It had become leatherlike, with no fur on it. He had no parents. He lived all alone and was quite ugly. The night he decided to climb the post, he waited until others had all gone to sleep. He thought the girl was too beautiful for him and he was too poor for her. He was also very shy. Anyway, he climbed up the post, got the ring, but he didn't take the ring to the girl. He sewed it inside his parka so that others wouldn't see it. In the meanwhile, other men still kept trying to reach the top of the post to get at the ring because he told no one he had already gotten it.

One day, he told one of his friends that he had the ring of the rich girl. The person to whom he told the story was a rich man. The latter asked if he could buy the ring from him, but the orphan refused. The young rich man wanted to buy the ring badly and kept insisting, allowing the orphan no sleep. Finally the orphan let the rich young man have the ring in exchange for a piece of his ear.

The latter brought out a very sharp knife, trying cut off his own ear, but he was faint-hearted. Finally he managed to cut his ear and gave it to the poor orphan. The rich young man waited until his ear was healed before he married the rich girl. When he showed her the ring, she married him.

The orphan dried the rich man's ear, then sewed it onto his parka like the ring.

Once in a while when the orphan was starving, he'd go to the young couple. The rich man would tell his wife to give him food to eat. As he continued to come to see the couple, he grew more and more jealous of his friend.

One day when he came to visit, the wife was combing her husband's hair. The orphan was so overwhelmed with jealousy that he told the woman that he could have been her husband. He told her that he was actually the person who obtained the ring from the top of the post and had sold the ring to the rich man for his ear. He showed her the ear. The woman checked her husband's ears. When she discovered that her husband had one ear missing, she chased him out of the house. After the rich man left, the orphan told her why he had sold the ring.

The woman took clothing from her parents' house for the poor orphan to wear. She let him use her father's hunting equipment. She found that he was a good hunter and was strong in hunting. That was the reason why she set up the post. She wanted to marry a man who would always go hunting so that the family would never starve.

Kinnaq, the Kotzebue Wife

Nora Paniikaaluk Norton

~~~~~~

Before the contact period, polygamy was a normal marriage pattern among the Iñupiat (see also the legends "Siaksruktaq" and "Isiqiak"). Having multiple wives was a functional economic and social arrrangement, enabling the family to gain economic resources from diverse ecological zones and helping to establish a wider kin network beyond their place of residence. "Kinnaq, the Kotzebue Wife" tells how a wife tactfully handled the situation. The storyteller's identifications of Kinnaq at the beginning of the story as a Kotzebue woman and members of her family by names establish Kinnaq as a real-life person.

RECORDED IN SELAWIK, MAY 7, 1972

~~~~~~

I'M GOING TO TELL ANOTHER STORY. THIS IS ABOUT A KOTZEBUE WOMAN who married a man from the Selawik area.

A woman named Kinnaq married a Selawik person. They made their living upriver from Selawik, the current Selawik village. They became parents of a baby boy. When the boy grew older, he followed his father on hunting trips.

Sometime during this period the family moved downriver to live at Kiitaaq. This area where we are living in now was called Kiitaaq. After the move, for most of the winter, the husband was gone. To make a living, the mother, Kinnaq, set her snares to catch rabbits and ptarmigans. The amount of her catch varied from day to day. Her son always accompanied his mother on these snaring trips, for the two of them lived by themselves. Although there were other people living in the area, these people didn't visit Kinnaq.

Then the long days arrived.

One day Kinnaq saw a man coming. He turned out to be her husband. He arrived—with a young woman in his sled. Her husband had married that young woman. That was why he didn't come home when he left during winter.

Kinnaq brought out her choicest food and fed them. She didn't ask, "What are you two up to? What are you two doing?"

When evening arrived, the couple, tired from the travel, went to bed. The husband went to bed with the young woman. Kinnaq said nothing. She acted as if she were the mother of the couple.

After a period of living in this manner, the husband told Kinnaq, "Kinnaq, I shall not leave you without food."

Kinnaq said nothing. It was up to him to choose his way of living.

After some time, the husband took off again—with his new wife. He told Kinnaq that they would come back later on.

When they returned, they had all kinds of food with them. They gave food to the mother and her son. Then the husband went away again—with his new wife.

Kinnaq lived like that for a while. There were people living upriver from her place. When it was the time for them to go downriver, they took Kinnaq along with them. They all traveled to Kotzebue, the village where Kinnaq came from.

Many people from Selawik traveled to Kotzebue. It was a Selawik man who took Kinnaq to be his wife. He brought her up the Selawik River to live. The couple first lived at Inland Lake where the ancestors of Qatluraq had been living. Kinnaq was married to an ancestor of Qatluraq.

Spring arrived and the ice went out. Kinnaq's husband came back. He began to set his fishing net, saying he wanted to catch some sheefish [a fish abundant in the Selawik River]. He said he was hungry for a taste of sheefish. The husband had a qayaq for going around. The young wife was still in bed when he left in his qayaq to check the net.

At some distance from the shore, he accidentally fell into the river. It was also possible that he was pulled overboard by a fish caught in the net. Kinnaq was with him but she didn't know how to save him. She shouted instructions to her husband to hold onto the net and then pull himself ashore. But her husband panicked. He didn't hold onto the net. He disappeared underwater for a while, then came up again. He probably didn't know how to swim. When he was about to lose his strength, he tried to hold onto the net. But he failed and was consequently drowned.

There was another couple living not too far away from them. At the time of Kinnaq's husband's death, the woman who was the wife was already a widow. Kinnaq ran over to the widow to ask for her help. Her neighbor went in her small boat and helped Kinnaq retrieve her husband. Together they got Kinnaq's husband out of the water and dragged him up the bank.

Kinnaq took off his clothes and dried them. That was at the time of the year when clothing could dry fast because it was going toward the summer. As soon as the clothing was dry, Kinnaq put them back on her husband. Then she pulled the body to a spot and set something heavy on top of the body. From time to time, Kinnaq would visit her husband's grave. After some time her husband's body got infested with maggots. Kinnaq would remove those maggots, but it eventually became useless. The flies had laid too many eggs in his body.

Kinnaq endured her loneliness. She remained strong despite her grief. The woman who was also widowed later invited Kinnaq to go to stay with her. The widow took Kinnaq to her house and the two women made a living together. The relatives of Kinnaq's husband, on the other hand, hated her and made no move at all to help her. When they found out that their relative was drowned, they came to Kinnaq's house, but didn't stay long with her.

When the ice in Selawik Lake melted, people from around here would travel to Kotzebue. They sailed or pulled the boat with a rope. Kinnaq decided to leave on a boat going to Kotzebue. When the relatives of Kinnaq's husband heard that she was leaving, they told her not to come back. They told her, "Just go and don't come back." They told her they didn't want her as their relative. That was what they said to their in-law. *Arii*! Kinnaq left with the boat, heading for Kotzebue.

Kinnaq spent that summer and the following winter in Kotzebue. During the second summer probably, another man from Selawik married her. His name was Aakataq. They called him Aakataġruaq. When my husband and I came to live in this area, I met him. I had never met Kinnaq. She had already passed away by then.

In Kotzebue, people from all over would get together, dance, and play the blanket toss. When Kinnaq was still alive, my Grandpa Utiqruuraq would pay her to dance. People from all over the Kobuk River paid money just to see her dance. People came and paid her to dance for them because Kinnaq was so skilled as a dancer.

Kinnaq was Kukik's mother. Aakataq took Kinnaq to live in Selawik. They had together a daughter named Sikik. She was their only daughter. Kinnaq's descendents are Nuiraaq, Kapisruk, Suuyuk. These are all children of Sikik, and grandchildren of Kinnaq. I heard this story from Sikik.

The Lost Husband

John Patkuraq Brown

"The Lost Husband" portrays a range of characters: wicked shamans, kind villagers, a young struggling family, and the protagonist who finally made it home after a series of adventures. The scene where he fought a ptarmigan, studded with rocks, resembles an episode in the Qayaq cycle, "Qayaq Fought the Rock Ptarmigan."

RECORDED IN SELAWIK, SEPTEMBER 6, 1968

LONG AGO IN KOTZEBUE SHAMANISM WAS PRACTICED. VISITORS WHO came into the area would not be able to make it home. One shaman lived at the site where the CAA building is currently located. Another shaman lived at the point of Kotzebue.

The shaman living at the point didn't kill any Qikiqtaġruŋmiut, the Kotzebue people, but he would kill visitors coming into Kotzebue from the outside. This shaman had two polar bears as his dogs. He was physically massive and used to pull in a walrus from the ocean all by himself. However, he didn't bother Kotzebue people.

The other shaman who lived at the site of the current CAA building on the other hand had a pet alligator. He built an enclosure next his house to contain his pet. When the alligator was hungry, he would feed it with the visitors he had killed. When no visitors were around, he would feed it with Kotzebue people. He fed it with healthy, strong boys or young men. The people of Kotzebue were terrified of these two shamans.

One day a young man and his wife came. The people of Kotzebue didn't want to see them killed, but they themselves were terrified of the two shaman killers. The people got together and discussed the problem. Eventually they were able to come up with a plan that would assist the young man and his wife to escape.

Wanting to stay alive, the young man and his wife willingly followed the people's advice. They left Kotzebue in the darkness of the night so that Kotzebue people wouldn't be able to see which direction they had taken. That way the people wouldn't be forced by the shamans to tell their escape route. The couple headed toward land. Neither of them knew the land they were

108 · THE DALL SHEEP DINNER GUEST

heading to. They had no knowledge of where to stay. They walked a long way before stopping to put up a camp. They saw no visitors while camping at that location. When the husband needed to hunt for food, he would sit on a hill, waiting for a game animal to come by.

One day the wife gave birth to a baby boy. The father hunted harder for his family. They continued to live there because they didn't know where else to live. All they had was a camp, not a house.

One day the husband went hunting again and, as usual, he sat on a hill waiting. While sitting there, something happened. When the husband woke up, he found himself in the wilderness somewhere else. He saw a house nearby, but he had no idea where he was. He kept thinking about his wife and his son, but he had no idea where he was. He walked over to the house, the only house visible around there. Inside the house, he saw a couple. They had a daughter. The family gave him food to eat. When it was time to go to sleep, the couple wanted him to go to bed with their daughter. The young man didn't know what to do, so he stayed there.

One day his father-in-law wanted to have some fresh food to eat. He told the young man that there was a ptarmigan on a hill. At that point the young man didn't care what could happen to him. He was missing his wife and his son so badly. So he just left the house to look for the ptarmigan his father-in-law wanted. When he reached the top of the hill, he saw a ptarmigan. The ptarmigan saw him too. It was so afraid of him that it decided to crawl under the snow and turned itself into a weasel. When the young man reached it, he shot it in the head. He had a difficult time getting the ptarmigan because the ptarmigan was at the time of the kill a weasel. The ptarmigan was so big that he was out of breath. But he managed to kill the ptarmigan.

Arriving home, he overheard his father-in-law commenting, "Amazing! My son-in-law thinks all animals are alike!"

When the young man entered the house, the father-in-law acted happy to see him back. He said he had been worrying because the son-in-law was so late returning home. However, the young man didn't bring back the ptarmigan his father-in-law asked for. Later on, his new wife confided to him that her father always behaved like that. After he allowed her to marry a young man, he would send his son-in-law out to hunt for him. None had returned home. The young man understood what his wife was trying to tell him.

The young man stayed there the whole winter. Then one day his father-in-law again asked him to go out to hunt. The young man left. He tried to see if he could recognize something of the land he was in, but found that he could not.

While he was out there, a woman came to him. She wore fox fur clothing. They talked. The woman informed him that her mother wanted to see him.

He followed the girl to her house. When he met her mother, her mother let him eat everything there was to eat. After he was fed, the mother told him she knew who he was. She also told him that his father-in-law ate humans. He would get a husband for his daughter, but never would let his son-in-law live long. She told the young man that his father-in-law was about to make him go out on a hunt again. She told the young man that the father-in-law would let him take along a knife. He had two knives. The young man would be allowed to choose whichever knife he wanted. The girl's mother told the young man to select the older knife. She also told him that the animal he was about to be sent to hunt was extremely dangerous and the beast's foot was the only place he could attack. The young man left her house after the talk and headed home.

The next morning the father-in-law told the young man that he should go to hunt an animal with big feet because he wanted to eat the animal's feet. He told the young man that there was an animal with big feet up on the hill. The young man could choose one of the knives he had in his cache to take along. The young man went to get it. His father-in-law certainly had big knives, he thought as he saw them in the cache.

The young man chose an old knife and took off. He went up a hill and spotted a big animal. But when he took a good look at it, he noticed that the animal had only one foot. He got ready and went toward the animal. As he went closer, he saw that it had flat teeth in its mouth. Instantly, the animal fought back. The young man tried to kill the animal with his knife, but the animal was made of hard rocks. He didn't know where to stab it to kill it. Then he discovered that the animal's ankle wasn't covered with rocks like other parts. Just when he was about to lose his strength, he was able to sever its ankle. The beast fought back no more. It dropped dead. After the animal was killed, he returned home.

The young man continued to live with his new wife.

One year passed.

One day, the father-in-law asked the young man to go to check his fishing net for him. The young man left the house, following his father-in-law's trail. He spotted a trap on the trail but he stepped gingerly over the trap and was able to return home safely. As he was arriving at the house, he overheard his father-in-law saying that his son-in-law wouldn't be coming back. Seeing him entering the house, his father-in-law was quite surprised. However, he told his son-in-law that he had been worrying about his return.

The next day, the husband missed his wife and his son so much that he ceased to care what could happen to him. When his father-in-law asked him to go to check his net for him again, the young man took off, taking along his bow and arrows. When he reached the trap on the trail, he stepped on it and this time he fell into it. The ditch was very deep. He stayed in the ditch for a long time and got very thin. Once in a while his father-in-law would come over to check if he was still down in the trap.

The young man missed his family he had left behind. Down in the trap, he got thinner and thinner. One day he untied a braided sinew from his bow, tied it to an arrow, and shot the arrow. When the arrow caught, he pulled himself up from the ditch. At first he thought the sinew might break, but it held because he had become so thin.

So the young man was able to get out of the ditch. He went back to his father-in-law's house. His father-in-law lied again, saying how much he had been worrying about his son-in-law. His wife fed him food, and, little by little, he regained his health.

One day after he was well again, he stepped out of the house. The girl whom he had met once before came to him again and told him that her mother wanted to have a talk with him. He went to her. When he entered the house, the girl's mother was sitting by the hearth with her back toward him. After her daughter had fed the young man, the mother told him that his family he had left behind had been living in poverty. If he wanted to return home, he was to follow her instructions. She then told him to come back the next morning.

The next morning the young man returned. The old woman told him that after he walked down the hill, he should turn around to see her true identity and that of her daughter. Then he should close his eyes, turn around four times before stepping forward and before opening his eyes again.

The young man did as the old woman had instructed. When he looked back he saw two foxes. Because he did what the old woman had told him, he was able to make it home safely.

Once the young man arrived back home, he went hunting and took the seals he had hunted to the foxes. They had asked him to get them some seals. The young man was so happy to see his family again that he gave the foxes many, many seals.

The Cannibal Child

Nora Paniikaaluk Norton

~~~~~~

> *The figure of a cannibal features in many versions of the Qayaq cycle.
> It appears also in the following two stories in different forms: as a child
> in the first story, and as an arm without a body in the second story.
> "The Cannibal Child" legend appears to have provided a guideline for
> a family practice in the Norton family. Whenever they make* akutuq
> *(creamed fat made with diced caribou fat mixed with berries and seal
> oil), they always make sure to dab a little bit on their child's lip.*

RECORDED IN SELAWIK, MAY 7, 1972

~~~~~~

FLORA CLEVELAND HAS TOLD HER STORY. I'M GOING TO TELL A SHORT story.

There was a family living in Kotzebue. They had a daughter. The daughter married and gave birth to a child.

Whenever the family had a craving for *akutuq*, the women would prepare the *akutuq* dish. When the dish was ready, each would help himself to a portion. On that occasion it was customary for Kotzebue and coastal people to dab a little bit of *akutuq* on their child's lips. (My husband was from that area. That's why I learned this story well from him. In our family, whenever we make *akutuq*, my father always dabbed some on the lips of the child in the family.)

Near the area where the family was living there was a lagoon with a bridge spanning the narrowest part of the lagoon. By crossing the bridge, one could go on to the hills on the other side of the lagoon.

After some time, the family had a craving for *akutuq* again. The grandmother made the *akutuq*, but this time she totally forgot to dab it on the lips of the child, her grandson.

After dinner and after spending the evening together, the whole family went to sleep. They lived in a house with two bedrooms. This style of house is called *akiḷḷiġiilik*. During the night while they were all asleep, the grandfather woke up. He heard a sound. He looked around and heard a sound of someone eating coming from his daughter's area. The sound was that of an adult eating something. He got up and went to investigate.

In the first light of the day just breaking through the window, he saw a small child. It had a mouth so huge that it stretched from ear to ear. The child was eating his mother, beginning with her breasts. He was eating her and she was dead. He woke up his wife and his son-in-law, shouting, "Hurry! Leave the house quickly!"

They put on their parkas and mukluks and quickly ran out of the house. They all ran for the bridge to try to cross over to the hills on the other side.

After eating his mother, the child went after other members of the family. He hopped, going after them. He could swallow big things when he opened his mouth because his mouth was so huge. As the family was running across the bridge, the child reached the edge of the bridge. When the child set his feet on it, they all grabbed the bridge and pulled. The child fell into the water. He came up several times, but ultimately he disappeared under the water.

To this day the lagoon is said to be haunted. People would see things, and no one would live alone around that area.

One time my husband had to bring his boat over to moor in this lagoon because huge waves were beating in the bay in front of Kotzebue. He was afraid that his boat might be swallowed by those big waves if he moored it in the bay. Later on, he went to the lagoon to check his boat and to bail out water from the bottom of the boat. There he heard someone getting into the boat. He looked around, thinking someone had followed him there, but there was no one.

It is said that that lagoon has someone living in it.

The Arm

John Patkuraq Brown

RECORDED IN SELAWIK, SEPTEMBER 6, 1968

MANY PEOPLE MADE A LIVING NEAR THE OCEAN. THIS GROUP OF PEOPLE lived in a village located between Point Hope and Kotzebue.

During winter when there was nothing else to do, the villagers would dance all night—for many nights. They would dance and dance in the community hall till the next morning arrived. While older people assembled for their dances in the community hall, the young people would get together too in one of the houses and hold their own dances. They too stayed up all night. Among the young group was an orphan who was more mature than the other children. Like their parents, the children danced every night.

One night during the dances the orphan happened to step out of the house. While standing outside, he heard something coming in from the ocean. He went back into the house and found the children still enjoying themselves. He stepped out again, and there it was again—that noise. This time it was louder and he could hear a human voice. The voice knew his name. It sang and approached closer and closer. The children in the house finally heard the voice too, but they couldn't get out of the house and flee to their parents. When the thing was at the door, the children were so terrified that they huddled together in one corner of the house.

The orphan tried to find a place to hide too. He hid above the door, lying on top of the door in order to see what was coming through. When the door opened, an arm came in. It was a human arm. It entered, then it started to grope around for things. When it came to a child, it would grab and eat the child. The Arm ate all of the children like that. It had a mouth on the palm of the hand. It ate all the children inside the house except the orphan. When the Arm went toward the orphan, it almost got him. But fortunately, it went above him, missing him, and not touching him. When it finished eating the children, it went away.

The orphan ran to the children's parents after the Arm left. There were no childhood friends left in the village for the orphan to play with or to eat with. He kept thinking about his little friends. When he realized that he could never forget them, he began to make a weapon from a piece of stone. He sharpened his weapon carefully.

When winter arrived, the orphan placed the stone weapon he had sharpened above the door. The stone was placed in such a way that it would drop down if the Arm were to come through the door again. When it was close to the time when the Arm came into the house the year before, the orphan collected inside the house the little children who had grown up somewhat since then. There, inside the house, he kept watch for the Arm.

One night when the orphan stepped out, again he heard it coming. He got ready and told the children not to be afraid. When the Arm arrived close, the orphan was ready for it. He pushed down the hidden stone when the Arm came through the door. The stone fell on the Arm and cut it off at the wrist. The wrist moved around the floor, but after a few minutes, it stopped.

The children left the house to tell their parents what happened and the parents learned who had eaten their children the year before.

This arm was a human arm. It had a big hand with a mouth on the palm of the hand!

Half Squirrel and Half Beaver

John Patkuraq Brown

~~~~~~

Strange creatures, threatening and dangerous to humans, abound in Inuit and Iñupiaq stories. The creature in this legend is a cross between a beaver and a squirrel. Another Iñupiaq version of this predator story can be found in Lore of the Iñupiat: The Elders Speak, *vol. 1 (Mendenhall et al. 1989:169–173). It was told by Truman Cleveland of Ambler and was named "The Forbidden Lake." Another version, "The Half-Marmot Half-Beaver Creatures," told by Robert Cleveland, appears in* Stories of the Black River People *(Cleveland 1980:105–111). Storyteller John Brown referred to this story by the name I am using here.*

RECORDED IN SELAWIK, SEPTEMBER 6, 1968

~~~~~~

THERE WERE THREE MEN TRAVELING IN THEIR QAYAQS ON THE KOBUK River.

When the men arrived at a narrow part of the river, they decided to go up a hill. On the hill they found a lake with all sorts of animals in it. They saw animals that looked half squirrel and half beaver near the lake. The third man told the others not to bother the animals, but his two friends wouldn't listen. They kept chasing them. They were having a lot of fun chasing. The third man did no chasing.

When the two men quit the chase, they went out into the lake in their qayaqs. Both men who had chased after the half-squirrel and half-beaver animals were killed by the animals they had chased. The animals ate them. The third man was, however, left unharmed.

So at all times people are told never to go to this lake. Even today. Anyone who goes there might get eaten by these half-squirrel and half-beaver animals. Once two men went up to the lake. They saw willows and trees being cut down. After having seen that themselves, the two men believed the story.

The Legend of Magic

Leslie Tusraġviuraq Burnett

Christianity and proselytizing by missionaries in northwest Alaska have obvious influence on the theme of this legend, told by a parishioner of the Selawik Quaker Friends Church. Here God's power has been presented as more efficacious than shamanic power.

RECORDED IN SELAWIK, FEBRUARY 11, 1972

AT A TIME IN THE PAST WHEN THE MISSIONARIES HADN'T COME IN YET, a group of people went hunting in the ocean. They were hunting in a walrus boat with several men in the boat.

When the hunters reached a location with a lot of ice pans floating, a strong gust of wind hit. The hunters had to pull the boat up on an ice pan. The wind blew so strongly that it made the ice pan float to a location where no land was in sight. The hunters were at a loss of how to find their way home. As that piece of ice pan grew smaller, they grew more and more anxious about finding a passage home.

One by one, the men attempted their magic, but none was of any help. One man in the group knew not a single bit of magic and the rest of the group disliked him. He himself was also afraid of them. That man walked away from the group and started thinking. He thought about the creator of the land, the sky, and other things on earth. He walked to a cliff and called out loud, "Whoever created all things on earth, please help us."

When he walked back to the group of hunters, nobody talked to him.

A while later, the ice pan the men were on started to move toward land. When the ice pan reached the shallow water, it stopped moving. The men pushed their boat onto the beach and were able to return home.

When the boat was off the ice pan, the ice pan floated away with the wind.

Tomitchiałuk and His Brothers

John Patkuraq Brown

~~~~~~

> *The actions that transpire in this story suggest Iñupiaq ideals of sibling and marital relationships. Brothers should work together and support each other instead of quarreling with each other. Wives should remain loyal to their husbands despite their long absence. In this legend the brother and the wife who did not veer from these cultural norms found fulfillment and community approval. The legend provides the only source available on the Iñupiaq ritual "to be touched by others."*

RECORDED IN SELAWIK, SEPTEMBER 7, 1968

~~~~~~

THERE WERE FOUR KOBUK RIVER MEN WHO WENT OUT HUNTING DURING the summer.

They walked to the north by way of the main trail used by the Kuuvaŋmiut [Kobuk River people]. But before they were able to reach their destination, it turned foggy. Having no visible landmark to guide them, one man got dispirited.

He decided to split and took off by himself in another direction. He left his brothers and walked in the direction where there was no fog. The other brothers trudged on even though they had no idea where they were heading. They could no longer recognize the landscape. Even when the fog lifted later on, they still couldn't recognize where they were.

The three brothers trudged on. When winter was near, they built a house to live in. During the winter while making clothing for themselves they could hear wolverines outside, trying to dig their way in. The wolverines wanted to come in to stay inside the house too.

They lived like that for a long time. One day when the brothers were on the trek again they came across a group of people. At the time the three Kobuk River brothers had no idea where they were. When the two groups met, their greetings to each other were less than friendly. A man from the other group shot an arrow at the brothers. Fortunately the older Kobuk River brother turned his chin aside in time and escaped being shot. But the arrow took his scarf. The brother who was shot reached into his parka and took out a wing feather of a goose.

The other group of people calmed down somewhat. Finally when they came face to face with the three brothers, they said they were Kuuvaŋmiut.

Strangely, the two groups of Kuuvaŋmiut couldn't understand each other's language!

A muscular man from the other group pointed toward the sun. He made a moving motion with his hand the way the sun traveled in the sky, saying, "*Anayugaa, anayugaa, anayugaa*," then mimicked the sun disappearing over the horizon. The man was trying to tell the brothers that the Kobuk River was in the direction of the setting sun.

The three brothers walked toward the direction of the setting sun. They still weren't able to recognize the landscape. They continued walking in that direction for a long time.

One night they stopped to make their camp for the night. One of the brothers had in his backpack a small wolverine hide he carried for crisis situations. He took out the hide.

"Wolverine hide, point us to the Kobuk River!"

He then threw the hide a long distance, beyond anyone's reach.

The next morning, they walked in the direction the head of the wolverine hide was pointing. Every night the wolverine hide would again be thrown in the same manner. They continued to travel like that all summer. The only time they stayed in one spot was when they needed to make new clothes. There they would build themselves a house.

One morning, two of the brothers started to argue with each other. They weren't able to agree on anything. During all those years of living and traveling together the brothers never had disagreements, but that morning they argued and argued. The third brother just listened, saying nothing. Then he just strapped on his backpack and took off in another direction. He no longer wanted to travel with his brothers. He no longer cared what happened.

The lone man traveled for several days. The other three brothers were in the meantime also hiking along somewhere in the countryside.

The lone brother finally arrived at a knoll at the end of a creek. He sat down, looked around, but couldn't recognize the landscape. He kept scrutinizing every part of his surroundings when gradually he began to recognize the headwater of the Natmaktuġiaq. For a moment he felt sad and lonely. He remembered his parents and his wife living at the mouth of a creek, branching out from this head-water. Hitching his backpack, he walked back to the place where he came from.

Even though home was still some distance away yet, he wanted to do some hunting before heading home. He also had to raft some distance. He started to hunt and packed the meat to take back home. At a location where he could build a raft, he built it and rafted down the creek. He knew then that he would be able to reach the Kobuk River.

Coming around a bend at the mouth of the river, this brother all of a sudden came across a group of people. While he was debating with himself whether to draw out his weapon or to jump into the water, a man jumped on him from the riverbank.

The latter had recognized him. He took hold of this brother and led him ashore. The group had been camping at that place all through the summer. The man who had jumped on him later left in a qayaq to tell this brother's parents living downriver about his return. The other campers kept the brother at the camp.

All through the years, during his three-year absence, the young man's wife had been living with his parents. The whole family came upriver to welcome the young man, Tomitchialuk. While the people were all excited over the young man's return, a qayaq arrived from upriver with the news that two of the brothers Tomitchialuk had left behind had also returned. The messenger also said that the two brothers' wives had already remarried. All of the belongings of these brothers had been buried because everyone thought they were both dead. Tomitchialuk's family living above the Ambler River had, on the other hand, continued to live in the same place for the past three years waiting for Tomitchialuk's return. The family was finally reunited.

One day, Tomitchiałuk announced that he planned on going downriver to Kotzebue in spring. When he arrived there, he would undergo the ritual "to be touched by others."

When spring arrived, Tomitchiałuk traveled downriver with a group. After reaching Kotzebue, he went across to Sisualik. The people of Sisualik heard that Tomitchiałuk was being brought across the bay from Kotzebue. When Tomitchiałuk's group arrived, many people were waiting for him on the shore.

Tomitchiałuk, a knife in his hand, jumped off his boat. The people gave him passage to come ashore. No one seized Tomitchiałuk because he had a knife in his hand as a weapon. When Tomitchiałuk spotted a good firm ground, he threw his knife a long way from everyone. At that point people rushed at him. Some tried to protect him; others tried to beat him. Poor Tomitchiałuk was beaten!

After some beating, they let him be. They didn't kill him because they knew why he decided to come downriver. They had all heard that Tomitchiałuk had decided to come downriver for this very purpose—"to be touched by others." He had used his knife only as a means of getting through the crowd. He didn't use his knife on others. He discarded it after he passed through the crowd.

Tomitchiałuk who went through this ritual lived a long life. The other two brothers didn't; they died early. The main reason was that their possessions had already been buried. The people at Sisualik had all thought that all the four brothers were dead because none had made their way back during the past three years. Actually they were still alive.

Tomitchiałuk later went back up the Kobuk River and lived for a long time. The third brother who first left the group was later found beaten up. He had made his decision against his own brothers.

The four brothers were away for three winters. The dried wolverine hide knew the direction back to the Kobuk River. It was probably a spring-caught hide. Or maybe it was not.

Isiqiak

Robert Nasruk Cleveland

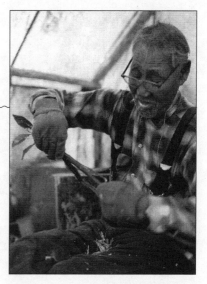

FIGURE 11 ~ *Robert Cleveland making a mudshark trap, Onion Portage, 1968.* PHOTO BY WANNI W. ANDERSON.

Robert Nasruk Cleveland, the storyteller, is one of the three Kobuk Cleveland brothers: Robert Nasruk, Johnny Inuqtuaq, and Charlie Qupilġuuraq. Born toward the end of the 1800s, Robert, as a young boy, had personally participated in the historic Sisualik trading meets where Iñupiat from coastal and riverine settlements met each spring to trade. A prolific storyteller, Robert spent a great deal of his growing-up years in a qargi *where he acquired his Iñupiaq subsistence skills and stories from the elders. He lived most of his life around Black River, a tributary of the Kobuk, and moved to live in Shungnak after the village was established. Robert's wife was Flora Sanmiġana (Copper) Cleveland from Qala. They had thirteen children.*

Robert Cleveland was honored posthumously in 2004 as the "Iñupiaq Storyteller" in the Alaska Indigenous Literature Celebration and the Native Educator's Conference in Anchorage.

RECORDED AT ONION PORTAGE, JULY 30, 1967

THIS IS NASRUK, WITH THE ENGLISH NAME ROBERT CLEVELAND. I'M going to tell this story at Onion Portage. With the first story I just told ["The Woman with Long Hair"], I couldn't say where the story came from.

There was a man named Isiqiak. He lived at a place called Aanaruaġik. He had two wives.

One fall season after the ground was frozen, Isiqiak told his wives that he wanted to go to Uluksruq Mountain to find some *uluun* [new slate] for making a new saw blade for cutting firewood. His wives consented, so he took off the next morning.

Isiqiak started up the Shungnak Creek. As he was approaching the waterfall, he heard voices. It sounded like some people were having fun playing some kind of games. Since it was turning dark, he wasn't able to see too far ahead. He came around a bend, treading on the edge of the fresh ice instead of walking in the middle of the river. He thought that by walking that way he would be able to hide quickly if he was spotted.

As Isiqiak was coming around the bend, he heard the people shouting, warning each other of someone approaching. "Hey, someone is down there!"

The people playing the game turned to look, but Isiqiak quickly hid among the thickets. Failing to spot him, they all ran toward the location where he was last seen. Many, many people were assembled there and they were all having fun playing *aqsrautraq* [Iñupiaq football]. They ran to the location where Isiqiak made his appearance, but his footprints were obscured and they couldn't find anybody.

A man named Tulugaq (Raven) was questioned.

"Tulugaq, where did you see this man?"

"I saw him around here. Somehow he simply disappeared."

"You're lying again. You are a liar!" they told Tulugaq.

"I didn't lie. I really saw a man. Maybe he's hiding somewhere. Or maybe he has started to walk back to the place where he comes from. I ran here as soon as I saw him. I didn't see where he went. I wasn't really keeping my eyes peeled for where he was going."

The people continued to search, but they weren't able to find the person Tulugaq had seen. They called Tulugaq names, pushed him, and shoved him. They also beat and kicked him. Although Tulugaq was a grown-up man, this rough handling made him cry. They beat him because he made them believe there was a man there. After a while, they left him. Tulugaq was still crying when they took off without him. Alone, Tulugaq made a song which he sang. I'm going to sing it:

Where, oh where is the man I saw?
Where is the man who disappeared?
I, i, i, i [sobbing sound].

Tulugaq was crying while singing. He sang the song, pleading the man he saw to take pity on him because he actually did see a man there. But nothing happened.

So Tulugaq sang his song again and started walking along the edge of the river. He should have gone into the woods to look, but, once again as usual, Tulugaq was afraid. (I'm going to sing the song again because I want people who are listening to this story to know how the song was sung. This was how Tulugaq sang the song.)

Where, oh where is the man I saw?
Where is the man who disappeared?
I, i, i, i.

Tulugaq was sobbing while singing the song.

The rest of the people went home. They had stopped playing football.

Sitting among the thick brushes and listening, Isiqiak felt sorry for the sobbing man. He came out to meet the crying man. Then together the two of them headed back to Tulugaq's home. While walking slowly home, Tulugaq informed Isiqiak that a large group of people from all over would assemble for a large feast. They would gather in a large house. Tulugaq told Isiqiak that the people there were always happy to organize a large gathering. The two of them should attend it, Tulugaq said.

"When the people saw you, you went into hiding. They accused me of lying and beat me. But I'm going to take you there so that they will all see you. After the feast they'll have many Iñupiaq games of skill. These games would be fun to watch. And that's where I'm going to take you."

At the large house, even from outside the house, they could hear lots of voices inside. It was also brightly lit inside.

Tulugaq took Isiqiak inside the house. When they climbed up through the entrance, the people again liked their Tulugaq because they realized that Tulugaq hadn't lied to them. They had beaten him up unfairly. Perhaps they were sorry for having beaten him up.

The people in the house seated Tulugaq on a high bench above the entrance. People had high benches in their houses in the old days. They were made as seats. Tulugaq looked around. Food was being served—to everyone in the house. There was plenty of sumptuous food including berries, Iñupiaq potatoes, and all sorts of food gathered during the summer. He took a portion of each kind of food to eat.

After everyone was through with the meal, they began playing Iñupiaq games. They played Iñupiaq games inside the house. The games were very entertaining, a lot of fun to watch. After a while Isiqiak began to feel drowsy. He made himself comfortable, placing his arms inside his parka. He then lost consciousness.

It was during the fall when Isiqiak went into the house. He didn't know what happened afterwards. But when he was conscious again, he could hear the "drip, drip, drip" of the water dripping down from the skylight window onto the floor. He could hear the sound of dripping water. He heard no other sounds and saw no one else around. Everybody was gone. He thought about the large crowd that assembled there before he went to sleep the night before. He listened some more to the drip, drip sound of the water. It was the skylight window thawing and dripping. When he arrived during the fall—when the river was also frozen—there had been no dripping in this house. Now, somehow, there were drippings in the house.

For a while, Isiqiak watched the water dripping. Then slowly he put his arms into the sleeves of his parka, intending to go back to sleep. That's what he always did before he went to sleep. After a while Isiqiak woke up. But he found himself still seated on a bench. And this time when he looked beside him, he saw a seagull. Its neck was hunched in. Isiqiak watched what the seagull was doing. He turned to look at his other side, and lo and behold, there was another seagull. There were two seagulls, one on each side of him!

One of the seagulls spoke. "You've awakened just at the right time. After you've eaten this trout for breakfast, you can leave here." The seagull then added, "Last summer while I was flying over your two wives, one of your wives had given me this trout. You can have this trout for breakfast. You can leave here after eating this fish for breakfast."

The seagull gave the trout to Isiqiak. Isiqiak ate the trout and ate it slowly. When he finished his breakfast, he stepped down from the bench he was sitting on.

One of the seagulls told Isiqiak as Isiqiak was about to leave the house, "We're about to take off from here too. It won't be long before we leave too."

When Isiqiak went outside he saw that the sun was rising. He also noticed that the snow that had frozen during the night began to melt. He left the house and saw the sun high up in the sky. Spring had arrived. Isiqiak had fallen asleep during the fall. When he woke up, spring was there.

Isiqiak started to walk home. He walked down to the river, then followed the river.

His wives happened to be downriver, past a long stretch of the river. They saw him coming from the distance, for both of them had been on the lookout for him all winter since his disappearance. Seeing him coming downriver, both rushed to meet him. When they reached him, each went to stand by his side. The two women had finally found their lost husband. They took him home.

Once home, Isiqiak told his wives the story of his adventure. He told them how he had come across a group of people. He told them how he went into a house, planned to spend the night there, and the people had made him fall asleep. He told them there were many people and that they were playing many, many games. He had slept and then walked back home when he woke up, he said. He had slept all winter. And, upon waking up in that house, he had seen two seagulls.

This is how the story of Isiqiak was told. Isiqiak had returned home. He had slept like those creatures that sleep all through winter, like the black bears and the marmots. He had slept all winter and left the house he had slept in when spring arrived. And that is the story of Isiqiak.

Niġlaaqtuuġmiut and Kuukpigmiut

Nora Paniikaaluk Norton

This is a Selawik legend that tells about two groups of people who lived in the areas that are now part of the present Selawik village. The conflict between the two groups attests to the significance of viable subsistence sites and how two groups were willing to fight over the rights to a fishing ground. This is the legend that was told to my husband and me as the current inhabitants of the Niġlaaq, the creek that connects the Niġlaaqtuuq to the Selawik River. The storyteller wanted to tell us who had lived around there before us, now referred to around Selawik also as Niġlaaqmiut. The legend also helped us to understand why an elderly Selawik woman sought our permission before she put her fishnet on the river beside our house and offered us a fish from her net.

RECORDED IN SELAWIK, MAY 8, 1972

THIS IS A STORY ABOUT THE SELAWIK AREA.

A long time ago the terrain around here was quite different. Across the river at Niġlaaqtuuq there was a group of people making a living. There were several families living there. Niġlaaqtuuq at that time had a good slough. It was deep and it was a good place to fish. In spring, as soon as the water flowed again the people living there could set small fishnets. They would catch many fish. They would catch many fish especially during fall. That's why this group of people lived there.

There was another large group of people living at Kuukpik. When the Niġlaaqtuuġmiut, that is the Niġlaaqtuuq people, set their fishnets, the Kuukpigmiut would be envious.

One day a shaman got angry. He made a large piece of sod float up the slough. From then on, the slough that had been deep became shallow. During the spring flood, the slough would be deep, but as soon as the water receded, the slough turned shallow. It turned so shallow during the summer that it could be walked on as though one were walking on land. That particular incident occurred because people were fighting over it. Every woman liked to set her fishnet there. I heard the story about this place from another person. The Kuukpigmiut were people living also along a slough, another slough.

That's what happened to the Niġlaaqtuuq. It had been a good slough for fishing at one time. If these two groups of people hadn't been fighting over it, it might still be a good fishing place nowadays. They used to be able to fish there especially in the fall when the fish swam out of the slough. In the fall, after staying in the lakes all through summer, the fish would come down the slough from the lakes. When a fisherwoman fished during that time of the year, she could catch a lot of fish. That's what I heard from the storyteller. The story is probably longer, but I had to do something and was interrupted during the listening.

After some time, the people in the area started to fight each other. They were shooting at each other with arrows. From that time on, the river in front where the fighting took place was called "Siktagvik." They shot at each other, thus the name "Siktagvik." A long time ago before Selawik was settled as a village, there were many old graves. I hadn't known before why the river was called "Siktagvik" until I heard this story.

Akpaġialuk of Iqsiuġvik

Nora Paniikaaluk Norton

~~~~~~

The following twelve legends told by Nora Norton, Robert Cleveland, John Brown, and Wesley Woods are grouped together in this section as warfare legends describing group conflicts or personal conflicts that subsequently led to skirmishes, raids, destructions, and killings. Three stories with Aagruukaaluk as the main character are versions of the same story as told by three different storytellers. Which version is closer to the historical fact cannot be determined since no written historical record of the happening exists.

What becomes clear is that the historicity of the period was marked as much by friendship and marriage alliances as by warfare between Iñupiaq groups or between Iñupiat and Koyukon Athabascans. Close connections across groups did occur beyond economic trading and casual meetings. What occurred as a positive or a negative relationship depends on the particular historical moment, a particular group decision, and, at times, on the actions of a particular individual. In the first story, for example, a marriage alliance was formed when Akpaġialuk's son married a woman from the Seward Peninsula. But later when the people of the Seward Peninsula developed a dislike for Akpaġialuk and decided to go after him, the skirmish was launched.

RECORDED IN SELAWIK, DECEMBER 18, 1971

~~~~~~

I HEARD THIS STORY FROM MY FATHER. HIS NAME IS SUUĠUUNUUQUU. His father's name is Saaluq. I'm one of their descendents. This story I heard from my father is probably part of a much longer story. I'm going to tell it as I know it. This short story tells what happened to the Siiḷaviŋmiut [the Selawik people].

Upriver from here, there are two small hills. The people of Selawik will recognize them when they hear about them.

A man named Akpaġialuk used to live close to these hills at Iqsiuġvik. He lived there a long time ago. He liked everyone to do what he wanted. Those who tried to harm him found that he couldn't be beaten. Perhaps he had some kind of power that shielded him from harm. Whenever he was shot at, the wound would heal by itself. The people of Seward Peninsula were also after Akpaġialuk. Although he was pursued by his foe, Akpaġialuk managed to live a long life.

One time while Akpaġialuk was living at Iqsiuġvik and the days were getting longer, he went to fish at Selawik Lake. While fishing, Akpaġialuk grew aware of the presence of some men on land. He figured that most likely the men were the Seward Peninsula people. He saw them coming toward him. They probably went first to his house, but when they couldn't find him there, had followed his tracks to Selawik Lake.

Akpaġialuk got up, acting as if he were crippled. He pretended he had something wrong with his leg. He then took off toward the middle of Selawik Lake. He continued to act like a cripple. The raiders were happy. They thought that Akpaġialuk had turned weak—that's why he moved like that. When they got closer, they took a shot at Akpaġialuk. But Akpaġialuk was one of these men who couldn't be shot. They couldn't shoot him to kill him.

Akpaġialuk wasn't afraid. He wasn't crippled. He went after the raiders. And when the raiders ran out of arrows, he abandoned his cripple act, and, picking up the arrows that were shot at him, shot them back at the raiders. There were one or two persons he didn't kill. (The people of long ago didn't kill everyone. They would leave a person alive to serve as the "messenger" of the news.) So, the raiders didn't succeed in killing Akpaġialuk.

The way it was told in the story, Akpaġialuk's son had married a woman from Seward Peninsula. When summer arrived, Akpaġialuk's son went trekking. At the time Akpaġialuk's daughter-in-law had already given birth to a child. While Akpaġialuk's son was away, Akpaġialuk, his daughter-in-law, and his grandson were the three persons home. Akpaġialuk went out to gather wild rhubarb and stored it in his underground cellar where it wouldn't rot. He was quite worried about raiders because he was aware that many people were trying to kill him.

One evening, Akpaġialuk's daughter-in-law stepped out of the house with her son. The walls of Akpaġialuk's house were built in a way that he could look out and see things. During the summer he also dug a tunnel next to his house as a hiding place. While the daughter-in-law was outside carrying her son on her back, Akpaġialuk kept his eyes on her. He saw her smiling at someone behind the house. Akpaġialuk realized then and there that the raiders were nearby. He suspected that they might strike sometime during the night, so he was on full alert that evening and didn't step out of the house.

When it turned dark, the daughter-in-law put her sleeping son down on the bedding. However, she didn't remove her clothes before going to bed. Neither did she take off her parka. She only wrapped her child and then lay down beside him on the bedding. Akpaġialuk realized what was happening. He didn't fall asleep. As his daughter-in-law was sleeping, he could hear people outside. Akpaġialuk went into the prepared tunnel and disappeared. The raiders entered the house, looked for him, but they weren't able to locate him. They searched for a long time but they weren't able to get him that day.

Akpaġialuk was quite intimidated by the people of Seward Peninsula. He lived in fearful expectation of the raid of the Seward Peninsula people for a long time. I wonder if finally he got killed. I didn't ask anyone about this part of the story.

One summer, Akpaġialuk went upriver to camp at Kuuruaq. There at Kuuruaq Akpaġialuk had set up his spring and summer camp. One day as he was qayaq-ing downriver, he saw people coming up the river toward him in a skin boat. (A bearded seal-skin boat is called an *umiaqpiak*.) He saw them coming up the river in this kind of boat. Akpaġialuk immediately backtracked and paddled upriver. He beached his qayaq, then went into the willow brush and began to shout. He shouted, "Go above them! Go above them!" Upriver, where there were plenty of willows, one could hear the echoes.

When Akpaġialuk shouted, the other group of people heard the echoes. They thought many people were present. So they turned back and left, down the river. They knew there were many people living in that area. There were families living on the riverbanks. This person, Akpaġialuk, deceived them with echoes. The raiders turned back and he was able to escape.

That is all. In this story I've combined incidents together. This story is a true story, not a lie. True stories aren't fairy tales. They are the lore of the people who lived a long time ago. Akpaġialuk has descendents who are still living here in Selawik. Tikisaruq is one of Akpaġialuk's descendents.

The Raid and the Kobuk River Grandmother

Nora Paniikaaluk Norton

Recorded in Selawik, May 8, 1972

I'm going to tell another story. I'll tell the story with as much details as I know them. This is how I tell stories. This story is a Kobuk River story, I think.

A group of people was spending their summer at their summer camp. One of the people at the camp was Qaluvik, the daughter of a widow. Qaluvik had a son even though she wasn't married. He was a very demanding child. He had a habit of crying long and loud, and it was trying to make him stop crying. He wouldn't stop once he started crying.

The people living at the camp didn't like the situation. They consulted each other and came to a consensus that they should all leave quietly, leaving the crying baby behind. They all felt that the baby would endanger them. Among themselves, they voiced their concern, "Whenever he starts crying, he doesn't stop. As it is, the raiders will easily locate us."

The people were catching salmon. (That's why I think this is a Kobuk River story.) They were camping there to do their summer fishing. After it turned dark, the raiders arrived near their camp. They came to fight the camp people. Probably they were Indians. The Kobuk River people were constantly on the watch for the Indians.

All the campers prepared to abandon the camp. The boy's grandmother knew that the villagers didn't want her grandson with them. She told her daughter to leave with others who were fleeing. "I'll stay behind with my grandson. If he goes along, he'll bring shame upon us. The raiders will be able to do whatever they want with us."

The child's mother didn't want to leave, but she eventually left because her mother adamantly insisted that she leave with the group. She got into a boat. And the people took off, down the river.

The grandmother grabbed a piece of dried salmon and a parka with which she wrapped the child. While she was gathering wood downriver one time, she noticed a spot where the ice had dug into the bank. (That was during spring when the ice was breaking up. The Kobuk River is fierce when the ice is breaking up. The ice can dig into the banks in some places.) The old woman knew where that place was.

She took her grandson there and hid under the cut in the bank. She told her grandson not to cry. The child obeyed her. The child was told that if he cried, the raiders would find their hiding place. She told him, "They will torture us or else they'll take us with them. So, don't cry! Not even a wee bit!"

The grandmother tore off a piece of dried salmon and gave it to the grandson. Sucking on the dried salmon, the child fell asleep. She cradled him on her lap because she didn't want him to cry. When the child fell asleep, the rest of the group had already left the camp and were on their way by boats.

After a while, the grandmother heard people running about near her hiding place. They made a lot of noise looking for people in the camp. The raiders found no one. From her hiding place, the old woman could also hear people walking on the ground above her. The raiders continued to search for people, but they didn't come down the riverbank. After a period of consternation, all became quiet. The grandmother didn't go to sleep at all because she didn't want her grandson to cry. The boy would wake up every once in a while and then go back to sleep again. He thrashed about, but he didn't cry.

Daylight returned. The grandmother was still hidden in her hiding place. Not a sound was heard anywhere. The boy began to wake up. Hearing no sound, the old woman decided to go out to check. She advised the boy to stay put and not to cry. She left her hiding place, looked around, but saw no one. She took her grandson out of the hiding place. Then as she was looking around some more, she spotted a boat. The campers had left that boat behind. The raiders who came into the camp had destroyed their gear, but didn't damage the boat. She picked through the things the fleeing campers had left behind and carried them to the boat. She put her grandson and some supplies into the boat, then took off downriver. Whenever she felt drowsy, she would beach the boat and sleep for a while. She didn't want to travel in the dark. When daylight broke again, she set off. Although she had been traveling all day, she couldn't see the rest of her group. Already they had fled a long way.

After a period of traveling, finally they saw people. Finally they met the rest of the group who had fled from the camp. They were all safe. Everyone had thought that the grandmother and her grandson would be dead by then. All through the trip, the old woman's daughter was sad because she too thought they would never survive. The grandmother had saved the baby. Most likely, the boy, not seeing his mother around, was more accommodating.

The Kobuk River Massacre

Nora Paniikaaluk Norton

Recorded in Selawik, July 1, 1977

~~~~~~

I'M GOING TO TELL A STORY ABOUT THE KUUVAŊMIUT [THE KOBUK RIVER people].

A group of people lived along the Kobuk River a long time ago. Normally during the summer, each family tried not to go camping by themselves. This group of Kuuvaŋmiut likewise followed the practice because they were afraid of raiders. They were constantly on the watch for raiders. A certain family might perhaps camp alone once in a while, but generally several families camped together. They camped out to collect their food for the coming winter. It wasn't like nowadays. In the past they had only whatever food they were able to collect. They didn't have the white man's food. They collected fish during the summer. That was the way this group of Kobuk River people lived.

One day, all of a sudden, the raiders arrived behind their camp. The raiders had come all the way from the Yukon River. When they arrived at the camp, they waited until all the campers were asleep. Then they killed almost everyone in the camp.

The only survivor to this massacre was a woman. This poor woman had a baby. The raiders made off with her, with her baby boy on her back. After traveling a long way, the raiders stopped and raped the woman. The baby was set on the ground, but they didn't kill him. They raped the poor woman, and there was no one there to help her. The baby wasn't aware of what was going on.

The raiders left the woman after the rape. After they departed, the woman struggled to get up because she was concerned for her baby, left lying on the ground. As she was trying to flee from the area, she overheard the raiders telling each other that they shouldn't have left her alive. It would have been better to kill her. Upon hearing this, the woman pried the ground open and became part of the ground. She was able to do that.

The raiders returned to look for her. They looked, but they couldn't locate her. For a long time after they left, the woman remained hidden. When things quieted down again, she headed home. Arriving back at the camp, she found that there was nothing she could do. She found all her people killed. She realized that she couldn't continue to live there for she couldn't possibly live among the dead. She proceeded to collect things she would need to survive and left in a boat. She took a net and different kinds of gear from the camp. All the people were dead, so she selected the best gear she could find. (If this happened to me, I wouldn't be looking for the best things! This woman was brave!)

The woman took off downriver. She found a place to live, a place to rear her son. The baby grew. He became a boy, then he became a young man. During the summer she would set her fishnets and pick berries. She utilized all kinds of means to collect their food. That was how she raised her son.

When the boy became a young man, his mother told him what had happened. She told him about the time when he was still a baby. The young man reflected on what happened to his mother. Whenever he sat down, his thought would be on the incident. He probably saw in his mind's eye what the raiders did to his mother. At the time his mother was raped he was unable to help her because he was still a baby. He wasn't yet able to understand what was happening.

One day, while traveling around, he found a group of people. When he approached them, they didn't harm him. The group he came across was probably his relatives, the Kobuk River people. He told them who he and his mother were and that both of them had been living by themselves some distance away. He talked about what happened to him and his mother. The people felt sorry for him and told him to bring his mother over to live with them. The young man did that and made his living with the group.

After they had been living there for a while, spring arrived.

The young man's mother began to prepare for her son's departure. She made him mukluks as well as other traveling gear he might need. (Up at the Kobuk River, if a person is traveling overland, they make low-cut mukluks for walking on land. When a husband is about to hike overland, his wife says she is making low-cut mukluks. If the mukluks have long leggings, it's a waste of the materials.) The rest of the people likewise had their relatives make traveling gear for them. They would never travel anywhere without being well prepared.

It was early spring when everything was ready. The creeks weren't yet filled with water. The group took off while the ground was good to walk on and the creeks easy to cross. Right after the ice went out, the creeks wouldn't be filled yet with water.

The group traveled until summer arrived. When they reached the Yukon River, they began to look for people. There they located a group of people. They observed the group and tried to find out whatever they could about them and what they were doing there at that location. The Yukon River people were probably Indians.

They watched and observed the Yukon River people for a long time. One day, listening to them having a lot of fun, the young man was enraged. Other men who were there with him tried to calm him down, saying he should wait and be patient. He would get his revenge, they assured him—when the Yukon people went to sleep.

When the Yukon River people were asleep, the Kobuk River group entered their camp and the young man had his revenge. He avenged his mother. He left one young woman alive and took her back with him. He took her home to be his wife.

The couple lived for a long time. They had children. The wife didn't miss her home and the young man made a good living with her. He didn't tell his wife how her people had mistreated his mother. He had a good life with her when she became his wife.

I heard this story from my father. I think I have only parts of the story. Perhaps I fell asleep while he was telling the story.

The Old Woman of Quliruq

Nora Paniikaaluk Norton

RECORDED IN SELAWIK, JULY 21, 1977

DOWN AT QULIRUQ THERE LIVED AN OLD WOMAN. SHE USUALLY CAMPED at that particular place during the summer. She lived alone. No other people were around. Once in a while, she would set her fishnet. During those days, they didn't have twine for making nets. They made their own nets for fishing. The old woman probably had one of those nets. That was how she did her fishing. (Poor old woman, living all by herself! Quliruq, the place where she lived, is our fish camp. We don't go there now every summer. But when our father was still alive, we used to live there.)

One day while the old woman was sleeping in her summer house, her qayaq was taken to the other side of the slough. When she got up the next morning and went out, she saw it sitting on the other side of the slough. I heard that long ago that slough was narrow. When people were rowing during that time, the oar would touch the bank if they rowed too close to one side. It was that narrow. Nowadays it has gotten wider because of the current and because there are two lakes at the end.

The old woman was at a loss to know what to do. She could see her small qayaq across the slough. All day while she was doing her chores she thought about how to bring her qayaq back. She thought about draping herself over her wooden tub to see if she could float over to the other side of the slough. She had a wooden tub.

(During those days they didn't have metal tubs. The wooden tub was made from a tree split to the desired thickness. The side and the bottom of the tub were then made from the split wood. They made buckets too the same way. My grandfather, Ulugaruk, had made this kind of tub. One time he gave me a pot like this to use when I was making sourdough. That was what the poor woman in the story was using.)

The old woman draped herself over her tub, hoping to cross the slough. She took off her tattered old clothing and placed her chest against the tub. She was able to make it across and reach her qayaq. She was so happy and brought her qayaq home.

That was how the poor woman lived. The raiders had probably taken her qayaq. They didn't kill her and didn't beat her up. They just took her qayaq across the slough while she was still asleep. But she could cross over to retrieve it. She floated across, using the tub as her floatation device.

Aagruukaaluk

Robert Nasruk Cleveland

RECORDED AT ONION PORTAGE, AUGUST 15, 1967

THIS IS ANOTHER *ATUUTILGAUTRAQ* [A SONG IN A SONG DUEL EVENT, A song sung as a challenge song, or as a message sent to another person].

Aagruukaaluk was spooked by a band of Indian raiders. When he was spooked, this person named Aagruukaaluk left. The raiders were not able to get him.

Although the raiders weren't able to get Aagruukaaluk, they killed almost all of his family. The only person they didn't kill was his son, a young boy who was on the hunting trip. Later when the raiders came across him, they stabbed the son's eyes and drove him out of the camp. He died somewhere after leaving the camp, possibly from starvation.

The father heard what the raiders did to his son. He heard that they stabbed his son's eyes and left him to wander blindly all by himself.

At a place called Coalmine on the Kobuk, after spending part of the winter, this group of raiders organized the game of blanket toss. They were singing a blanket toss song. In the meanwhile the father Aagruukaaluk and his friends were searching for the men who had harmed his son. He was looking for them to take his revenge. They stopped above the group that gathered for the game of blanket toss. That was near Coalmine.

Aagruukaaluk found that the group was about to start playing blanket toss. The group down below had the blanket toss all night. I'm going to sing the song. This is how they sang the song:

Whose son is that,
That took off?
It must be Aagruukaaluk's son.

This is the whole song. I shall sing it again:

Whose son is that,
That took off?
It must be Aagruukaaluk's son.

The father listened to the song about his son. During the singing, he got up and was about to charge into that group of Indians when his two friends grabbed him. They were singing about his son whose eyes they had stabbed and was left to wander. Aagruukaaluk's friends told him that he wouldn't get his revenge if he went after them too soon. He might get shot if he set off after them then. They also said that when morning arrived and everyone was asleep, he could go down to their camp. "We'll get things ready for you," they told him.

They reasoned with him and managed to calm Aagruukaaluk down somewhat. They listened to the group having fun all night.

This is what the song is about. After the raiders did that to Aagruukaaluk's family, they sang about his son and Aagruukaaluk heard the song.

Whose son is that,
That took off?
It must be Aagruukaaluk's son.

That's all. I sang the song accurately.

Aagruukaaluk and Kippaġiak

Nora Paniikaaluk Norton

RECORDED IN SELAWIK, SEPTEMBER 9, 1968

THERE WAS A PERSON NAMED AAGRUUKAALUK WHOSE SON WAS TAKEN away from him. The raiders who took his son made the son live with them. I think the family was Kobuk River people. Let them be for the time being Kobuk River people. We'll find out later. My father told me this story, but I hadn't learned all of it. Maybe they are Kobuk River people or maybe they are coastal people. The people of Shishmaref have people named Aagruk. Perhaps he was from there. Perhaps he was from Deering.

Aagruk's son was named Kippaġiak. When the raiders abducted his son, Aagruk was inconsolable even though people around him tried to console him. Aagruk thought his son was killed. Others consoled him, saying that they would all go to look and find his son when summer arrived.

One day the time came for the group to begin the promised search. They prepared their supplies for traveling overland. They consoled Aagruk, saying they would surely find his son and Aagruk believed them. Aagruk and the men left on their search. They trekked up the Yukon River and came upon a group of people who were traveling upriver in a canoe. The time of the year was early summer. When the people in the canoe proceeded upriver, the men who were looking for Kippaġiak tracked them from the bank. The people on the river had no idea that there were other men around, looking for Aagruk's son.

One day the people traveling along the river stopped to camp. The tracking men watched and listened as the campers went about with their 'chores. That day the campers decided to have some fun. They could be heard dancing and having a good time. The dances were followed by the blanket toss game. The campers played their blanket toss amidst a lot of laughter and shouting. They sang blanket-tossing songs, hooting and hollering.

After a period of singing, they sang a song:
Whose son is this, always trying to sneak away?
Maybe he is Aagruk's son?
Maybe he is Kippaġaana?

At the end of the song they hooted and hollered; they were having so much fun. They didn't suspect that others might be listening to them. Aagruk understood that the song they were singing was about his son. They were singing about Kippaġaana, who wanted to return home. The men who were with Aagruk grasped him, advising him to be patient. "If we wait a little longer, they'll get sleepy. They won't blanket toss all day. When they go to sleep, we'll take you there. You'll get to avenge your son when they're asleep." The father calmed down.

The people continued with their fun all through the night. Soon the sun came up and it started to warm up. That large group of campers blanket tossed some more, then all turned quiet. The tracking party waited for them to fall asleep. The sun rose and the weather grew hot. The people were quiet. They were all exhausted from all the blanket tossing and having fun all night.

When they were all asleep, the tracking party prepared to strike. After all, that was the goal of their mission. They were looking for Aagruk's son who had been abducted. They sneaked down to the camp where the campers were fast asleep, exhausted from the last evening's fun. Aagruk started from one side of the camp with his knife. When he came across a person who wasn't his son, he would kill him. After some time, he found his son. Aagruk didn't kill all of them, but he killed many.

Aagruukaaluk's Revenge

Wesley Qaulġutailaq Woods

~~~~~~

Storyteller Wesley Qaulġutailaq Woods lived in Shungnak. He was a member of the old trading Woods family on the Kobuk, who early on had been trading with the whites. His father was Paaraq, younger brother of Riley Jim Woods, Nora Norton's father. Wesley's last name became Woods through a recording error in a government document. Wesley's wife was Josephine Qupilġuuraq Woods. They had nine children. Wesley passed away in 2003.

Wesley came to visit the Pah River archeological site that Douglas D. Anderson was excavating in 1996. While talking to Anderson in the expedition's cook tent about the historic Eskimo-Indian conflict in the area, he mentioned that there are stories about it. He told two Kobuk legends, which Anderson recorded on video. His Aagruukaaluk version describes Aagruukaaluk as a mixed-blood Eskimo and Indian.

RECORDED AT PAH RIVER, JULY 24, 1992

I'M GOING TO TELL ANOTHER STORY THAT TOOK PLACE IN THIS AREA too. The event occurred when wars were still going on—that is, before the last war was fought.

The story is about a man, half Kobuk Eskimo and half Indian, named Aagruukaaluk. He was a capable man, making his living between the Koyukuk and the Kobuk, maybe at Nanyatuuq. When the Lower Kuuvaŋmiut [Lower Kobuk people] heard rumors of his alleged mistreatment of some Kobuk people, the Lower Kuuvaŋmiut decided to raid his place. The raiders could very well be those people from Igliqtiqsiuġvik again. As usual they recruited the war party from the Upper Kobuk and searched for Aagruukaaluk's place. But when they got there, they found only his wife and her family home. The man they wanted was nowhere to be found. They killed his wife and all of his children except the oldest. This son was still a youngster, not quite an adult yet. The raiders damaged both of his eyes and then let him go. What a way to make people suffer! And this boy was an Iñupiat from the Kobuk of their own kind, even though he was of mixed blood!

When Aagruukaaluk returned home, he saw what happened. He had no family left and one son was missing. He had no idea where his son was.

It is known that when a person was seeking revenge, he would never carry it out immediately. The avenger would wait for years before finally attempting it. That was the way our ancestors dealt with vengeance. They were people who lived with the wars and the conflicts of their time.

When Aagruukaaluk thought that those who had killed his family were no longer expecting him, he planned his revenge. He waited until spring and took two other young men with him. They started down the Kobuk River. On the way they came across some camps, but somehow they knew that those campers weren't the people they were looking for.

As they proceeded down the Kobuk, they arrived at a place they thought they found the raiders who murdered his family. They stopped at a summer camp on the lower part of the Kobuk. There were many dwellings and one large tent. They waited nearby, waiting for people to go to sleep. There were festivities going on and there was a *nalukataq* [blanket toss]. Usually a song accompanied a blanket toss. The words of the song of the blanket toss were:

> When the eyes of Aagruukaaluk's son were damaged
> I wonder where he wandered to after that.

Aagruukaaluk's companions had to restrain Aagruukaaluk because Aagruukaaluk went into a rage. They wanted to wait for the right moment to take the revenge and were able to calm him down.

These people had *nalukataq* all night and ate until morning arrived and the sun was high in the sky. That was when they quieted down and went to bed.

Aagruukaaluk had a knife with a blade that was sharp on both sides called *igluktuulik*. The knife was fastened with a rope to his hand so that it would not slip off. When Aagruukaaluk went down to the camp, the big tent was his target. He placed his partners at the exit with an order to kill should any man come out. When Aagruukaaluk entered the tent, there was a sound of an object penetrating flesh and a man crying out in pain. A man ran out, but he was killed by Aagruukaaluk's partners. When Aagruukaaluk came out, his knife was dripping blood. That was the way he killed all of them, entering every house. His revenge was accomplished.

After that Aagruukaaluk continued to live in the Kobuk area. A half-Eskimo, half-Indian man. Maybe he lived near Alatna for a while.

The False Alarm at Kobuk

Nora Paniikaaluk Norton

Recorded in Selawik, July 21, 1977

~~~~~~

I'm going to tell a true story. The incident occurred before I was born. The incident occurred to the Kobuk River people. An incident might occur to a person when he was young. It became a legend when he grew old.

Before I was born, there was a time when my father was away from home on his hunting trip. Our mother was home with the children while he was away. The event took place before my parents moved to live in other places.

At that place where my parents spent their winter, the people organized a messenger feast. They had a messenger named Alutuun. They were getting him ready for leaving with their messages. He was supposed to leave to carry those messages to the Indians. They provided him with travel provisions. They made him a new parka and a new pair of mukluks. They made for him a new set of clothing that was good and warm for cold weather. He was traveling to another place where another group of people were making their living.

Alutuun took off. But after he passed the Qalamiut (the people of Qala), he spotted a group of raiders. He saw them coming toward him. He thought that surely he would be killed. He was so terrified that he quickly ran back home. It was dusk when he arrived back. Alutuun was sent off as a messenger, but he hadn't traveled very far. He turned back. Running back from the east, Alutuun reached the families living on the eastern end of the village. When they saw him, they noticed that he had a different expression on his face. That's because Alutuun felt differently than he did when he left.

Alutuun entered the house he departed from that morning. Surprised, the people in the house asked him, "What happened?"

Alutuun told them he came back because he wanted to live.

Alutuun's words spread throughout the village.

The villagers began to warn each other about the impending raid and tried to prepare themselves for it. They devised a strategy sending out two men to spy on the raiders. (I've forgotten the names of the two men.) The villagers sent out the two men, but the two didn't come back right away. As the villagers were waiting nervously, Alutuun commented that the two men would never come back alive. "I myself had to use every trick I know to make it home," he said.

Upon hearing that, everybody prepared to abandon the village. The women spread out their best food to eat as their last meal. They all thought they weren't going to survive the raid. They were so terrified.

My mother prepared to leave too. At the time she was living in a two-story house. Living with her were Pauline and Hadley, my two older sisters. They were the two oldest children but they weren't yet grown up. My mother instructed Pauline and Hadley to make some holes into the walls of the upper floor of the house. Through these she could push her rifle barrel. The children made several holes around the house. When you had a log house, moss was used to fill the chinks. Then she got the two girls ready. She made the oldest daughter put on her bearded seal-bottom mukluks. It was cold then and they were all very frightened.

The villagers spread out their best food to eat even though they weren't at all hungry. They were ready but frightened. When the two scouts came back, the villagers were informed that they had found no one—no footprints. Both had followed the messenger's tracks to the spot where he turned around to run home. (I wonder what Alutuun had seen. Perhaps he saw ghosts that turned into people. That was before the days of the Gospel.)

This is how people told this story. The story is probably a long story, but I didn't learn all of it. When my mother and Putuluq got together, they used to joke, "I had such and such to eat as my last meal!" They were not even hungry then. They were so terrified.

During this incident, Kakiaq, a Selawik man, brother of Yaayyii and Paniikauraq, who had married a Kobuk River wife was also living there. When his body became weak, most of the time he wasn't up and around. When the scare was on, he and his wife got ready, put on all of their warm clothes, and took off for the mountains. Some people were said to flee to the mountains. Kakiaq caught pneumonia. Perhaps they took shelter in a tent. Perhaps they lived outside. Anyway, when he returned home, he got worse and passed away.

My grandmother, Narvaugauraq, was living then at the place where she had always lived. She had no idea what happened at the village. When it was all over, a man went down to her place and told her the story. Upon hearing the story, my grandmother ran her dog team back to the village. She left from her place immediately the very next morning because she was concerned about her frightened grandchildren. She traveled upriver to the village untouched by the raid.

The women of the village had stored all of their good food. They had all kinds of game animals, like the fat of grizzly or black bear. They had caribou and all sorts of other food, maybe berries. They took out all of this good food to eat as their last meal, but they were so frightened that they lost their appetite. The incident happened before I was born. That was before people at Kobuk moved to live in different villages.

Satluk, the Man Who Could Not Be Killed

John Patkuraq Brown

RECORDED IN SELAWIK, SEPTEMBER 6, 1968

THERE WAS A MAN WHO WAS A TROUBLEMAKER. THE PEOPLE IN THE community one day decided to get rid of him.

A group of men left with a man named Uularaġauraq. He was from a place across the river from Kiana. The group traveled north to the end of the Kobuk River, looking for the man they intended to kill.

When the group found the people they were looking for, a young man was sent up a hill to stake a lookout. They waited for the people to go to sleep. When it was time, Uularaġauraq left with three arrows—only three arrows to shoot with. He was sent to where the people were fast asleep, under a shade. The person to be killed was a man who wouldn't die upon being shot. He had two other young men with him.

Uularaġauraq selected one young man and shot him with an arrow. He then shot the second man. The last man seized a bucket full of water, twirled it around, making it difficult for Uularaġauraq to have a good shot at him. Uularaġauraq took his last arrow and shot. The arrow went through the bladder of the last man. But the man had a power of healing. When the arrow hit him, the arrow just dropped off and the wound healed by itself. The tip of the arrow was however lodged in his pelvis. Only the shaft of the arrow dropped. He crawled away.

The pursuing group of men entered the cache, found some sheepskins, and began to toss the skins down to the ground. One man spotted a man with arrows hiding in the cache. He tried to warn others. The two men who were tossing down the sheepskins saw an arrow coming straight at them. One was able to dodge it, but the other couldn't and was killed. The shooter shouted. He still had the tip of an arrow in his pelvis, lodged to the bone. In the ensuing confusion, the people of the Kobuk River almost ended up fighting with each other.

After a while, two men resumed the search for their man. They went up the slope of a hill to a small thicket where they finally located the man and shot him.

But again nothing happened! When an arrow hit him, the arrow dropped off and the wound immediately healed. Neither had the man's strength diminished. After several attempts, one man took out his arrow and sang a song—a song we don't sing nowadays. After that he shot the man who was hard to kill. The arrow hit the man's nostril. The flint point pierced his nose while the shaft fell. The man shot cried out in pain, spun around, and fell down.

The man who was shot lived all winter. When they tried to chip the flint point away, it would always come back. It would grow the way a loaf of bread rose. The man survived most of the winter before he finally passed away.

That man is an Iyaġaaġmiut [literally People of the Rocks, an Athabascan Indian group]. He died probably that winter, somewhere between the Noatak River and Aalaasuk River [Alatna River]. His name was Satluk. Uularaġauraq inflicted that wound on him. Uularaġauraq set off from his place across the river from Kiana. Either Aakałqpak or Piruqtichat sang the song before shooting him in the nostril. The only way to shoot him was with a song. I wonder what kind of song it was. It isn't any of our songs.

The Old Woman Who Vanquished Indian Raiders

John Patkuraq Brown

RECORDED IN SELAWIK, SEPTEMBER 9, 1968

A GROUP OF KOBUK RIVER PEOPLE WAS MAKING A LIVING AROUND THE upper part of the Kobuk River.

A group of Indians came and killed a number of them. The Indians didn't know that a young man from the group managed to escape and went to warn the people living at the mouth of the creek called Quġluqtuq. The Quġluqtuqmiut fled up the valley to the Tulukkam Siyyuuk Mountain [Raven's Beak Mountain]. They all fled in fear of the raiders.

One old woman decided to leave her dog behind. She tied her dog to a caribou snare and told the dog before leaving, "You're not to lie here by yourself!" She wanted her dog to kill at least one raider. She knew that the raiders would kill the dog when they arrived, but she wanted her dog to make the kill first before he got killed. She thought that if she took the dog along with her, it might be troublesome for the rest of the group. It might bite them.

The people fled up a wooded valley. They abandoned their homes. The young man who had escaped the raiding party had warned them about the raiders' arrival. The group stopped to make camp at a spot facing Tulukkam Siyyuuk Mountain. Then they saw the raiders coming down the bank of the creek. (Why did they do their raids during the day, in broad daylight?) The raiders discovered that everyone had fled from their settlement. When the raiding party came into view at Sivuqaqpuk, a long stretch of the river, an old river, the old woman who had fled with the group pointed at the raiders coming down the riverbank. She clutched her fist in the air, then put whatever she had grasped onto the ground. Then she did it again. The second time she did that, she put whatever she had grasped into her mouth. She did that repeatedly. Soon blood began to spurt out of her mouth. What she was doing was eating the souls of the raiders. She was killing all the raiders.

When the old lady clutched her fist the first time and put what she had grasped onto the ground, she was holding at that time the soul of one raider in her fist. He was the only raider to survive. She had killed all but one raider.

The raiders arrived at the abandoned village. The dog the old woman had left behind killed a raider as he was told. The raiders were going to ransack all the houses in the village, but they began to get sick. The old woman had eaten their souls. Except for the first man whose soul she had clasped, the rest of this large party of raiders perished. When they left the houses they ransacked, they were already beginning to drop dead. They died without incurring any wounds. The old woman at Tulukkam Siyyuuk was eating them. She was eating their souls. She was eating their hearts. The raiders perished.

The Indians didn't realize that the escaped young man had given the group a warning about the impending raid. The raiding party had already killed people living farthest up the river. The Quġluqtuq people retreated to the face of Tulukkam Siyyuuk. They would have had a trying time had the old woman not ruined the raiders' plan. The raiders tried to return to where they came from, but they were dying, with no wounds. (I hope Anigniq doesn't hear this story. She might say I'm lying.) What happened was devastating to the Indians. The raiders were returning home, but they were dying. Their souls were gone. Maybe they ate the food the people left behind before they fled.

There is a big point up the Kobuk River. A large qayaq of solid stone sits higher up at that point. Its location is above the mouth of Quġluqtuq, upriver and at the end of the mountains. The qayaq has stone figures of people in it. That is the *umiaqviġak*. There are wave-like patterns on the ground. These came from way, way back.

The creek named Quġluqtuq has a high waterfall. People rafting home on that creek would normally beach their rafts above the fall and then walk home.

When the Raiders Got Killed at the Waterfall

John Patkuraq Brown

RECORDED IN SELAWIK, SEPTEMBER 9, 1968

ONE TIME THE SIḺALLIÑIĠMIUT [THE NORTHERN PEOPLE] WERE RAFT-ing down the canyon on a raid. The banks of the canyon were steep like house walls. Those sheer banks of solid rocks looked as if they had been cut by a saw. There was no way to escape up the steep banks.

The Northern People rafted quietly down the river. When the raft slid down a small incline, they would let out a yelp. Then they continued to drift down the river. The current wasn't swift downriver. It was quiet. As they were drifting down, all of a sudden their raft rose up in the air, and the water was far below them. The raft flipped over and landed upside down. The raiders fell into the waterfall. Only one person survived. That person had been watching the progress of the raft quite closely. The raft was turned upside down and blood was oozing up between the logs. Almost all of the raiders were smashed under the raft as it fell from the high waterfall. The people who were spending their summer below the waterfall saw bodies and arrows floating down to the place where they were camping. The dead were raiders from the north.

There are two creeks like this up there. These are the Shungnak River and the Quġluqtuq. Only these two creeks have waterfalls. People who raft down the Quġluqtuq beach their rafts upriver. They would then walk home—only a short distance that doesn't take long to walk. People who live around there know about these waterfalls. In the old days, the shamans would use these falls to trap their victims. That's why it was so quiet around there.

The Last War with the Indians

Wesley Qauluġtaiḷaq Woods

*This legend provides an important oral account of inter-group rela-
tions on the Kobuk at a period when the Lower Kobuk people are said
to have been involved with the Upper Kobuk people and a number of
Koyukon Indians were living side by side with the Pah River Iñupiat. It
should be noted that at the end of the account, Wesley Woods made a
remark about current Eskimo-Indian relations. His statement reflects
the changed political and social climate. Former Eskimo-Indian antag-
onism has now been smoothed over. Present-day Iñupiat view Alaska
Indians as fellow Native Alaskans.*

Recorded at Pah River, July 24, 1992

I'm going to tell a story about the last war with the Indians
as I heard it. It happened up the river, a little below the mouth of Siiqalauraq,
on Silaniq. The place where the war took place is somewhere around there,
according to the story. At that time many other settlements were located above
the Pah River. I'm not certain about the exact location of the last Indian war,
but when people talked about it they always mentioned "below Siiqalauraq,
near Silaniq."

In those days the Iñupiat lived side by side with the Indians. They were known
to live well with each other, speaking the Indian dialect more than speaking their
own Iñupiaq tongue. They got along very well indeed.

The people of Igliqtiqsiuġvik, above Kiana, with Iqsiuġvik located nearby,
were known to be the people who oversaw or perhaps controlled Upper Kobuk
inhabitants. They were concerned that the Upper Kobuk people would permit
the arrival of too many Indians.

When the Igliqtiqsiuġvik people kept hearing rumors about the Indian popu-
lation increase, they set off for the Upper Kobuk. Along the way they recruited
more men, increasing the number of men in their war party.

When they reached the Pah River people, they were informed that the people
they were looking for were living at Salukpaugaqtuq. Among those who used

to live with the Indians was a person named Unaliinguraq. Unaliinguraq was selected to be the messenger. The message that was sent to the Indians said that there was a disease, an epidemic of some sort, spreading up the villages along the Kobuk River. Those who succumbed to the disease would die quickly. No one would be able to survive it. The message also said that the Indians should leave before the disease struck their villages. But this was false information. It was a ruse to get rid of the Indians around the Upper Kobuk. The Indians, known to be trusting, left as soon as they were able to leave.

The Indian group was known to have two strong men, famed for their strength and unbeatable feats. I don't know their names because the storyteller didn't identify them by names. He only said that these two Indians were powerful fighters. One of them had a girlfriend from the Kobuk. When the news came he was rather reluctant to leave, but he left with his group when they all took off. This occurred during winter.

Their route went overland. When they reached the Pah River, they followed the river all the way to their own territory on the Koyukuk. Not long after the Indians' departure, the men from Igliqtiqsiuġvik who were coming up the Kobuk arrived at the Pah River. But by the time they arrived, the Indians had already departed.

At that point the Iñupiat felt intimidated by the presence of the two strong men among the Indians. They asked Unaliinguraq, a wheeler-dealer, friendly, and good at small lies, to follow the Indians with a message. "Your girlfriend wishes you to have the last feast of sheefish eggs before leaving. You must come back for the feast." It was of course a lie.

When Unaliinguraq was given the order, he didn't want to travel alone. He was fearful now that the Indians were grouped together. He was afraid even though one of the two strong men, the one with the Kobuk girlfriend, was his *suunaaq* [male friend of the same age]. Unaliinguraq persuaded another man to go with him because he didn't want to take the risk all by himself. At this point the Indians were thought to be somewhere upriver, on the Pah River still. Unaliinguraq waited for his partner, then took off. Not long afterwards, they overtook the Indians somewhere along the river where the Indians had stopped to camp and take a rest.

Without wasting time, Unaliinguraq went to the man with the Kobuk girlfriend. "Your girlfriend in the Kobuk wishes to give you a farewell feast of sheefish eggs."

That man was already reluctant to leave with the group, so upon receiving this message he didn't need much persuasion. That was all he needed to hear.

He was ready to leave immediately. The other strong man somehow sensed that something wasn't quite right. He hinted that he felt uneasy about the whole thing, but all his friend could think about was his Kobuk girl.

Unaliinguraq and his partner went back to the Iñupiaq village with one of the Indian strong men as planned. The Iñupiat carried out a vile scheme because they couldn't handle two Indian strong men. When the three men came back close, the Iñupiaq group with spears went across the river near a bluff and hid. They had set up a watch for their return. This occurred at Salukpaugaqtuq, near the trail that ran by it. When the three men reached the knoll there, they only had to walk down the hill before arriving back at the village. Unaliinguraq, always cunning, told his friend, "*Suunaaq*, let's hold on to each other while going downhill."

From that spot they could see the village below. The area is somewhere near the mouth of Siiqalauraq as I understand it. The other Kobuk friend of Unaliinguraq held on to the Indian's other arm. The Indian grumbled, "*Suunaaq*! What's going on?"

Unaliinguraq answered, "Let's have some fun. Let's go down the hill holding on to each other."

And they went down the slope. As they arrived at a smooth area before the riverbank, the hidden men rose, spears in their hands. The strong Indian broke away from the hold. The three travelers were traveling on snowshoes. One attacker stepped on the Indian's snowshoes and made him trip. They pinned him down to the ground. Several spears landed on him, killing him. He was not even allowed to go home to see his girlfriend. They killed him under the bluff. After that, they made preparations to go after the rest of the Indians because there was then only one strong Indian left to cope with.

When the raiders left for the war, Unaliinguraq didn't go along with them. There was only the last encounter to be fought and it was easy for the Iñupiaq group to follow the tracks and find the rest of the Indians. It wasn't mentioned in the legend how far they had to travel to overtake the Indians. The Indians were camping, resting somewhere along the river. The Iñupiat didn't know how many Indians there were, but their goal was to follow them all the way to the Indian home village, somewhere on the Koyukuk River.

At dusk, the Iñupiat spotted the Indians' camp. They set up a watch and waited for daybreak. At early dawn, raiders usually "spook the victims" in a surprise attack, hence the expression "spook the victim." As the Kobuk raiders were killing the Indians, the strong Indian ran to their temporary cache and snatched his snowshoes, bow, and arrows. Being very agile, he tossed down his snowshoes and slipped his feet through the laces. He took off so swiftly that it was impossible for Kobuk raiders to hit him with bow and arrows. Much to their disappointment, that strong man managed to get away. All the other victims were killed. They were mostly families and children who weren't able to put up much resistance.

The legend doesn't tell about the number of victims killed. What is important is that this was the very last conflict between the Athabascans and the Iñupiat. After this incident they became friends again. During later years, in their own Indian villages, whenever Kobuk people visit them, only a few Indians would hold the grudge still. Most are willing to "bury the hatchet" and become friends again. This friendship survives till present. There has been a lot of mingling of peoples during potlatches, most noticeably in Huslia, Allakaket, and Hughes. That is not true of the Athabascan villages farther down the Yukon, probably due to greater distance. Cooperation between the two groups of peoples is good nowadays.

Old Stories

Unipchaat Utuqqat

One Who Walked Against the Wind

Nora Paniikaaluk Norton

~~~~~~

The young man who trained himself to walk against the wind is a prime example of the Iñupiaq self-made hero. He was resourceful and disciplined and used his skills and strength to assist others.

The story was narrated in Nora Norton's house, built by her husband, Edward, in the 1920s after the family decided to settle in Selawik. This occurred after the Baptist Church, which Edward was in charge of, was built. During the last part of her life, Nora lived with her daughter, Emma, and her grandchildren in a two-bedroom government house on the school side of the Selawik River.

RECORDED IN SELAWIK, FEBRUARY 28, 1969

~~~~~~

A YOUNG BOY BECAME AWARE OF HIS SURROUNDINGS.

As soon as he was able to walk considerable distance, he took off.

The wind was blowing when the young boy left. He walked against the wind and walked all day. Sometimes he would fall down because he had difficulty fighting the wind. But when he picked himself up again, he would continue to walk. At the time he was just learning how to walk. He would walk all day—against the wind. Whenever he felt exhausted and sleepy, he would go to sleep.

When the little boy woke up, he found food, already cooked, spread out for him. There was a new set of clothing for him too and the clothing fit. After the boy finished his meal, he put on the new clothes and continued to walk. He was still going against the wind. He never walked when the weather was calm. He kept going against the wind, falling down, picking himself up, falling down, picking himself up, again and again, still going against the wind.

After having walked against the wind all day, the boy was so exhausted that he fell asleep—who knows for how long. When he woke up, again there was food—breakfast—waiting for him. (He probably had help from somewhere. It was probably God. After all he had no other helpers.) After the meal, the young boy pushed on, still walking against the wind.

The boy left on his journey while he was still a boy. He kept on traveling until he became a young man. Who knows where it was that he started from. When he became aware of his surroundings, his earliest memory was of walking against the wind. There was never a day when he was walking that the wind was calm. Always he walked against the wind.

The boy became a young man. Whenever he felt exhausted he would stop for the night and sleep. He slept soundly after such a long walk against the wind. When he woke up the next morning, there was again a new set of clothing. He was traveling against the wind so much and so long that his clothing was quickly torn to shreds.

When the young boy became a young man, he was poised at the threshold of manhood. Because he had been growing up walking against the wind, nothing could harm him. He put on the new clothes that were left for him. Who knows what kind of clothes they were. (I wonder what they looked like.) The clothes fitted him perfectly.

One day, as usual, the young man had been traveling against the wind all day. Toward evening he heard voices of people farther up from where he was heading. Before then the young man knew nothing about other people. He had no knowledge of what other people did to make a living. His earliest memory was that he had always been walking against the wind. He had been walking as soon as he was able to walk. There was never a day when he was walking that the wind was calm. Hearing people's voices, he stopped several times to listen. Then he continued on, still walking against the wind.

After a while, he approached closer. The voices he had been hearing seemed to be those of not simply a few people, but of many, many people. He kept on walking and when he arrived closer to the sources of the voices, he was able to hear clearly people having a lot of fun. Going still against the wind, he climbed up a ridge to take a look. He was then quite close to the people making all those noises. What he saw in front of him was many people, playing Eskimo football. They were all having great fun playing the game.

The people saw him arriving. They saw a man—the One Who Had Been Walking—coming toward them against the wind. Never was there a day he was walking when the wind was calm. They all began racing toward him. Whenever the people saw someone arriving, they would race to be the first to touch him. The first person to touch the newcomer would serve as his host. That was their tradition.

The people raced toward him. They all wanted to be the first to touch him. The person who managed to touch him first was a man living at the far end of the village. He took the young man home as his guest and gave him a meal.

As the young man was about to begin his meal, a messenger jumped up from the *qanisaq* [storm shed, lower than the living part of the house]. He delivered a message that the manslayer wanted to see him. But the young man didn't respond. He started to eat. During the meal, another messenger arrived with the message that the manslayer wanted to see him immediately. His host informed him that every time a newcomer came into the village, the manslayer always demanded to see the newcomer immediately. His host also mentioned that there were very few young men left in the village. The manslayer had been killing those who disobeyed his order.

The young man ignored the command.

When another messenger was again sent over, saying the manslayer demanded to see him immediately, the young man left the house. He went to the manslayer's house, accompanied by his host. As they were approaching the manslayer's house, they heard someone groaning intermittently in pain. Who knows what the manslayer had done to that person. Then they noticed a woman, perched on the roof of the manslayer's house. The manslayer hadn't killed her, but he inflicted this punishment on her because she failed to follow his order. Up there, on the roof, she was left to suffer.

The two men entered the manslayer's house. The manslayer was seated inside, way at the back. Instead of rudely walking inside, the traveler sat down when someone gave him a seat near the entrance.

The manslayer gave his order. "Call everyone here."

Not long afterwards there were men and women inside the house. But only a few young men could be seen. After a while the big *qargi* was filled with people. When everyone was there, the manslayer ordered, "Bring in the big boulder."

The boulder was huge.

Inspecting the boulder, the visitor saw that it had dark stains on it. It was caked with blood! It was the boulder the manslayer had used to kill people.

The manslayer ordered a woman to give the visitor his last meal. He then went to stand by the boulder and summoned the visitor.

A woman came out and placed a dish of food in front of the visitor. "I've already eaten. I ate at my host's house. I'm not hungry," the visitor said.

He took a few bites but didn't eat much.

"I really can't enjoy my meal. The noise that person makes on the roof spoiled my appetite. Please bring her down and take her elsewhere," he said.

No one made a move to do what he asked.

He repeated his request. "I really can't enjoy my meal. Please take her elsewhere. As it is I can't taste this food."

Again no one made a move to take away the groaning woman. When nothing happened, the visitor stopped eating. He waited.

The manslayer walked to the boulder and summoned the visitor. As suspected, the boulder was his murder weapon.

"I will smash you against this boulder!"

The young man had no hesitation to meet the threat. The two men wrapped their arms around each other and wrestled. At first the young man didn't apply his full strength. When the manslayer seized him and tried to smash him against the boulder, the young man was able to maneuver and land on the floor, still standing, away from the boulder. The manslayer wasn't able to knock him down.

The people assembled in the *qargi* gawked at the young man, totally taken by surprise that, for the first time, the manslayer was unable to smash and kill the young man on the boulder.

The manslayer wanted to have another throw, but the young man reminded him that it was his turn. He wrapped his arms around the manslayer, tightened his grip, and the manslayer grunted in pain.

The manslayer asked for a chance to say a few words. He was allowed to. What he said were pleas for mercy. He offered the young man everything he owned, whatever the young man wanted. The manslayer made those offers but the young man remembered what his host had informed him earlier, what the manslayer had done. At that point, the manslayer begged for mercy fervently, but the people who had been watching and listening told the young man, "If you can kill him, do it! He has made us cry. He has made us grieve. He has killed our sons. He has killed our brothers-in-law. He has killed our relatives and our brothers. He has taken our belongings."

The manslayer continued to beg for mercy, telling the young man he could have everything he owned or anything at all the young man wished to have.

Instead of listening to the manslayer, the young man listened to the people. Because the people didn't want him to free the manslayer, he tightened his grip. He didn't smash the manslayer against the boulder. But as he tightened his grip, the manslayer's legs buckled. When he finally let go of the manslayer, the latter was lying on the ground, dead. The young man neither fought nor smashed the manslayer against the boulder. He just tightened his grip and that killed the manslayer.

Earlier, when the people told him, "If you can kill him, do it," he had answered, "I will." He had promised them that he wouldn't let the manslayer get away with what he had done.

The young man had grown up walking against the wind in the freezing cold since he was a child. He told the people there that his earliest memory was that of spending his life outdoors. He told the villagers, "Go home, those of you who live here. Also those of you from other places. Go home and live your life as you used to live. The tyrant is dead. Now he can do nothing. The only remaining task to do is getting rid of his body. From now on you can freely live your own lives."

The Woman with Long Hair

Robert Nasruk Cleveland

~~~~~~

This story, identified by Robert Cleveland as an old story, is composed of several episodes. The story tells how an Iñupiaq young man proves his worth as a prospective spouse. The magical power that the woman with long hair has is implied rather than explicitly stated. The story ends happily with the reunion of the young couple.

This story was first recorded in 1967. It is not included in other story collections of Robert Cleveland (i.e., Cleveland 1980; Giddings 1961).

RECORDED AT ONION PORTAGE, JULY 30, 1967

~~~~~~

I AM GOING TO TELL A STORY HERE AT ONION PORTAGE WHERE ARCHE-ologists are excavating. My name is Nasruk. My English name is Robert Cleveland. Robert N. Cleveland is my name. The middle initial is the clue to my identity. There is another person with the name Robert P. Cleveland. You can distinguish us by our middle initials. This is Nasruk telling a story. It is an old story [*unipchaaq utuqqaq*].

Do you want to know from whom I had learned this story? The story was told by a Kobuk River man named Akatauraq, Mabel Brown's father. I had learned this story from him.

I don't know where the story came from or where the events took place. It might be a story of a Kobuk River person. It might be a story of someone who had moved to live in this area. I don't think it was learned from elsewhere. I think that since the story is about a person who was threatened by people of this area as well as by people from the coast, the origin of the story might therefore be from one of these two areas. The storyteller, Akatauraq, didn't say where the story came from. He didn't say from where he had learned it. The old man had many, many stories.

This is a long story. I want to tell another story too, but maybe I shall not. The second story tells about a person who lived along the Kobuk River, on the main channel of the Black River. It seems that the second story is not too old.

Along a seacoast a large group of people made their living. The people had an *umialik* and the *umialik* had a son. The son was his oldest child and he had also two younger daughters. The *umialik* had all together three children. The young woman, the older daughter, was *naviaqsiġaatchiaq* [woman ready for marriage], but the younger girl, I think, was still too young to be married.

Living also among this large group of people were a grandmother and her granddaughter of marriageable age. Their house was farthest away from the main part of the village. (That was how they lived as described in the story.) The villagers made their living both from the land and from the sea. Life was good for them. That was how they lived, as told in the story.

One day the *umialik* and his wife told their son who was approaching the marriageable age that he should marry and live his life with a wife. The son didn't respond, but after several nights he told his parents, "I've been considering the granddaughter of the old woman living on the outskirt of the village. If she'd have me, she is my choice. I'd like her to be the woman to take care of me."

It was in the morning when the *umialik*'s son gave his reply. Then he took off to hunt.

Without hesitation, his mother walked up the hill to see the old woman and her granddaughter. When she entered the house, the grandmother was kneeling on the floor, bending and calmly working. Her granddaughter was lying in bed, her back turned. The old woman chuckled when she saw the *umialik*'s wife come in.

"I wonder what happens to bring the *umialik*'s wife all the way to my house? The wife of the *umialik* rarely came over."

"My son wants that young woman to be his wife. That's why I'm here."

"Oh, so is that why you're here? But this woman might not be a suitable wife."

The grandmother didn't praise her own granddaughter. "I really doubt if she'd make a good wife. Look, she doesn't even talk. It doesn't look like she welcomes company."

While the two women chatted, the young woman remained silent. She simply lay there with her back turned as the two women talked on.

Around the middle of the day, the *umialik*'s two daughters also arrived at the house. When their mother asked why they came, they replied that they were sent by their father. He wanted to know what was happening. The two girls stayed for a while, then left.

After some time the *umialik* himself casually walked into the house. He sat down beside his wife. The old woman continued to chuckle to herself. Each time one of them came in, she would chuckle. They talked, and talked all day.

As the day turned into dusk, their two daughters again came back. The *umialik*'s wife told her daughters to bring over some food for dinner, and also their bedding. The two girls immediately returned home for what their mother wanted and brought back the bedding as well as food for dinner. The *umialik* and his wife spent the night at the house of the old woman and her granddaughter.

They woke up in the morning, then continued to spend the next day there. Since the arrival of the *umialik*'s wife the day before, the granddaughter hadn't got up at all. She just lay there with her back turned. Neither did she eat.

The *umialik* and his wife spent the next day at the old woman's house. When their daughters came over again, they told their daughters to bring over more food. Again the girls brought over the food.

The day passed. When evening approached, still the granddaughter didn't get up. She didn't get up that day and neither did she get up the day before. She didn't get up for two days and two nights. At that point, the *umialik* and his wife became quite concerned. They thought there was something odd with the girl.

"What if she is hungry or something!"

With that comment they left the house and returned home. They failed to get their daughter-in-law.

Back home, their son had been hanging around, doing nothing.

Seeing their son, the *umialik* couple said, "When one wishes to have a certain woman and considers marrying her, when he thinks that a certain girl is exactly the person he wants to live with, he should approach her and find out about her himself. Perhaps you'll be able to understand her if you go there yourself. Perhaps you can talk to her. If she responds to you, most likely you'll learn more about her."

When the *umialik* said so to him, the *umialik*'s son went hunting the next morning. He hunted all day. When it was time for him to come home, he didn't return.

The *umialik* told his daughters, "I don't know what happened to your brother. He didn't come home at his usual time. Perhaps he went to see the girl living back there. Why don't you two go over to check."

The two girls were never hesitant whenever they were asked by their parents to do something. They immediately went up to the old woman's house and entered. There, inside the house, they saw their older brother with the young woman. He was lying down. They returned home with their discovery, telling their parents, "He's there all right."

The *umialik*'s wife prepared dinner for the young couple and the two sisters carried the food back to their brother.

The young man spent the night. He also spent the next day there. He stayed there even though she neither got up nor ate nor drank. When evening approached and she neither got up nor ate nor drank, he too returned home.

With their son's return, one of the parents had a talk with their daughters.

"You girls should go to see your *uuma* [female friend of the same age]. Find out why she's acting like that. Surely, there must be something that caused her to behave so oddly like that. Find out what it is. You two should go there, sit beside her, and try to make her talk. If she talks to you, answers you, find out what's going on."

The two girls followed their father's advice and walked over to the old woman's house. They went into the house and sat beside the young woman. One girl called her, "*Uuma*." Wouldn't you know, the granddaughter got up from her bed and talked to the girls.

The three girls chatted. One of the sisters suggested, "*Uuma*, the weather outside is really beautiful. We should all go out and *tupiŋŋualiguta* [to play house]." The young woman agreed. She was by then talking comfortably with the two sisters.

When the two sisters had come to the house, they had brought along special caribou hides for making a caribou-hide tent and to use as mats. They built a *tupiŋŋuaq* [play house]. While playing house, the older sister said that her mother had given her an instruction to say "*Uuma*, we can make a new set of clothing for you. Would you like to have a change of clothing?"

The young woman accepted the offer. "Yes, please. I really don't have anything to wear."

The older sister told her, "All right. We'll make you new clothing."

They returned home to get the needed materials. They brought back fawn hides. Immediately they proceeded to scrape the hides, removed the top membrane layer, then moistened the tanning solution over them. The hides were set to tan overnight. The next morning when they woke up they began tanning the hides. After the hides were tanned, they were cut to the clothing size of the young woman. The three girls then sewed together. The old woman's granddaughter also knew how to sew.

When the sewing was finished, the two sisters tried to pull the old pair of mukluks off the feet of the young woman, but they had a hard time pulling them off. They kept trying. Finally one side of the mukluks came off. They had to wiggle her ankles before they were able to remove the mukluks.

When one mukluk came off, the two sisters found that it was covered with hair. Her hair had grown so long that half of her hair had wound its way into her mukluk and had become like an insole, wrapping around her feet. The two girls untangled the hair from one foot and from her lower leg, and put on one side of the mukluks for her. Then they struggled with the other foot and succeeded in doing it. After the mukluk was removed, they did the same as with the other side. They put on her the new pair of mukluks. And when her trousers were finished, they put on her the new set of clothing. Afterwards they also worked on her hair, all tangled up and long. They unbraided, untangled both braids, then rebraided her hair, and coiled it on top of her head. She had very, very long hair.

When the two sisters finished fixing the young woman's hair, they returned home.

Upon arriving home, the two sisters gave the news to the family. They talked about the young woman's long hair, so entangled and long that it was like an insole. "That's probably the cause of her embarrassment. We helped to clean and fix her hair. Now she's ready for your visit," they told their brother.

"Most likely, that's the reason why she didn't want to talk to you earlier," the older sister added.

Later the young man went to see the young woman. And so he married her.

The young married couple began to make their living. They didn't move away from her grandmother's place, located somewhat behind the *umialik*'s house. Since her grandmother was old and frail, they stayed with her to help her and nurse her.

The grandmother later got ill and passed away. Before her death, she told them that at her death they were to place her on her platform cache.

"Place me on the platform cache. Make sure nothing gets blown off by the wind. Also tie me down. You two will not stay on at this place with me after you've finished placing me on the platform. Go down and live at your parents' house."

The young couple did as she had instructed. Then they went home, to the home of the husband's parents. At the *umialik*'s big house, they were set up in the back part of the house. The *umialik*, his wife, and their daughters lived in the front part of the house. There the couple began making a living.

While living with the *umialik*'s family, whenever there was a game of football in the village, the young *umialik*'s son and his wife would be playing—but on opposing teams. The wife didn't join her husband's team. She was a skilled player and her husband was likewise a skilled player. The wife was furthermore a fast runner. If they were to play on the same team, no one would ever want to play against them on the opposing team. During the football game, the two of them would be so far ahead of other players, each trying hard to win. The wife played against her husband.

After living in this manner for a long time, the husband one day teased his wife, "We don't seem to be able to have a child. We're both past child-bearing age. Aren't we ever going to have a child?"

His wife replied, "If you really want a child, how about racing me to Grandma's storage platform? If you can reach and touch the platform first, we'll have a child. If you cannot, we won't."

The husband really wanted a child, but he knew full well he couldn't outrun his wife. Whenever they raced, she would always be ahead of him and he never was able to catch up with her. His wife was very fleet-footed.

After giving more thought to his wife's challenge, the husband eventually agreed. "Yes, let's do it. Or else we'll never have any children!"

An announcement went out to all villagers that the *umialik*'s son would run a foot race—with a child as the prize. He had to beat his wife in this race. The race would take place the next day and the two of them, husband and wife, would race to touch their grandmother's platform. The couple wanted everyone in the village to know about the race. They wanted the villagers to be witnesses at the race.

When morning arrived, both got ready. (I'm hurrying this story. I've another story to tell. The next story I'm going to tell is easier to believe in. This one isn't as easy. It's an old story. The one that is new is probably true, it is a legend.)

Early next morning, without taking any breakfast, both got ready. The prize was a child. Once ready for the race, they came out of their house. The villagers were already there waiting. They marked the starting line. The finish line they were running to was some distance away, a long way away from the river.

The competitors flexed there on the starting line for a while. Then both took off, running swiftly. Right away after taking off, the wife was ahead of her husband. He could see his wife out of the corner of his eye. He ran as fast as he could. They were coming up fast to the finish line and it looked as if the wife would touch the platform first. She was ahead of him. They both sprinted fast as they approached closer to the finish line. The wife was about to touch the pole when the husband hurled himself forward, and touched the post first. His wife lost. She didn't bother to reach out to touch the post.

When they were standing straight again, the wife said, "You've won. We will have a child." They then walked back home.

Before long, the wife was pregnant. When the pregnancy term was up, she gave birth. She gave birth to a boy who they named after their grandmother.

The child grew up. Soon he was old enough to play by himself. They lived there, I don't know how many winters.

After several winters, well into a fall season when the weather turned quite cold and ice was beginning to form in the sea, the daughter-in-law, upon waking up, told her husband, "Out there from the coast, another couple like us are coming!"

The next morning when everyone in the *umialik*'s family woke up, they noticed that the wife of the *umialik*'s son seemed distraught. She put on her old clothes when she got up. She was quiet, wouldn't say a word. She pulled up the hood of her parka over her head and just sat there, offering no explanation. Noticing her unusual behavior, her husband asked, "What's wrong? What are you thinking about? What's worrying you?"

His wife replied, "Today a couple will come here from the deep sea. The couple had a son."

Her husband had never known that she had this power.

"You'll be able to hear them when evening arrives, when they come ashore. When they come in here, they'll attack us. But don't be afraid. When they arrive, don't stay around inside the house. Climb up to the top of the house. From up there, stay still and watch what happens. I'll take care of them myself."

The husband accepted her instruction. The wife ate nothing all day. She confined herself to the back room of the *umialik*'s large house.

As darkness fell, the sea ice froze more and more, far out into the sea.

From a long distance, from the direction of the sea, a noise was heard. It was the noise of the ice. It was the noise of the ice being ripped apart in the sea.

"Now, you and your son, follow me. Your parents should be high up on the side of the house. No one stays on the ground floor," the wife told her husband.

The noise came closer and the people grew more alert. They heard the noise coming in from the sea. It was the noise of the ice being ripped apart. As the darkness of the night approached fast, they heard the noise coming closer and closer. They saw ice chunks piling up as the chunks moved closer to shore. The people grew jittery and frightened. The ice continued to move closer and closer to the shore. When it turned pitch dark, the ice landed on the shore! They could hear it stop moving.

They all waited inside the house. A couple entered. They were about the same age as the *umialik*'s son and his wife. They also had a son. They came into the house. The *umialik*'s family watched them, saying nothing. They didn't utter a word of welcome because they had heard from their daughter-in-law that these people were awful. The three of them sat down beside the entrance, next to the entrance from the tunnel, near the door. (In a traditional house, the door to the main living area was covered by a bear skin.) They sat there, saying nothing. When they sat down, the sloshing sound of water entering the house could be heard from the entrance tunnel. Soon they heard the water beating in, in waves. The water entered the house, in waves.

The *umialik*'s family waited.

Another wave tore in. They waited. The wife of the *umialik*'s son had given them advice. She had told them to stay put. She had instructed them not to try anything. She had also comforted them not to be frightened. So the family was prepared for what was happening.

Soon the waves came up to the floor of the house. The waves were rushing in from the sea. The house had its flooring made of logs. The floor logs were as thick as the trees.

Another surge of waves tore in. It was so strong that it swept everything off the floor. As the wave surged in, a piece of sod dropped from the top of the house. It made a big splash in the water. After a while, an even bigger wave surged in. As it washed over into the other room, another piece of sod dropped into the water again. When the wave entered the back room, again another piece of sod dropped. The sod dropped from the roof of the back room.

The husband was outside the house. All of a sudden he found himself standing next to his wife's grandmother's house. He heard her grandmother calling him. He listened.

"The person you're looking for is high up above you. But by yourself, you've no way of reaching her."

The husband looked up. He saw his wife, high up in the sky, looking down at him. She was a long, long way up in the sky.

The grandmother told him again, "There's no way you'd be able to reach her. But if you really want to have her back, you should untie me and remove my belt. Stand next to my body, then close your eyes. You can attempt to rope her in with my belt. You'll probably be able to reach quite close. If you're able to catch her, if something happens, like she's splitting in half, you can put her back together. I'm telling you what you should do—and that's all I can say."

The grandmother acted like she was displeased with her granddaughter, the one who was high up in the sky. She told her son-in-law what she knew was going to happen.

The son-in-law climbed up the cache and untied the grandmother's body. When he saw her belt, he pulled it out from her under her disintegrating clothing. The grandmother had told him earlier that afterwards she wanted everything put back the way it was.

The son-in-law took the belt, then jumped down from the cache and closed his eyes. He threw up the belt to rope in his wife. He felt the belt catching his wife. As he was pulling her down, he cut her in half. He put the two halves together and she became whole again. When she was all healed and breathing, he sat her down and took care of her.

Afterwards they both got up. They had a talk, then hurried over to the grandmother's body to put everything back the way it was and tied up her body well. This time he also wrapped her body. After that they both headed home.

The people had noticed what happened. They had seen his wife floating in the sky. They had seen how he had brought her down. The young couple returned home and continued to live their life. They lived a good life after this incident. They had nothing to worry about from then on. And that's where the story ends.

The Girl Who Had No Wish to Marry

Willie Panik Goodwin, Sr.

This story is a good example of how an individual storyteller tells a story in his or her own style. It was told in English to the Brown University archeological crew one evening during the summer of 1967. To draw the audience's participation, Willie posed questions to his audience. The responses given that evening occasioned a great deal of merriment and laughter. The story text is presented below with the lively interaction between Willie and his audience. To accommodate his audience, Willie appropriated the Western formulaic story opening "once upon a time" for the occasion.

Willie heard this story from his grandmother. He gave his grandmother's cultural explanation of why this story was told. Whether her explanation applies to all stories with "the girl who had no wish to marry" character type is still debated among female Iñupiat.

RECORDED AT ONION PORTAGE IN ENGLISH, JULY 30, 1967

ONCE UPON A TIME THERE WAS A VILLAGE—A TOWN, A LITTLE TOWN. This story is about a man and a woman who had a daughter. The girl was fully grown but she didn't want to marry. People from all over came over to the village to see her, to marry her, but all returned to their villages without her.

Her family, her father and her mother, were worried. Their daughter didn't care for men! Other people also talked about her. "If she lives on like this, it will do her no good! She must be married because everyone else is. She is the only girl here who doesn't care for any man!"

Her family was worried. At that time they had a place, a community house where people came to eat, talk, and sometimes hold a big dance. One evening her father mentioned to older people in the community house, "Do you think it's good for girls to be married?"

Well, everybody kind of felt sorry for the girl. She didn't care for anyone. Many good people, many good hunters, and many great men were after her, but she wouldn't take any of them. So the old people kept talking, consulting with each other. They tried to figure out how to persuade her to marry. They talked it over and finally decided that one of them should ask her if she would take the man she liked best to be her husband.

One of them suggested, "Maybe you should ask her if she wishes to marry the strongest man in the world. Maybe she would be interested in this type of man."

They all agreed. "Yes. There's something to that idea."

The father returned home and asked his daughter, "Why don't you marry? I'm sad when a man comes to see you and doesn't take you home with him. I'd like to see you married."

His daughter told him she didn't care to. So her father said, "How about this? Would you like to marry a man who is the strongest man in the world?"

The girl thought about it. The old man, and maybe the mother, kept asking for her answer. Finally she said, "Yes."

Her parents felt happy, went out of the house, and told everyone about it. Everyone was happy that she agreed to the suggestion.

They all tried to help the parents figure out how to find the strongest man in the world. The older people, like the medicine men and the Silalliŋiġmiut [the Northern People] who knew the world, tried to decide which man was the strongest. They kept talking. One person posed the question, "Which person is the strongest man in the world?

Someone suggested a man strongest in games of strength while others suggested other men they knew and thought as great. They kept talking, but couldn't agree on what is the best thing to be strongest at.

What do you think is the greatest thing in the world to be strongest at? Can you think of the answer?

"U-r-r-r." [From a listener.]

"Just guess," [prompted Willie]. "Well, Doug, what is the greatest thing in the world to be strongest at? Can you guess? Just guess. Just guess. Keep thinking."

"Sivak." [A listener's answer.]

"Sivak! What's that?" [Willie's response.]

The story that I had heard tells it like this.

One old man said, "Don't you think, people, that the sun is the greatest thing in the world? Who can beat that guy?"

Everyone agreed that they knew no one who could. So it was agreed then that the sun was the strongest. They couldn't think of anyone who could beat the sun. And so they assembled the doctors who knew how to call the man from the sun.

"What do you call the doctors?" [A listener's question.]

"*Aŋatkuk*" [Willie's reply, referring to the medicine man]. "These were the people who could kill others. They could do whatever they wanted. They could travel around and so on. So they got three or four of these people."

The medicine men came together at the community house, the *qargi*, and started to call the Sun Man. They kept calling and calling and finally they heard someone at the door. It could be him. They heard loud noises in the storm shed, then a man entered.

He was a huge man, husky and fat, with big arms. He looked like he was an important man and he also looked huge. The man asked, "Why do you call me down? What for?"

They asked him, "Do you think you're the strongest man in the world? We have a girl here who likes to marry the strongest man in the world."

The man thought for a while, then answered, "Well, I used to be strong, but there is one man I know I cannot beat."

Can you guess who that man is?

"The clouds." [A listener's answer.]

"You are right." [Willie's response.]

The Sun Man said, "I'd like to have the whole world filled with bright sunshine. But whenever this man shows up, I cannot make the whole world bathe in the bright sunlight as I wish. He is the only person I cannot beat. Sometimes I can beat him all right, but at other times I can't."

So the Sun Man went out and they lost a good, strong man.

Those men in the *qargi* didn't have to ask each other which man to call next. They knew which one they had to call. So for a while they concentrated on calling the Cloud Man. It didn't take them as long as calling the Sun Man. When the Cloud Man came, he made loud noises in the storm shed like the Sun Man. He was big and husky, a strong man like the Sun Man. He looked big and strong. He asked, "Why do you have to call me down? What's going on?"

They told him the same thing as they told the Sun Man earlier. They then asked him if he was the strongest man in the world.

"Well, not so strong," the Cloud Man said. "I used to beat the sun, covering the whole world. But there's a man, one man I cannot beat. I've tried as hard as I can, but I can't beat him."

Can you guess who that man is?

"Well, that's hard! Let's see."[One listener.]

"How about the wind?"[Another listener.]

"The wind blows in the clouds. If we don't have the wind, we won't have the clouds, would we?" [Willie's response, laughing good-naturedly, followed by voiced agreement from the audience.]

"Keep guessing. We have quite a bit to go yet." [Willie's prompt.]

"The rain." [One listener.]

"Yes, the rain." [Another listener.]

"Well, the rain is a brother and helper of the clouds, isn't it. It doesn't fight the clouds. If we don't have the clouds, we won't have the rain, would we?" [Willie's response.]

"How about the fog?" [Another listener.]

Well, it's time for me to tell you who the man is.

The Cloud Man said, "Just as I was going out, I came to a mountain. I tried as hard as I could to cover the mountain, but the top of the mountain still could peek out to look at the whole world."

The men felt bad. The poor girl just lost another good man again [laugh], but they still had another choice to try. When the Cloud Man left, the medicine men called on the Mountain Man.

Every medicine man went through the same procedure, calling and calling.

This time it didn't take long for the Mountain Man to arrive. He too made some noises in the storm shed like the others. He came in, a big husky man, stronger than the other two men. He asked, "Why do you have to call me? I have important work to do."

They told him, "There's a girl here who wants to marry the strongest man in the world. Are you the strongest man in the world? Is there anyone else who can beat you?"

The Mountain Man said, "Well, there's one person whom I cannot beat. I'm standing still in one place and there is that person whom I just can't beat!" Can you guess again who that person is? This is the last one. Can you guess? Anyone know who can beat the Mountain Man?

"The river." [One listener's answer.]

"Jean Joiner!" [Another person quipped with an insider's joke, prompting laughter. Jean Joiner was a legendary figure in the area, a white man and adventurer and owner of the Jade Mountain behind the cabin where the storytelling session was taking place. Everyone knew him.]

"How about earthquake?" [Another listener's answer.]

"Keep guessing. Keep guessing." [Willie's encouragement.]

"How about a bird?

"How about the snow?"

"A mouse?"

"Who said that?" [asked Willie].

Well, this is about the time I continue with the story.

The Mountain Man said, "I'm standing still in one place and cannot go anywhere. There's a man who lives with me, but I can't get rid of him if he doesn't want to go himself. He's still living with me. He's destroying me, but I just can't do anything to him. He must be stronger than I am."

"Who is that man?" someone asked.

"That's the mouse who lives on the mountain," the Mountain Man answered.

The girl lost the chance of getting her husband again. That girl certainly had many suitors—all the hunters and also these Sun Man, Cloud Man, and Mountain Man! [Laughter.]

So the Mountain Man left.

The medicine men started calling the Mouse Man. It didn't take long for the Mouse Man to arrive. He must have been somewhere in the house. He made tiny, tiny noises.

"Come in."

A little man, a tiny guy, came in and asked why they wanted him there. The men told him the same thing as they had told others and then asked if he was the strongest man in the world.

The Mouse Man answered, "I don't know anyone who can beat me. I think I'm the strongest man. I live on top of the mountain. No matter what kind of weather—cold weather or bum weather, no matter who comes over—animal, bird, or anything else—I am still here. I don't think anyone can beat me."

Everyone felt funny about the whole thing. Here was a mouse. And the girl was to marry a mouse. [Laughter.]

This is the end of the story.

My grandmother used to tell us children this story. I was the youngest.

Now that I am old, I can say what she also said then. She said that the story informs people that if a girl is too choosy about her man, this is what she might end up with—a man whom people don't really care for.

The Brother Who Rescued His Lost Sister

Maude Kanayuqpak Cleveland

~~~~~~

Storyteller Maude Kanayuqpak Cleveland of the Kobuk Cleveland family was a daughter of Aakałuk and Aumałuk. She was married to Johnny Inuqtuaq, brother of Robert Nasruk Cleveland. They had five children.

Maude's stories were recorded when she came to Onion Portage to visit her adopted daughter, Clara Lee, and her family (several of them worked as crew members of the Brown University Archeological Expedition). Maude was also one of the Ambler villagers who boated to celebrate the 1967 Onion Portage Fourth of July with the Brown University archeological team and the Iñupiaq crew.

RECORDED AT ONION PORTAGE, SUMMER 1967

~~~~~~

FIGURE 12 ~ *Maude Cleveland (center right), Minnie Gray (far right), Edna Greist (center left), and several children at Onion Portage, summer 1969.* PHOTO: DOUGLAS D. ANDERSON.

THERE WAS A LARGE GROUP OF PEOPLE MAKING A LIVING ALONG A RIVER. Living among them was an *agliñguaq*, a girl who was secluded upon reaching her puberty. Her seclusion period was not yet over.

As the group lived there, a young man married a young woman within the group. The young man at first didn't want to marry. His wife had a younger brother. As the three of them were making a living at that location, the men would go hunting, on land as well as in the sea. When they were hunting on land, the wife would at times disappear. Having been able to marry one of the very few eligible women in the community, the husband didn't want to risk taking his wife hunting with him because he feared her disappearance.

But, one day, the husband decided to take her along. They were out hunting all day and at the end of the day he managed to bring her back home. Several days passed, then the wife set off to pick up the hunted game animals they had left behind. She went alone; her husband allowed her to go by herself. And she disappeared on her way to the game cache.

Her brothers and her husband searched for her. Her disappearance occurred sometime during the fall after the first snow. While searching for her, they came upon the location where her footprints disappeared. Her husband didn't want to leave the area and wanted to continue searching for his wife, but his brother-in-law convinced him to return home. The brother-in-law consoled the husband that they could still be out searching for her every day. The brother-in-law took him home.

The young husband was out every day searching for his wife. He couldn't eat. He and his brother-in-law continued to live there by themselves after the rest of the group departed. The two continued to live there—just by themselves. The young man was so absorbed with his own worries that he was not aware that sometime during the night his brother-in-law had slipped off from the house.

Outside, in the dark by himself, the young boy pulled up bunches of grass and small willows. Later, every night, he would pull up small birch trees and spruce trees by their roots. His route took him farther and farther away from the area. When daylight wasn't too far off, he would return home and return to bed. During these periods his brother-in-law thought he was sleeping.

Within the village, occasionally the villagers would receive invitations from the people living on the other side of the sea. Whenever an invitation arrived, a group would set off from the village and travel across the sea as invited guests of the other village. The people across the sea, on the other hand, also crossed over to their village and became their guests.

When the invitation to visit the village across the sea came again, the husband and his young brother-in-law didn't join others on the trip. But then someone from the village across the sea sent a messenger to the young husband, personally inviting the husband to go over. The message that came with the messenger also said, "During the fall when there was only snow dust on the ground, my wife also disappeared." The message came during the first snowfall. But the young husband said he wouldn't be summoned across the sea and that the other husband should come over to see him. The two of them then could grieve together. Realizing that the husband wouldn't change his mind, the sender of the message traveled over to the young husband's village. The two husbands shared their grief over their lost wives. The brother-in-law, the younger brother of the lost wife, put up with the two grieving husbands.

One day the young boy decided to visit the Secluded One, that is, the young girl who was secluded from other villagers and was living by herself. For some time she had been living alone in her dwelling. At her place, the young boy asked, "Do you know anything about my older sister?"

(In those days, secluded girls wore birch bark hats. They would put the hat on the instant they heard people entering their dwelling. They would also bow their heads low to avoid looking at the person entering. They would wear the birch bark hats to protect others.)

"Do you know what happened to my older sister?" he asked.

The short young man visited the Secluded One not only once, but many, many times. In the meantime, he continued to pull grasses, willows, and trees during the nights to build up his strength. He did this exercise both during the summer and during the fall while his brother-in-law was sleeping. After pulling up willows, he progressed to pulling up birch trees. He built up more strength by pulling up birch trees as well as spruce trees. He built up his strength with pulling up all kinds of trees, including cottonwood trees. He toppled them and he carried them. His brother-in-law had no idea that he was building up his strength in this manner. His exercises started because he was worried about his lost older sister.

After building up his strength for a while, the boy again went to visit the girl who was secluded. He had already been visiting her several times. The girl was secluded, living by herself up in the hills and couldn't return to the village because she was having her first menstrual cycle. He approached her and again asked her where his older sister was. He told her the whole story and this time she replied that she knew about his older sister.

"I know what happened to her. The Formidable One got her!"

The young boy asked her to tell him everything. He told her he wanted to go to the place where his sister's abductor lived no matter how difficult the trip might be. The girl told the young boy that if they really wanted to go to the place where his sister was held, she would give him a staff. The young boy said he was determined to go, so the girl told him that she would give him the staff whenever they were ready to leave.

Before their departure, the Secluded One gave the young boy instructions. "Stake this staff on the ground beyond people's living area. Stake it at the spot where no one has stepped on. When you check on the staff in the morning, head off in the direction where the fallen staff is pointing."

The young boy did as he was told. He went beyond the village area where everyone was living and staked the staff. He did that during the night and told no one about it. Once the staff was staked, he returned home and went to bed.

The next morning, the young boy told the two worrying men who had lost their wives what had transpired. The three of them began their preparations for the trip. They had new mukluks made.

The three men set off with the young boy leading the way in the direction pointed by the fallen staff. They traveled all day. When it was time to stop for the night, the young boy would go outside the camping area and stake the staff. They took off again the next day in the direction of the fallen staff.

They continued to travel in the direction the staff had pointed out for them.

One day, they ran out of food but they kept pushing on. When it was time to stop to rest, they stopped at a clump of trees that could serve as a natural wind breaker. While walking toward this camping spot, they spotted a jackrabbit darting away. One of the men ran after the rabbit but wasn't able to catch it. That night they had nothing to eat. Maybe they ate a little something.

The next morning they took off again. Always they took off in the direction of the fallen staff. They were walking toward another clump of trees when the same thing occurred. Again a jackrabbit scurried away.

This time the young boy commented, "If I were the person to go after the rabbit, I'd get it. I wouldn't fail to catch it." He was trying to challenge the two men to try harder. But the two men were not fast runners and weren't able to catch the rabbit. They spent their night there and the young boy again staked the staff. He was in charge of the staff.

The next morning they started off in the direction pointed by the staff. That night as they were walking toward a clump of trees, they saw a jackrabbit dart-ing away again. This time the young boy bolted after it. He was able to catch up with the jackrabbit. He kicked it and killed it. He took it back to their camp as their dinner.

The next morning they took off again in the direction pointed by the staff. As they walked toward a clump of trees, the young boy again caught a jackrabbit, killed it, and they had it for dinner.

For a long time the three men traveled. Winter arrived. They had been traveling always in the direction of the fallen staff. The boy would stake it. He was the person handling the staff. After traveling in this manner till winter, they finally came upon a group of people. They walked toward a river. There in front of them were two large villages, each one standing on one side of the river.

The three men waited until it turned dark. The people had been playing football. When they stopped playing, the three men proceeded to the village closest to them. They approached the first house they came upon.

A woman came out of that house and invited the three men inside. Inside they saw several young men and their sisters. The father of these men and women greeted the guests, "Ah, what fine young men we have with us here, despite the Evil One."

They settled down for the night. The father proceeded to tell them, "By now the evil man probably knows that you're here. We've a manslayer among us."

The three men had left the staff at a place outside the living area. That staff wasn't supposed to be brought in among people. The three men stayed there.

And when morning arrived, as expected, they heard someone's voice from the skylight window. "The manslayer wants to see the visitors."

The old man began to give them warnings. He told them, "Go. Go with him."

That wasn't the first time someone stopped there to spend the night with the family. The three men were also informed that the first thing to occur would be a football match.

When they all stepped outside, the opponents were already on the [frozen] river. The people on one side of the river were on one team. Those on the other side of the river were on the other team. The two teams from the two sides of the river began to compete at a football match. The family with whom the three men had stayed pointed out the manslayer playing in the other team. The manslayer ran swiftly. He shouted as he ran, way ahead of everyone else.

The father of the family with whom the three men had stayed had a son of the same age as the young boy looking for his lost sister. In the football game the two boys played as a team. They ran together, becoming inseparable. As they were enjoying themselves playing together, the people were shouting and cheering.

When the young boy was told that his team was about to lose the game, he proceeded to beat the opponent.

"What an arrogant visitor!" exclaimed the manslayer, exasperated.

The losing team challenged the winning team to play again. The two teams competed in a rematch. The team in which the young boy was a team member again beat the other team. They took the ball and they succeeded in beating their opponent.

When that happened, they knew that the next day a foot race would take place. The racers were to run to the marker barely visible from the village and then turn around and run back to the starting point.

The next morning someone called down the skylight that the manslayer wanted to see the new visitors at the race.

The three men didn't hesitate. They immediately went outside and joined the foot race. The racers took off. The two young boys were so attuned to each other that they didn't pay much attention to the race. They were busily playing with each other as they were running. They passed other racers along the way. Some had already stopped running; others were running back. The young boy caught up with his companion.

People reminded him, "The manslayer should be beaten."

The manslayer was already ahead of them. He disappeared out of sight.

The young boy swiftly ran off. He caught up with the large manslayer who had by then went around the marker. The young boy ran abreast of him. The manslayer, seeing him, quickened his pace. The young boy, running beside him, surged ahead from time to time. He did this intentionally to make the manslayer work extra hard. The manslayer had to really exert himself. When they approached closer to the finish line, the boy surged ahead again, leaving the manslayer behind.

At the end of the race the young boy didn't proceed to the *qargi*, the community house. Instead he returned to his host's house. He had left the large manslayer behind as well as everyone else who ran the race with him.

After everyone returned home, the father of the family told them, "Tomorrow he'll try to kill all of you. He'll summon you to the *qargi*."

Sure enough, the next morning they were summoned. A man was sent. "The manslayer wants to see the new visitors."

The three visitors didn't hesitate to go. Their hosts accompanied them. People from both settlements assembled inside the *qargi*. They gave the visitors a place to sit near the entrance. There was a big boulder near it. The boulder had blood-stains and strands of hair stuck to it. It was the manslayer's weapon for killing people. The large manslayer sat near the boulder. He called out, "Why aren't the visitors served some food? They should have some food to eat first."

It wasn't long before a person emerged from the back room with a curtain hanging in front. A woman coming out from behind the curtain was totally covered in clothing made from wolverine and wolf hides. She entered carrying the food, but her face remained hidden. She placed the platter steaming with food on the floor. In the platter, the visitors saw human's feet, hands, and parts of human's body. They were cooked human parts.

The young boy's brother-in-law was the first person to be called. He was about to jump down from his seat when the young boy told his brother-in-law that he would take care of it. The young boy jumped down and when he reached the food platter, he kicked it.

"We don't eat things like this!"

The platter flew, the food splattering all over the floor of tree branches.

"*Yaiy*, what an arrogant visitor!" cried the manslayer. He wanted the man sitting up there. He ignored the boy.

The young boy challenged, "Don't bother to call down the two men. Let's fight."

The boy tried to seize the manslayer but couldn't. The manslayer was so huge. Instead the manslayer seized the boy, swirled him around, then threw him toward the boulder. The boy nimbly landed beside it. Again the manslayer seized the boy and threw him toward the boulder. But the boy again landed on his feet beside the rock.

The boy announced that it was his turn. "You've already tried twice. It's now my turn to give it back to you. I'm going to give you what you tried to give me!"

They seized each other. The boy seized the large manslayer by his skin, swung him around, and smacked his head against the boulder. The manslayer's head began to bleed. His head was crushed.

The people in the *qargi* had been watching what was happening. From among the seated people, an old man began to weep. "You should have arrived here earlier. He had just killed my only son! You should have come here sooner. He had killed our only son!" He was weeping as he talked.

The boy asked the people assembled if anyone wanted to avenge the dead manslayer.

"Anyone wanting to avenge this man's death? Come on down. We can fight." The boy was not done with wrestling.

But the people told him, "You've killed the man who has been suppressing us for years. No one here wants to revenge his death. You can do whatever you want with his body. Do to him what he did to others he murdered. Do to him what he did to visitors and to people from other villages."

The boy became the leader. Some young men jumped down, wrapped up the manslayer, and took his body outside. They also took out the rock. After these were done, the young boy told the two men who came with him, "You two go to check and see if your wives are here."

The villagers told them that the manslayer had brought home two women not too long ago. The visitors gave them the names of the two women they were looking for. The young boy himself had earlier recognized his older sister when she brought in the food platter. He recognized her by her mannerism.

"Come on out," he called.

The two lost wives came out. The two husbands took the two women home, but the young boy stayed on.

The people in the two villages continued with their lives. The young boy, a little man, decided to marry one of the women there. He hadn't planned on having a change of clothing for his wedding because he had with him only one set of clothing, the one he was wearing. But the villagers decided to make him a new set, and the women, the makers of the clothing, weren't in want of the needed materials. They had the new set of clothing made, brought it over to him, and made him change into his new clothes.

With the new set of clothing on, the little man became a fine young man. There standing before them was a large, handsome man. The old set of clothing he had been wearing had constrained him and made him look small.

So the young boy, the small man, became a fine-looking young man. He married one of the women in the village.

The married couple lived there for a long time. The young man's father-in-law, considerate of the young man's family, one day told him, "We've been hunting and harvesting many sea mammals. We got both the game animals from the sea and from land. But you yourself have a home of your own. You should return home. You can of course come back here to visit once in a while."

The couple prepared to leave. The young man wanted his *suunaaq* [male friend of the same age] to go with them. They collected food to take on the trip. Who knows what they used for food and transportation. They left (they probably didn't drive a car!). They left (they probably didn't leave in a sno-go!).

When they arrived at the home village of the brother-in-law, they built a house to live in. The woman, the Secluded One, was still living in that village.

The young man told his *suunaaq* that there was a woman in his village who would be a good wife for him. He told his buddy that he too should be married, but his buddy said he didn't want to marry.

Eventually, after the two men had finished building their new house, the young man's buddy agreed to marry the Secluded One, the one who had given the staff to the young man. The buddy had also turned into a good-looking young man after he changed his clothing. The Secluded One was a beautiful young woman herself. She had given the boy the staff so that he would find her a good husband. She knew that the three men leaving on the trip could do it.

The story doesn't go on once they arrived back home. The story only said that the people of the two villages visited each other, traveling back and forth between the two villages, and marrying each other.

The Lost Little Brother

Nora Paniikaaluk Norton

Two key issues in Iñupiaq family relations are explored in this story. What should an Iñupiaq do when a sibling under his care encounters mishap? What should he do when his own sibling commits murder? How the siblings in this story confronted these social issues and how they responded to them creates a poignant tale of community responsibility and family tragedy.

RECORDED IN SELAWIK, AUGUST 8, 1968

AN OLD MAN [ROBERT CLEVELAND] HAS TOLD HIS STORIES. I'M GOING TO tell a short story after him. Thank you, I'm happy now. This summer I was sick. I'm still quite weak but my thoughts can still be expressed. I'm happy my God gave me this opportunity to talk today. I hope all of you people of the Kobuk River can hear my voice. Our God is watching over us even though we're far apart.

Since Robert N. Cleveland had been telling stories, I'll try my best too, even though I'm not a good storyteller. If I could learn fast, I would have learned many more stories from my husband. Why hadn't I learned all of those stories?

I've always regretted not having learned all of his stories. But I can't do anything about that now.

I'll try to tell a story.

A couple had been making a living. They had three sons, two older sons and another youngest son. The small boy, the youngest son, always wanted to follow the two older boys whenever they went hunting, but the two older boys didn't like having him along.

One day—this was during the summer—the two boys went bird hunting. When they took off, the small boy followed them. The two older brothers weren't aware that their younger brother was following. They were so caught up in their bird hunting. Unbeknown to them, they had taken the youngest brother a long way away from home.

After the hunt, the two older brothers started back home but the small boy lost his bearings. He wanted to head home, but he had no idea which direction to take. When the two older boys arrived home and discovered that their young-est brother was missing, they concluded that he had followed them. The whole family searched for the small boy. They searched and searched everywhere, but they weren't able to find him. Soon it grew dark.

Meanwhile, the small boy was crying for help. "Mommy! Daddy!"

He cried and cried, but his parents couldn't hear him.

Night came. It turned dark. The small boy didn't know what to do. Finally he made himself a mat under a tree and sat there because he had no place to sleep. He cried and cried and tears were streaming down his cheeks. He was homesick. When he could no longer stay awake, he would doze off, then wake up again. That was how he spent his first night.

When he woke up, he saw sunlight. He took off walking again. He called out for his parents, he called out for his older brothers, but nothing happened. When he reached a place where berry bushes were growing, he picked the berries and ate them. He had no other food to eat, only the berries. (Who knows what kind of berries they were.) That day he couldn't find his parents. Neither could his parents find him even though they looked and looked for him.

The small boy spent the summer in this manner. Soon, the summer turned into fall. The weather later turned cold and after a certain time, the ground began to freeze. The soles of the boy's mukluks were torn and worn out. When that happened, he tried to walk on his knees. The trousers he was wearing then got also torn around the knees. The poor boy was in a pitiful dilemma. The family he had left behind also grieved his loss, but there was nothing they could do. They were not able find each other.

One night, the boy prepared a place to sleep under a tree. The weather was cold, but he fell asleep anyway. He slept all night. When he woke up, it was getting light, but the snow was falling. It was distressing. He knew that shouting and crying would be futile. There simply was nothing else he could do. There he was—sitting under a tree—and it was snowing!

When it turned bright again, he got up and walked around. His feet felt cold. He tried walking around but found that the berries were all buried under the snow. The berries had been his only food. As he was walking, he spotted something. Although he had no idea what it was, he proceeded toward it because he wanted to find out what it was. At that point he was shivering from the cold, but there was nothing he could do. He had been lost all summer.

When he approached closer to the thing he saw, he discovered a caribou that had been snared. Its skin was torn and part of its flesh was exposed and eaten into. The caribou carcass had been abandoned at that location. The boy didn't have anything else to eat, so he tried a small piece of the caribou meat. The meat tasted all right. He ate the raw caribou meat, cutting off a little piece at a time.

Then a thought occurred to him. "If I can tear its hide into pieces, I can wrap my feet with them."

Somehow he managed to tear a piece of hide off from the caribou. (He couldn't have done that by himself. He must have had a helper.) When he had enough of the hide, he wrapped his feet in it. He also decided to tear out a piece of hide to use as a seat cushion. He tore off the hide somehow and got his cushion. Now he had a caribou to eat and he put down the seat cushion on the ground to sit on in the evening when it turned dark. He felt better now that his feet were covered. Life continued for him. But he felt lonely.

When daylight broke, he woke up. When he walked beyond the carcass of the caribou he saw a mound. He set off toward the mound and kept on walking until he reached it. There he found a small house. The house wasn't very big. The boy thought, "I'm going to enter this house. At this point it doesn't matter what sort of people live in it."

The boy didn't hear anything from inside the house as he approached the entryway, so he entered. Inside he found no one. The house was a little house— just right for him. He stayed inside the house, thinking, "It doesn't matter who lives in this house and what kind of person he is. He can do whatever he wants with me when he comes back."

Dusk approached, but the boy wasn't about to leave the house. He wasn't going to allow himself to be frozen outside. Against all odds, he had found a house. As he felt drowsy, he noticed a rabbit blanket, his size, around there. The poor little boy covered himself with the blanket and went to sleep. The boy had been living in the open. There he still felt lonely but at least he was warm.

When daylight broke, he woke up. Since he couldn't go back to sleep anymore, he got up, looked around, and walked beyond the caribou carcass. On a mound he spotted clay plates. (They called this type of plate *alluiyaq*. I've never had a clay plate, so I don't know what it looks like.) There was food in a plate. The food was all cut up, ready for eating. Another plate was full of oil of some kind of animal. Who knows what kind of fat or oil it was. Who knows from where the food came. The boy proceeded to eat the food. He had a big meal. Since he hadn't eaten like that for a long time, he ate all the cooked food on the plate. He was sated and ended up spending his day at that location. (I wonder how sated and full he felt?)

Once in a while, living in that house, the boy would step outside the house but he could hear no one. There was no one around. When it was time for him to sleep, he would sleep. When he woke up the next morning and the following mornings, there were always different kinds of food for him to eat. Without having to procure food for himself, the boy had food. There were also clothes that fit him for him. There were wolf mukluks and a parka of ground-squirrel skins with fancy trim and wolf ruff. For a long time, the boy continued to live in this manner. And when he grew up and needed bigger-sized clothing, it would be there for him.

The boy became a young man. So far, he hadn't yet seen or heard another person.

One day he gave a lot of thoughts to the way he lived there. "I wonder if there are other people somewhere?"

When this thought occurred to him, he was by then a young man. He could do things for himself and he could even hunt for himself.

The next morning, just before daybreak, when the young man looked up at the skylight he saw the sky and noticed that the weather had changed. He grew wide awake. Soon he heard the sound of something walking in the snow. (When something was walking in the snow, it was audible from inside the house.) He could hear it coming closer and closer. Finally, it came to the front door. The young man already had his harpoon ready because he began to feel uneasy. Then he saw a person entering his house through the entry tunnel.

A woman with a big ruff came into view. She told the young man, "I've come with a message for you. My husband wants you to know that he's feeling weak. He's having a hard time hunting. We want you to be our hunter in his old age.

That's why we've been raising you. My husband is now weak and we want you to be our hunter. He asked me to give you this message."

The woman then went out of the house. The young man could hear her leave.

The young man came to a realization. "So, these are the people who made me homesick. So they are the ones who made me become lost to my brothers and my parents." He remembered how frightened he was when it turned dark. He remembered that as a little boy he was so afraid that some creatures might come and do things to him. After reflecting on his miseries all day and understanding all the facts, he had mixed emotions. From time to time, he cried. He felt worthless.

Night came. Since the woman had told him, "My husband will come to get you," he had very little sleep. He put his weapons—all kinds of harpoons—beside him and lay there, waiting.

Sure enough, just before daybreak, he heard footsteps crunching in the snow. They were footsteps of the person who was coming to get him. When that person arrived at the house, he didn't hesitate, he just entered the house. As soon as he was at the entryway, the young man threw his harpoon at him. He harpooned a large man. The man grunted, fell down, and died. The young man held on to his harpoon, determined to give another try because he knew that the large man didn't come by himself. The woman had told him that the man coming would be her husband.

The young man waited all morning. Then he heard the sound of crunching footsteps in the snow again. The young man seized his harpoon, ready to aim. As soon as the form was visible, he wasted no time in throwing his harpoon. Again he harpooned it. It grunted, then made no more noise.

The young man waited until daybreak before he stepped out to check. What he saw were two large wolves, male and female. He had killed both of them. He realized that the two wolves had raised him. But he also remembered his fright and his loneliness. He was torn with emotions. "They've raised me. I should have helped them for a while." He was in a situation in which his past experience had led him to act in that manner.

He took the two wolves out of the house and took them to the place where there was no sign of human habitation. Only his footprints were there. He buried the two bodies, the bodies of the two who had raised him.

The young man continued to live at that location. When he went out, nothing was too hard for him to accomplish. He started to hunt, for there was no longer someone to provide for him. After some time, he began to wonder if there were other people living somewhere inland. He prepared to leave. When the next morning arrived, he took off—early in the morning.

The young man traveled by way of a ridge. He climbed the ridge and from up there spotted a man. Before he left he had been nursing a wish. "I wish I could meet people." He wanted so much to meet other people. The short, little man he saw was chasing a ptarmigan. He was so engrossed in what he was doing that he paid no attention to anything else.

The two men met.

"I haven't seen a single person since I was a child. *Aarigaa* [how wonderful!], now I've found someone I can talk to," the young man said happily.

The young man he met heartily welcomed his company. He also told the young man about a group of people living down below. However, two young men living down there had become real embarrassments to villagers. The two men were manslayers. They killed people. Already they had killed many, many strangers from out of town. They had all sorts of young men and women working for them. The whole village lived under their command and poor strangers were always killed whenever they arrived.

The young man said it was all right with him, that he still wanted to go down to that village with him.

The man he met said, "We've a little old house on the downriver end of the village. My small children are too mischievous. I'm so embarrassed by their mischiefs that I decided to live on the other end of the village." (The children must be really mischievous!) He said he was trying to catch some ptarmigan to take home for food. He took the young man home.

They went home together and the young man saw that the entry tunnel to the house was a dirt tunnel. (How dirty and muddy the tunnel must be!) The man took his guest inside the house and told his wife that his guest was a welcome guest. But probably the two manslayers already knew about his arrival.

"Do get some food and feed him," he told his wife.

Quickly the wife did what she was asked.

As the wife was bringing out her food and was preparing to feed her guest, the young man noticed that the couple's children were certainly active as their father said. They were all over the place. As he was about to begin eating, they heard a man's voice from up the skylight. "The manslayers want to see the new visitor right away."

His host replied, "Wait until after he has his meal, then we'll go over. I'll come along too."

The host who took him home told his guest that the two manslayers had lost a small boy, their youngest brother. They started to kill people after their search for the lost brother had failed. They proclaimed, "Here comes the person who killed our younger brother," then killed the visitor.

The young man understood, for he was the lost child. He told his host, "I am the person they refer to! The two men are my brothers!"

As he was trying to finish his meal, another messenger came by.

"Hurry! The two brothers don't want to be kept waiting!"

The young man prepared to leave, but his host didn't want to lose him. "You're our cherished guest. Who knows what those men will do to you."

But the young man informed his host, "I must go to them."

So the two left together.

Inside the *qargi,* many people had assembled, including those who served as the two brothers' workers. There were all sorts of men and women. When the young man walked into the *qargi,* his host quickly sat down beside the entrance and told the young man to sit there with him.

"*Yaiy,* this man is arrogant!"

The first person to speak up was the young man's host. "This young man was lost when he followed his brothers to catch some birds. He was following them when he got lost."

One of the brothers told the young man's host to shut up.

"Shut up! Be quiet, you puny little man by the door! Don't butt in all the time! You are lying! You believe what he lied to you. There's no way our younger brother can survive because he has been lost during all these years since that summer. You, the visitor sitting by the door, you've probably killed our younger brother and pretend to be him. Go, bring over the two boulders."

The workers, hearing his command, rushed to follow his order as usual.

The young man explained, "I am your brother. That time when you two were catching birds, you didn't want me to follow you. I did and got lost. I couldn't find the clearing. All summer long I had been surviving on berries."

"Liar!" accused the two brothers.

"Where are our parents?" the young visitor asked.

"They are home," one manslayer said. "Would you recognize your parents?"

"Of course, I can."

"Go. Bring over our parents. Bring along other people too," the two brothers ordered their workers.

The workers brought back many people, including the parents, and seated them in a row. One of the manslayers looked at the young visitor. "Now, let's see if you can go directly to them."

The young man had no hesitation at all as he approached his mother.

"Where is your father?"

The young man pointed his finger at his father.

"However you used to treat other visitors, now go ahead and do it to me!" the young man told his older brothers.

The two manslayers retracted, saying they shouldn't have done what they did. They backed into the people there assembled. The young man didn't halt. He thought about being lost and he felt bad about his older brothers' crime of murder. He stripped down, ready for a fight. He told one of the brothers, "Come on. One of you!"

But the two brothers had no heart to fight.

The young man called out to the other brother, "Go on, do whatever you want with me!" He wasn't able to force himself to harm his older brothers either.

One brother tried to manhandle the young man, but failed.

"Let me!" the young man said.

He seized his brother and smashed him against the boulders.

The other brother started to *nuniaq* [sing endearments to] his younger brother, but words of endearment couldn't stop the latter. He seized his brother. He wanted his brother to manhandle him like he did the other murdered victims. But his older brother couldn't. The younger brother seized him and smashed him too on the boulders. Then, he faced the crowd, "Poor you! You're all free now to go home. This village no longer has terrorists. If you're from elsewhere, feel free to leave. I'm going follow my host home."

The Head

Lois Piŋalu Cleveland

~~~~~~

> *Lois Piŋalu Cleveland was a storyteller from Selawik. Born in 1913, daughter of Mike and Mabel Jones, Lois married a Selawik man, David Cleveland. She had with him four daughters and two sons and*

adopted another son. Lois was a first cousin of Emma Skin, another Selawik storyteller in this collection.

Lois told two stories: "The Head" and "Paałuk, the Klutz." "The Head" has many characteristics of a horror story.

RECORDED IN SELAWIK IN 1972

~~~~~~

THERE WAS A COUPLE LIVING IN A HOUSE WITH THEIR ONLY DAUGHTER. The house was located on the beachfront with a mountain next to it.

The daughter always worked hard for her parents. She got sea animals for her parents to eat. Her parents frequently told her that she should marry, but the daughter told them that she had no wish to marry.

One day, on her way back from picking up the sea animals, the daughter found a human head close to the beach. It was floating in the water. She was terrified. She tried to run away from it, but the head kept turning up in front of her. After repeated happenings and finding that she couldn't get away from it, she picked it up and took it home. Whenever she looked at the head, it would wink at her. She didn't show the head to her parents when she arrived home.

One night when the family turned in for the night, the parents heard their daughter's voice and a man whispering. The parents were glad, thinking their daughter had finally found a boyfriend.

A few days later her parents grew suspicious because they had never seen the man their daughter had been whispering to during the night. So the next day when the daughter went to hunt sea animals for their food, the parents consulted with each other. Afterwards the mother went to her daughter's bed and searched. She brought her daughter's bedding out of the house and started to clean it. Out rolled a human head!

The mother was terrified. Despite her fright, she picked up the head, walked away from the house, and flung it away. The head rolled away toward the north side.

When the daughter returned and found out that the head wasn't there, she wept. She tried to muffle her weeping so that her parents wouldn't hear it, but they heard it anyway. After having her cry, the daughter ran out of the house. She followed the trail her mother had taken when she went to throw the head away. She saw drops of blood on the trail. For many days the daughter kept searching for the head.

One day she came upon a house and saw a person standing next to it, chopping wood. The man didn't realize she was there until she spoke to him.

"Have you seen the head coming this way?" she asked.

"It went that way," the man told her.

The woman took off. A few minutes later she came upon another man. But this man knew nothing about the head. He, however, advised her, "You'd better go home. Don't follow it!"

The woman refused to turn back. She wanted to see her human head friend first.

She left him and kept on walking. She then came upon another house. Inside the house was an old lady. Again she asked the old lady about the head. The old lady advised her, "Go home. It's too dangerous for you to go on."

"I want to go on."

"There are cannibals along the way!" the old lady told her.

But the woman really wanted to see her human head friend. After she left the old lady, she kept on walking until she came upon another house. There she saw many human heads! Those heads all advised her to turn back. But she told them she really wanted to see her friend.

She went to a house. When she entered that house, there he was—her human head friend. The Head was the leader of the people who devoured other humans. The Head said, "When I found you, I had wanted you to be my wife. But your parents don't like me."

"Eat her!" the Head ordered one of his followers.

The woman ran out of the house. The Head's men weren't able to find her. When they had all left, the woman who had pulled her inside her own house gave her instructions. "When you set off from here, go in the direction the sun rises. Along the way you'll come across a trail. Don't ever stray from this trail."

The woman set off, walking for many days before she came across a trail. She followed the trail as instructed and came to a house. When she entered the house, she found a woman inside. The woman told her, "You won't be able to get away unless you follow the instruction I'm going to give you. Now, close your eyes."

But the woman disobeyed the instruction. She opened her eyes even though she was instructed not to. Since she disobeyed her instruction, the woman at the house told her to leave. The young woman had to lick away a piece of the ice window in order to be able to get out of that woman's house.

She took off and continued walking. Again she came across another house. It was exactly like the one she had come across earlier. When she reached this house, the place was pitch-black. She wanted to turn back but found that she couldn't because she was pushed forward by someone. It was pitch-black. She wasn't able to see and she was terrified, but she wasn't able to turn back.

Finally when she saw the light, she noticed two trails in front of her. The left trail was wide, but the right trail was very narrow. While trying to decide which trail to follow, she saw a skeleton. Its eye sockets were crawling with worms. The skeleton told her, "Take the wide road if you want to be like me."

The woman this time obeyed the skeleton and took the very narrow trail. But when she arrived at a place, quite dark, she began to regret following the narrow path. Again she couldn't turn back because someone was pushing her from behind. She continued to walk in the dark until she saw some light in front of her. She tried to walk fast, but the trail was too narrow.

Arriving finally at the bright spot, the woman was happy at what she saw. What she saw in front of her was a beautiful place with flowers growing everywhere. She looked around and saw a house. She walked toward it. As she approached closer, she saw a cache and a man's equipment. But when she entered the house, she found no one inside. Dried pieces of caribou meat were hanging inside the house.

When evening arrived, she heard someone outside the house. The arriving man, noticing her footprints, spoke. "Finally, I have a visitor!"

When the woman arrived at this house, she noticed two bags sitting in the storm shed. The bags were made of seal skins. One was sitting on one side of the shed and the other on the other side.

A man entered. He asked the woman if she had eaten. The woman answered, "I ate a little."

"Eat anything you like because you won't be able to leave here. Did you see the two bags sitting in the storm shed? Don't touch them! Don't ever think about opening them!"

The man told her that he would constantly be gone hunting or doing something. He wouldn't be home most of the time. "If you want something to do, there's enough work to do in the cache," he said.

Always the man hunted. Always he worked hard.

One day he asked the woman if she had seen anything unusual. She told him that a little man came and tried to persuade her to peek into the box sitting in the middle of the cache. He would let her see the hunters, the little man had told her. But she had refused to do what the little man said.

The man, the hunter, forbade her to do what the little man asked. He checked things in the house. "I can't catch that man. But if you don't do what he asked you to do, you'll live," the man told her.

And the woman continued to live in that house as the man had instructed.

One day, the man went hunting again. Staying by herself at home, the woman puzzled over the question why he didn't want his two bags opened.

The day after he left for the hunt, she could no longer contain her curiosity. She went to the storm shed and opened a bag. She untied the bag. Inside two polar bears were growling, trying to get out.

The woman screamed for help. The man rushed back and stomped the bears back into the bag with the snowshoes he was wearing.

"If I hadn't heard you, the polar bears would have killed you!" he told her. "They're my dogs! I use them whenever I have plenty of things to carry home."

The next day the man didn't go out to hunt. He was afraid the woman might disobey him again.

One day when the man left for his hunt again, the woman contemplated opening the other bag. The day after his departure, she opened the bag. When she untied the bag, she again saw two polar bears fighting. She screamed and the man heard her. He rushed home and forced the bears back into the bag. After both bears were put away, he told her, "You've been lucky I heard you. If I hadn't they would have killed you!"

The man didn't go hunting again after this last incident. He told the woman, "I like you a lot and want you to stay here. But you always do what you're not supposed to do. If you want to go home, you can leave now."

The man told her about the sinew he had. If she wanted to go home, she should braid the sinew into a head. The woman went to the cache, located the sinew, and started braiding. It took her a few days to braid it to the size of a head. She was next told to braid a harness her size. She made a harness like a dog harness that fit her, then made a bag for carrying food.

"When you land on the ground, you should go toward the ocean. You'll come to the place where you used to hunt. You'll recognize it once you arrive there. From there on you can go home to your parents."

The man's last instruction was that she should practice dancing once she arrived home.

When the woman was ready, she was told to enter the box in the middle of the cache. The man lowered her down to the ground by the braided sinew. When she landed, she walked and walked until she reached an ocean. As she followed the beach line, she began to recognize it as the place where she used to hunt sea animals. She proceeded toward her house, but no one was there. Her parents had already moved to live elsewhere.

The woman ended up staying with other people. When some of them came to get her to go dancing with them, the woman was so exhausted from the trip that she turned down the invitation. She told them she would do so the next day.

The next day arrived. But the woman had turned into an old woman—so old that she couldn't move. She had turned old overnight because she failed to do what the man had told her to do. She became so old that she finally passed away.

Nakasruktuuq, the Sleepyhead

Nora Paniikaaluk Norton

~~~~~~

The human position in the hierarchy of living things is presented here through the person and voice of a caribou. Nakasruktuuq, a lazy husband, learned the hard way how lucky he was to be human and have a loving family. Iñupiaq teaching methods are indirect. Among Iñupiat who know the story, Nakasruktuuq is often evoked in humorous self-deprecation or teasing reprimand of a person who is lazy or sleeps late.

RECORDED IN SELAWIK, MARCH 7, 1972

~~~~~~

THERE WAS A COUPLE WITH A DAUGHTER.

A man named Nakasruktuuq married their daughter. After the marriage Nakasruktuuq's wife gave birth to two sons. The young couple raised their sons, living with the wife's parents.

Often Nakasruktuuq's father-in-law would be irritated at his son-in-law because Nakasruktuuq had a habit of sleeping late.

One morning, when Nakasruktuuq finally got up, his father-in-law made a comment. "*Nanaa*, this guy sleeps too much! He's so lackadaisical at doing things!"

Nakasruktuuq's sons were already young boys by that time. Nakasruktuuq's wife heard what her father said, but she kept quiet. Actually the son-in-law's name wasn't Nakasruktuuq. His father-in-law gave him this name because he always slept late.

Nakasruktuuq, hurt by his father-in-law's criticism, felt depressed. He began to think of himself as worthless. He wondered where he should go because he no longer wanted to stay in his in-laws' house. Even though he loved his wife and his two sons, he decided to leave them. His wife didn't want him to leave, but he had lost his will to stay on.

Nakasruktuuq left. As he was traveling, he saw some caribou. He thought to himself, "Hmm, I wonder what it'd be like if I go with the caribou." He no longer wanted to see humans.

He traveled alongside the caribou herd. Whenever the caribou left him behind, Nakasruktuuq would later catch up with them. Finally, after traveling like that for some time, one of the caribou came toward him. When it reached him, it took off its hood and talked. The caribou told Nakasruktuuq, "My, my, you surely don't realize how easy you had it back home. You could sleep as long as you wished. Why are you following us? Being caribou, our life is hard by comparison. We always suffer. Whenever we want to snooze a little, the wolves would attack us. (The wolves would catch and eat the caribou found sleeping. That was how the caribou lived.) You had such an easy life. Why are you tagging along? If you continue to follow us, you'll discover that living our miserable life, sometimes we have to run off as fast as we can. Whenever we find wolves nearby, we have to run off faster—as fast as possible. When we're fleeing like that, you won't be able to keep up with us."

Nakasruktuuq told the caribou that it was all right with him. It mattered no more whether he lived or died because he felt so hurt. He told the caribou what his father-in-law had said. He would never return to his in-laws. He said that even though he loved his wife and his two sons, he had left them anyway.

When the caribou who came up to Nakasruktuuq realized that he couldn't talk Nakasruktuuq out of leaving, he showed Nakasruktuuq what to do.

"I'll show you what to do," the caribou said.

He put his hood back on and turned back into a caribou. Then the caribou pawed the ground with his left hoof. There, on the spot, dried fish roe appeared.

The caribou told Nakasruktuuq that he would show him more later on. He instructed Nakasruktuuq that when they ran off fast, Nakasruktuuq was not to look at the ground. Nakasruktuuq was to fix his gaze on the horizon. Nakasruktuuq became a caribou and he began living with them.

One day the wolves suddenly attacked the herd. The herd ran off, leaving Nakasruktuuq behind. Nakasruktuuq was running as fast as he could. No wonder they told him not to become a caribou! Noticing that Nakasruktuuq was lagging behind, one of the caribou came to him and told him "You're still distracted by the ground—that's why you're so slow." The caribou then showed him what to do.

Another morning, the herd heard a man coming toward them, making loud noises. It sounded like the man was walking on a flooring of willow branches. When the caribou heard this sound, they knew that the person coming toward them always slept late because he clumsily made too much noise. And later when another person approached, accompanied by the sound of metal, the caribou who heard it knew that this person had no water dipper and was drinking water from a bucket. Nakasruktuuq learned all of these while living as a caribou.

Summer approached and Nakasruktuuq was still living with the caribou. The heat became unbearable and there were lots of mosquitoes. The caribou, however, knew how to make their own breeze during the summer. They galloped to create a breeze to cool themselves.

One day, as the heat became more and more unbearable, Nakasruktuuq created a breeze. He galloped. While galloping, he didn't notice a snare that was set on the trail to catch caribou. He got caught in that snare. He tried to free himself but wasn't able to. He wanted to remove the snare, but the snare wouldn't come loose. After struggling for a while, he felt he was suffocating.

While he was in this unfortunate predicament, two young men approached. They had weapons with them and they both looked strong. One of the young men drew his weapon. Nakasruktuuq, the caribou, lifted his hood and spoke. "I'm not at all a caribou, good for eating! I didn't grow up a caribou! I was a human being, but my father-in-law caused me grief, so I left. My name is Nakasruktuuq. That was my name when I was a human being. I was so upset and so hurt that I left my poor two sons and their mother, my wife. I left because my father-in-law criticized that I slept too much. He said that within my hearing. If he had said so only once, it wouldn't have mattered. But he said it again and again. I left my two sons. I loved my sons very much, but I left them. Really, I'm not at all a caribou, good for eating! I was just trying to cool off when I got caught. I didn't see this snare. I came upon it so suddenly."

The two young men set down their weapons.

"You are our father! Most likely, you are our father!"

They told Nakasruktuuq that their mother had told them that their father had taken off from home because their grandfather talked ill of him. Their mother told them the story when they became young men.

"We are your sons!" said the two young men.

They took off the snare from Nakasruktuuq and Nakasruktuuq became a human being again. His snout, however, didn't recede all the way. It remained somewhat like the snout of a caribou.

You know how Nakasruktuuq became a caribou. His sons had found him before he died and took him home when they realized that he was their father. Nakasruktuuq's in-laws were already dead by then. Nakasruktuuq's wife and her two sons had been living still in the same place. The family continued to live together there. But for Nakasruktuuq, human's food no longer tasted good to him. He had been living like a caribou far too long. He had grown used to eating caribou's food. And this is as far as the story goes.

People of long ago used *aluq* to make snares to catch caribou. It was probably seal hide cut into strips as rope. Nakasruktuuq was probably caught at the neck by the seal hide rope.

Marie Clark [a member of the audience]: "Or it could have been walrus hide rope?"

Nora Norton [the storyteller]: "Maybe."

Paałuk, the Klutz

Lois Piŋalu Cleveland

~~~~~~

> *Although it is not overtly stated, the main character of this story is an orphan. As with many other orphans in Iñupiaq stories, he lived with his grandmother. Paałuk's grandmother appears to have certain magical powers, which she used to help her grandson win a village race despite his handicap.*
>
> *The following seven stories with an orphan as the main character form the orphan story complex. For a fuller analysis of the orphan stories, see the second introductory chapter "Iñupiaq Narratives and Culture: The Interplay."*
>
> RECORDED IN SELAWIK, 1972

~~~~~~

THERE WAS A MAN NAMED PAAŁUK. (THE NAME MEANS A PERSON WHO constantly falls down.) Every few seconds Paałuk would fall down.

Paałuk lived with his grandmother. One day as they were preparing to move to another location, his grandmother told Paałuk to climb up a snowbank and whistle for the dogs to come over. Paałuk climbed up the snowbank and then ran down, whistling. Two small wolves ran after him. He hadn't raised the two wolves, but when he whistled as his grandmother instructed him, those wolves acted as if they had known him for a long time.

His grandmother next told him to shovel the snowbank. When Paałuk did as he was told, he found many things he needed. He put food and all the needed things onto the sled and the two of them took off for their camp.

Paałuk and his grandmother were the first to reach the camp, ahead of other campers. Because of that, they were able to select a good spot to camp before others arrived. Other people didn't know that Paałuk and his grandmother had wolves as their dogs.

After camping there for a while, Paałuk and his grandmother traveled to another village. In that village, the villagers one day organized a game. The leader of the game told Paałuk to take his place in the foot race because Paałuk seemed to be stronger and more nimble than he was. With the name "Paałuk," meaning a person who always fell down whenever he walked or ran, his grandmother gave him light mukluks to wear for the race.

Paałuk joined the race.

When he was ready to take off from the starting line, his grandmother told him, "When you've warmed up along the race course and begin to pass other racers to the finishing line, you are to jump off the cliff. While you are in mid-air, clean your feet a little." That's what his grandmother instructed him before Paałuk took off on the race.

When the men ran from the starting line, Paałuk set off too. But he fell. The other racers ran and they were so much ahead of him that soon they were out of sight. Paałuk ran after them, falling every few seconds.

When Paałuk arrived at a place where he couldn't be seen by the spectators, he began to increase his speed. He didn't fall down—not even once. He felt stronger and more nimble as he ran along. When he caught up with the last racer, the latter asked him who he was. Paałuk told him he was Paałuk. The racer was really surprised because all of them thought Paałuk couldn't run as fast as they could. Every time Paałuk passed another racer, that racer would ask who he was.

Finally Paałuk managed to catch up with the racer who was the lead in the race. When Paałuk reached the cliff, he jumped off the cliff as his grandmother had instructed him. He remembered that he had to clean his feet, so he rubbed his feet against each other. Paałuk came in first at the finishing line. After that, other racers came in, one by one, but they all came in after Paałuk.

The Orphan in the Beaver House

John Patkuraq Brown

RECORDED IN SELAWIK, SEPTEMBER 7, 1968

A CHILD AND HIS UNCLE WENT HUNTING. THE CHILD WAS AN ORPHAN and the uncle was a young man. The two of them found a beaver house. They tore open the beaver's house.

On that hunting trip, while roasting rabbits for their meal, the orphan told his uncle, "I'm watching you, my uncle, through the eyes of a rabbit!"

The uncle was quite disturbed by his nephew's words.

After a while, the two decided to return again to the beaver house. The uncle instructed the orphan to take along some arrows and to go down the riverbank into the beaver house and wait for the beavers. The orphan followed his instruction. But once the orphan was at the beaver house, the uncle covered the house that they had torn open earlier. The orphan, a small boy still, started to cry. (I wonder if the orphan stayed there one night or two nights?) He cried every time he woke up because he had nothing to eat and it was pitch dark in the beaver house.

Inside the beaver house, the beavers had mats of wood shavings on the floor. (I wonder who made the wood shavings?) The orphan was sleeping when a woman woke him up.

"You! You are making my children go hungry. Move! Scoot closer to the wall."

The orphan opened his eyes and saw that the house was all lighted up. He moved up against the wall. He also saw a large woman in the house. Children began streaming into the house. A man entered. Another young man entered. As the orphan watched, they began to have their meal.

"That man shouldn't be left by himself like that. He too should have something to eat." Wouldn't you know, that's what the man of the house said.

They were eating fish and dried meat, so the orphan was invited to eat with them. Their children were all full of pep. They frolicked from place to place and wanted to play with the orphan. They wouldn't however permit the orphan to go out the entryway. The orphan himself knew nothing about the house entryway since he had come into the house from above.

For some time the orphan lived with the family. At all times, the man of the house wanted the light on in the house. "A large, crazy man might come into the house if we don't leave the light on," he explained.

One day a man appeared at the entryway. The orphan saw the man, a real person. But the man later went away. The man of the house told the orphan, "Had you not been here, that man would have taken one of my children as his food. That's the large, crazy man I had told you about earlier." The man in the house was referring to the land otter who probably would have taken one of the young beavers for food.

The orphan grew worried, but the man of the house who noticed him brooding told him, "Don't worry. When you hear the Canadian geese in the sky in spring, you'll be able to leave." Whenever the orphan was gloomy, they would reassure him that he would be able to leave.

The orphan lived there for a long time. He later discovered that the young man who stayed in the other room didn't eat any fish's head. He had gloves on at all times.

One day, they heard a Canadian goose honking. They heard it flying overhead. The man of the house took out a shiny new ax and cut a hole at the top of their house. The orphan had entered this house a long time ago since the time his uncle had dropped him there. When the hole at the top of the house was cut open, the man of the house said, "This person will not leave here without having any food to take along with him. He should take along one of my children as travel food."

"You are the one!" the children told one child before they dove into the water.

A girl, probably a little girl, slid her arms into her parka. She stood in front of the orphan. Then she toppled forward and lay still on the ground.

"When you leave, you'll see an owl sitting on a tree. Shoot it! Watch your arrow. Watch where your arrow hits, then walk to it," the man of the house instructed him.

(I wonder what the orphan did when he was about to leave the beaver house? Did he close his eyes or did he keep them open? I can't recall this part, what the storyteller actually said.)

"Take this girl and take her outside the house. When you're outside, hit her behind the head. You can use her as food while traveling," he was told.

When the orphan went outside, he saw that the little beaver he brought out of the house with him was the one born just the year before. He hit the little beaver behind the head as he was instructed to do.

And when the orphan stood up to survey his surroundings, he spotted an owl like he was told. He shot the owl with an arrow. He watched where his arrow had landed, then walked over. There he found that he was right in front of a black bear's den. He also killed the black bear. He hadn't forgotten his way home and so he was able to head home without difficulties.

The man of the house had given the orphan one of his children to eat. He told the orphan about the food he was to receive. He did what many people wouldn't have done.

The orphan used the bear hide as his sled and walked on home. As it happened, the orphan had been eating willows while he was living with the beavers. Afterwards whenever he ate something that upset his stomach, he would vomit willow. At the time he thought he was eating fish.

When the orphan arrived home, he killed his uncle.

(The person who gave one of his children as food to the orphan had extended himself beyond others, including me perhaps.)

The Orphan with Bear Helpers

Emma Atluk Skin

Emma Atluk Skin was born in 1889, a daughter of Nuqaqsrauraq and Tunnuq. Her half brothers were Frank and James Ramoth. Emma married Tommy Panitchiaq Skin and lived at Kuutchiaq before moving to the present Selawik village site. Emma was known as an excellent storyteller and once in a while would tell stories at the end of the Friends Church services to entertain the congregation. The couple had three children.

Emma passed away in 1984 at the age of ninety-five.

RECORDED IN SELAWIK, MARCH 7, 1972

THERE WAS AN OLD WOMAN AND HER GRANDSON LIVING AT THE MOUTH of a slough.

The grandmother was so old that she advised her grandson that upon her death he was to take her outside, out of the house, wrap her in something, then place her on top of a scaffold. She also instructed him to go toward the headwaters of the slough where, in a village, lived his *agnaqatigiik* [maternal parallel cousin]. "A manslayer lives there in the village," she warned him.

When the grandmother passed away, her grandson wrapped her according to her instruction, then placed her atop a scaffold. Afterwards he took off, making his trip up the slough.

The grandson traveled all day. When he felt so exhausted and was about to stop and take a rest, he saw a house with smoke curling up the top of the roof. For a moment he hesitated, but then he decided to enter. Inside the house, he found a couple. The grandson spent the night with them. Probably the couple didn't have any children of their own.

When daylight broke, the grandson left, still traveling toward the headwaters. After another whole day of traveling, the young man needed to stop for the night. He came upon a house that again had smoke billowing up the roof. When he reached the house, a large woman came out to greet him. She was so taken by his good looks that she picked him up and carried him into the house where a large old man was also present. They gave him food to eat. They had a lot of food and they were both fat. The young man spent the night there.

The couple told him about his maternal cousin who lived up at the village. They also told him about a manslayer who liked to challenge visitors coming into the village. After spending the night there and the young man was ready to leave, the couple told him, "Whenever you suspect that you're about to be killed, try to send us your thought."

With that advice, the young man set off. He was told to look back after walking for a while. After walking some distance, he looked back. What he saw were two grizzly bears standing in the open.

The young man traveled all day and came upon a village by nightfall. Carefully examining the village, he noticed a house sitting on one side of the village. "Maybe that's the house," he thought.

He decided to go into that house unannounced. Upon entering the house, he discovered that he just walked into the house of his maternal cousin who had once lived with his grandmother. So he arrived at the right house and that was where he decided to stay. Both he and his cousin were orphans, but his cousin was slightly older than he was. They enjoyed each other's company so much that they didn't pay much attention to others who came into the house later on, including a young man.

Soon people began to assemble in the *qargi*. The gathering took place whenever a visitor came into the village. There in the *qargi* the manslayer assembled all the villagers.

A man came for the visitor, saying that the manslayer wanted to see him. The cousin took the message, but the two of them were having such a great time with each other that they were in no rush to go to the *qargi*. After a while, another messenger arrived and told them to go to the *qargi* immediately. But the two cousins were so happy to see each other that they didn't hurry over. They talked with each other a while longer before leaving for the *qargi*.

In the *qargi* the crowd had assembled. Around the village, no one could be seen outside as all assembled inside the *qargi*. When the two cousins entered, they saw a hearth in the middle of the *qargi* with ashes in it.

The manslayer seized his drum, began beating it, then walked slowly around the ashes while beating his drum. As he was about to reach the spot where he started his walk, everyone heard some sounds out in the entry tunnel. They were the sound of a flounder or something and the sound of people splashing in the water.

After the feat, the manslayer dropped his drum and told the orphan to perform similarly. "Now, let's see you try it."

The orphan had never held a drum before. Nevertheless, he didn't hesitate because he was afraid of the manslayer.

The orphan took the drum in his hand and started to beat the drum the way the manslayer did. He walked around the hearth. He walked around slowly while beating the drum. When he was about to reach the spot where he started his walk, there appeared on a small piece of hide two small black-capped chickadees hopping about. They were hopping around, looking for something to eat. When the orphan let go of the drum, the two black-capped chickadees disappeared.

The manslayer remarked, "That's entertaining! Do it again!"

The manslayer was used to having people do whatever he ordered them to do. The orphan didn't hesitate. Again he picked up the drum and walked around the hearth while beating the drum. When he was about to reach the spot where he started his walk, there came creaking noises near the entry to the tunnel. They were terrifying noises. People could hear two creatures out there making the loud noises while trying to squeeze through the entry tunnel.

In came two grizzly bears!

The people were terrified. The orphan set down the drum. He pointed out the manslayer and told the bears to kill him. The two bears approached the manslayer, pulled out his arms and legs and killed him.

After the manslayer was killed, the orphan asked the villagers, "Are there more troublemakers in the village?"

His maternal cousin pointed out those troublemakers. With his cousin's verification of their wrongdoings, the orphan instructed the bears to go after them until all were killed. After getting rid of all the troublemakers, the bears disappeared.

The people of the village feared and respected the orphan. Who knows, maybe he became the *ataniq*, the head of the village.

The Orphan with the Doll

John Patkuraq Brown

RECORDED IN SELAWIK, SEPTEMBER 7, 1968

I'LL TELL A STORY ABOUT A POOR ORPHAN TOO.

An orphan lived in a village *qargi*, the place people used for getting together. A rich man's son, not yet married, had been a friend to the orphan.

Whenever the villagers left the village to hunt, the orphan would be the only person left in the *qargi*. When the villagers left during the summer, they would return home later on. And when spring came around, they would again leave the village. With each departure, they would come back.

("Was the orphan in the *qargi* alone?" asked a listener.

"Yes, he was all alone, living by himself—the only one left in the *qargi*," John Brown answered.)

There were people living in houses across from the *qargi*. During winter these people would make their trips across the sea. Those who were able to make the trip would leave, but those who weren't able to would be left behind.

One summer the orphan was again the only person left in the *qargi*. An idea occurred to him. He had an urge to make something. He wanted to work on something, but he couldn't at first decide what exactly he should be working on. One day he made his decision. He decided to carve a doll.

The orphan worked on the doll until it was finished. He stood it up, but the doll didn't move. The orphan disassembled it, then reassembled it. (I wonder if he sewed it up or he did something else to it?)

He stood the little doll up again. This time it took off running. He grabbed it and stored it behind the wall of the *qargi,* in the sod.

The orphan did nothing for a while. Then he started on a toy polar bear. After the polar bear was carved, he made a small spear with a spearpoint for his doll. When he set the toy polar bear down, the bear took off running. The doll ran after it and speared it. After the chase, the orphan put both of them away in his parka. This little orphan had a belly that wasn't like ours. He always kept his toys in his parka against his belly.

The villagers returned to the village and spent the fall time at home. When winter arrived, they prepared themselves for the trip across the sea.

Both the son and the daughter of the *aŋaayyuqaq*, the village chief, had no spouse. The orphan went to their house. He never visited with others. He told both of them about the things he had made. At first they didn't react, but later the older brother said, "You should have come here earlier." (What does this mean? Does it mean that he would then be able to get ready in a few days?)

But when the older brother finally agreed to make the trip, he let the orphan wear his clothing. The orphan went back to the *qargi*. He took nothing else with him except the doll and the toy polar bear in his parka. Those were all he took along with him.

They walked across the sea all day. Several times two young men who were also along on the trip would push and bully the orphan. They kept remarking, "Why does this idiot have to come along with us?" The orphan was trying his best to walk across the sea like the others. But that was his very first trip.

Who knows how long it took them to go across the sea. Arriving at the other side of the sea, they came to a large group of people with an *umialik* and *aŋaayyuqaq*, a rich man and chief, living among them. The two young men stopped there and when they were told to go to a gathering, they went. The young man had the orphan sit behind him by the entrance.

People began to bring in supplies they had been gathering all through the year. Everyone talked about the belongings he had brought along with him. When it was the turn of the *umialik*'s son to speak, he gave his talk. Then the man who was seated far inside, the chief, asked the little orphan what he brought with him. The orphan tried not to disclose what he had. As it was, they were all talking about what they were about to give to the person seated far inside.

The chief took something out of a double-layer bag. When he showed it to the crowd, what they saw was a doll. When the chief set down his doll, it took off. The doll belonged to the owner of the house, the one seated far inside. All through the years, people had been bringing things over to give to the man just to see his toy—the doll that could move by itself!

The orphan said nothing. He had similar things in his parka. He also had a toy polar bear. He noticed that the chief's doll had no weapon and neither did the chief have a polar bear.

The chief stood up his doll and it took off walking and running. After the performance, the chief put it away. He received many gifts from the people who came there just to see this doll. During all these years people had been traveling across the sea just to be able to see it.

When the chief's doll was put away, the orphan announced that he too wanted to show his. The chief told him that if he had something to show, he should do so.

The orphan had no bags. He had his toys in his parka. He took out the two toys he had been carrying all day inside his parka. He let them go. The doll caught up with the polar bear and speared it. After the spearing, they fell down. The orphan showed his toys, then put them back inside his parka. He told the chief that he wanted to see the chief's doll again.

The chief took out the doll he had shown earlier and had put away. When the chief made his doll walk around, the orphan took out his doll and placed it on the floor. It had a weapon. It followed the other doll, then speared it with its weapon. The orphan then lifted it up and put it back inside his parka. The orphan always kept his toys against his belly.

The chief picked up his doll and tried to stand it up again, but it wouldn't. It no longer moved. The orphan's doll had probably killed it. The chief wasn't angry at what happened to his doll. After inspecting his doll again, he decided to buy the orphan's doll. He offered the orphan half of the gifts he had accumulated all through the years. But the orphan didn't accept the offer and asked instead for the chief's daughter. The chief asked his daughter for her consent, and she agreed to be part of the deal. When she said "yes," the orphan gave his doll to her father.

The orphan had asked for the chief's daughter for his friend, the son of the *umialik* of his village who had brought him to this place across the sea. The way things worked out, the orphan had given the *umialik*'s son a gift. He gave the young woman to his *suunaaq* [friend of the same age]. (Who knows when the two returned home. I don't know when they made the trip back.)

For years the orphan had been thinking about this trip. He had made a doll similar to the one owned by the *umialik*. Then he made his doll kill the *umialik*'s doll.

The Orphan with No Clothes

Emma Atluk Skin

RECORDED IN SELAWIK, DECEMBER 18, 1971

~~~~~~

A GROUP OF MEN NORMALLY HAD THEIR MEALS IN THE *QARGI*, THE VILLAGE'S community house. Their wives cooked for them and brought them caribou meat to eat.

Living also in the *qargi* was a teenage boy. He lived there because he had no parents. Neither did he have any clothes to wear because he was so poor.

Whenever the women brought cooked caribou meat to the community house, the young boy would have the meat that was given to him as his meal. When everybody returned home, he would be the only one left in the *qargi*. He slept there naked because he had nothing to wear. And with no light in the *qargi*, it was pitch-black at night.

Time passed and the orphan became a young man.

Living in the *qargi*, the orphan would hear stories told by other young men who had traveled to different villages. These young men would be gone for a whole month, then return home when they ran out of travel food.

In another village, there lived an *umialik*. He had a daughter who had no wish to marry. Many young men wanted to marry her. These young men would travel to her village even though the trip was long, as long as a whole month. When these young men returned home, the poor orphan with no clothes would hear their stories about the trip.

When the orphan became a young man, he took a pair of discarded skin trousers from the cache of a childless couple. He also took from them a pair of thigh-high mukluks. He had no parka for his torso. He didn't inform the childless couple that he had taken their clothing. That night when everyone else went to sleep, the orphan put on this clothing, then took off on a trail. He wore nothing at all on his torso.

The next day when the men went to the *qargi*, they found the orphan gone. Well aware that the orphan wore no clothing, they all feared that he could freeze to death. They quickly launched a search party. They were able to locate his footprints along a trail. The orphan appeared to be running. The young men in the search team followed his footprints, thinking they would in the end find a frozen body. But these young men in the search party got so exhausted from the search that they eventually had to turn back home.

The orphan ran all the way and reached the second village in one night, a feat others couldn't accomplish. The village was that of the *umialik*'s daughter who had no wish to marry. When he reached the house of the *umialik*, he thought he was at the skylight of the house of the *umialik* with the unmarried daughter. But he was, in fact, at the entryway to the tunnel. There at the entryway he squatted.

Inside the house, the *umialik*'s young daughter was sewing. Her father was also there fast asleep. The orphan, hunched over all night, began to feel chilled. He shivered and his jaws clattered noisily. The sweating in his mukluks made him feel even colder.

The clattering of the orphan's jaws woke up the *umialik*. He told his daughter, "Daughter, some being is here as a human being. Go out and let him enter our house. He'll add a lot to our household even if the only thing he can do is to carry out our honey bucket!"

The daughter immediately went out and brought in the orphan. She made him lie down in her bed. He had no parka on his torso.

In the meanwhile, in the orphan's village, the villagers had all given up their search for the orphan. Only the couple who couldn't find their skin trousers and mukluks figured out that the orphan had taken them.

When the orphan was warmed again, the *umialik*'s daughter gave him the clothing she had been sewing to wear. The orphan married the *umialik*'s daughter. With the new clothing, the orphan went hunting and caught many caribou for these two people, father and daughter. It is said that the orphan got a lot of caribou because he was a lucky hunter.

After living together for some time, the orphan asked his father-in-law if he could take his wife back for a short visit to his home village. His father-in-law, not possessive of his own daughter, gave the orphan permission under the provision that his daughter would be brought back home after the visit.

The *umialik*'s daughter gave her husband a pair of wolf-skin mukluks and a fancy squirrel parka to wear. And he looked handsome wearing them.

In the morning the orphan seated his wife in the sled. They arrived at his home village in one day, without stopping to rest anywhere along the way. His fellow villagers didn't recognize him at all. "I wonder who this stranger is?" they all said.

The orphan went directly to the house of the couple from whom he had taken the trousers and the mukluks. He confessed to the couple that he was the person who took those clothing. He hunted so much caribou for the childless couple that they would never run out of food. He ran errands for them and did chores for them.

The orphan and his wife stayed in his village for a while. Who knows how long they stayed there. Then, towing his wife in the sled, the orphan left his village to return to his wife's village—without even stopping to camp.

The Orphan Who Won the Ring

Leslie Tusraġviuraq Burnett

~~~~~~

This story was told outside the storyteller's house while he was supervising Kignak, his son-in-law, repair his equipment. Observe the storyteller-audience interaction at the end of the story.

RECORDED IN SELAWIK, FEBRUARY 11, 1972

~~~~~~

I'M GOING TO TELL ANOTHER STORY. THERE WAS A YOUNG WOMAN WHO had no wish to marry. She erected a post and placed a ring on top of it.

All the young men were interested in her. They all wanted her for their wife. (Didn't I tell this story before? But anyway I'll tell it again.) The young woman declared that if any young man could climb up the post and get the ring, she would marry him. All the young men tried but none could climb up high enough. As each young man envisioned the image of the young woman he hoped to marry, he tried his very best to climb up the post.

There was an orphan who had been watching these young men making their attempts. After watching them for some time, the orphan decided to make a try himself. He thought he could do it. When everyone left, he climbed up the post, got the ring, and then sewed it onto his parka. He didn't take the ring to the young woman. In his own mind, he didn't consider himself worthy of the young woman.

The orphan, after obtaining the ring, frequently visited another young man who was living with his parents. He made all of these visits in the evenings. One evening on his visit, he told the other young man about the ring he had taken from the top of the post. He also told the other young man that he had the ring on his person.

That family was not poor. The other young man began to bargain with the orphan for the ring. After rejecting several offers, the orphan proposed trading the ring for the tip of the other man's ear. The latter agreed. He sharpened his knife, made an attempt to cut his ear, but the cut hurt so badly that he couldn't finish the job. But when he envisioned the image of the young woman, the desire to have her as his wife was so strong that he quickly grabbed his ear and cut off the tip. He gave the cut ear to the orphan and asked for the ring. The orphan gave him the ring sewn inside his parka. In its place he kept the tip of the young man's ear.

When the ear of the young man was healed (probably his ear wasn't cut with a clipper!) and no one could see the cut ear because his hair was long, he gave the ring to the young woman. He married the young woman after giving her the ring.

The orphan often visited the husband with whom he had traded the ring for an ear. The husband eventually grew jealous of the orphan even though the latter did nothing to provoke the jealousy. That upset the orphan.

One day the wife was either removing her husband's gray hair or was looking for lice in the hair of her husband who was lying with his head on her lap. The orphan told the wife, "Actually I am the person who had fetched the ring from the post. I traded it for the tip of the young man's ear. You should check his ear."

When the wife parted her husband's hair, she saw the missing ear tip. So the young woman discovered the truth. She asked the orphan, "When you got the ring, why didn't you bring it over to me?"

The orphan told her that he wasn't worthy to be her husband because he was just an orphan. He had doubts about himself. But he got the ring and traded it for the man's ear.

Upon discovering the truth, the young woman made her husband leave. The orphan had shown her the ear tip, all dried up.

"When you got the ring," the young woman asked the orphan, "why didn't you bring it to me right away? I had placed the ring that way to find a man who is tough, the man who can endure severe hardships when he goes hunting."

But the orphan kept insisting that he wasn't worthy to be her husband.

When I told this story in Kotzebue, David Adams said, "If I didn't get the ring on the first try, I'd rub tar on my legs and then try again!"

Perhaps we should rub tar on our hands too before trying to climb the post. We talked about the strategies and had a good laugh. I myself wouldn't be able to marry the young woman because I wouldn't be able to fetch that thing on the post.

I wonder what Kignaq [an audience member] would do? Maybe he would be lucky—because he's tough—and marry that young woman who had no wish to marry. Kignaq standing over there is big and tall. He is my son-in-law. I know him, but he won't talk into this tape. He should at least say "Hello" into the tape.

It's good to hear a person's adventures. It's good too to hear a story from elsewhere. It's good to hear stories from Barrow.

The Orphan Who Married an *Umialik's* Daughter

Nora Paniikaaluk Norton

RECORDED IN SELAWIK, SEPTEMBER 9, 1968

~~~~~~

I'M GOING TO TELL ANOTHER SHORT STORY. I HAD TOLD SOME STORIES yesterday. If I could have learned faster, I'd have more good stories to tell. I'll tell this story as I remember it.

There was a large group of people making a living in this area. Across the river from the main part of the village lived a grandmother and her grandson. The grandmother was raising the boy. They had a small, dilapidated house, probably an underground sod house. The orphan soon grew up. The children living across from their house, boys as well as girls, and the orphan boy always played together.

The people of the village had two rich families living among them. On the farthest side, up the river, was an *umialik* with a daughter. Farther down the river lived another *umialik*. He also had a daughter.

The poor orphan became a young man. One day he thought he wanted to marry the daughter of one of the *umialik*. He had been growing up playing with all the children in the village including the *umialik*'s daughters. So he told his grandmother, "Grandma, I want to marry the *umialik*'s daughter who lived farthest up the river. Would you go to tell them if you can make it all the way up to their house?"

His grandmother replied, "Dear boy, you don't have a chance! The rich family there would never accept you. They're hard to approach. To them you're not a suitable husband!"

The orphan didn't give up and whenever people were having fun outdoors, the orphan would be one of them.

One day, as evening was approaching, the orphan told his grandmother, "Grandma, it's time you go over to the *umialik* couple living up the river."

After a great deal of hesitation because she really didn't want to go, the grandmother prepared to leave, putting on her mukluks and her mittens. She crossed the river, then climbed up the riverbank. Humbly the poor little old woman entered the *umialik*'s house and knelt down by the entrance of the house.

The *umialik* was sitting inside the house. He was carving something and had no shirt on. His daughter was seated in her corner, making something. Her clothing, all fluffy with wolf and wolverine trimmings, was scattered all over the place. She was the daughter of an *umialik* couple.

The *umialik* finally asked, "What brings this old woman into my house?"

The poor old woman in the front part of the house replied, "I really don't want to come here, but my grandson kept pestering. I had told him, 'Dear boy, you don't have a chance. They won't have you. They're beyond your reach.' But he won't listen. He asked me to come across to your house to ask for your daughter."

When the old woman said that, the *umialik* bowed his head and was in that position for a long time. The mother of the daughter was also there in the room. For a long time the *umialik* remained quiet, his head bowed. Then he ordered, "Daughter, hang that woman by her nostrils!"

Hearing that, the poor old woman quickly fled—as fast as an old woman like her possibly could. When she reached the riverbank, she slid quickly down and darted toward home. She suspected that someone might be chasing after her, but she made it home across the river.

The grandmother, bursting into the house, told her grandson, "Grandson, that woman over there is not to be had. She's beyond your reach. Let her be. I barely made it home. The *umialik* was about to hang me by my nostrils!"

Her grandson said nothing.

When the young people were having fun, as usual the orphan would go to the river and join them. The grandmother and the grandson continued living.

One day the grandson pestered his grandmother again, "Grandma, how about the girl living downriver. I want to marry her."

He asked his grandmother to go over. Her response this time was, "Oh no! Really, you're delivering me into their hands this time! The one across there is even harder to get." But the young man wouldn't change his mind.

One day after the grandson's repeated insistence, the poor old woman crossed the river to another *umialik*'s house. The *umialik* was making something and his daughter was also busy, making something. When the poor little grandmother entered the house, the *umialik* asked, "What brings an old woman across?"

She answered, "My grandson kept pestering me to ask you for your daughter. He wants to marry your daughter. I tried to discourage him, but he won't change his mind."

The grandmother was ready to leave at a moment's notice. She thought this *umialik* might react toward her the same way the other *umialik* had done.

The *umialik* was quiet, his head bowed. After a while he looked up and said, "Daughter, life is unpredictable. An orphan might one day become someone to be reckoned with. Get ready and follow your grandmother home."

The grandmother was very happy. She was beaming.

When his grandmother left the house and went across the river, the orphan had kicked down the walls of their little sod house that was far too small for them. Before you know it, it became a large sod house. When his grandmother came home with the young woman, they discovered a large house. They made a living together. The orphan hunted, catching all sorts of game animals: caribou, wolves, wolverines, and different kinds of animals. He was able to catch everything he came across. After some time, there were all sorts of storage caches outside, next to their house. The orphan had so much food and supplies that there was no room left for storing things.

After a while the *umialik*'s daughter came across the river to visit her parents. The *umialik* father told his daughter, "Why don't you all move to live next to me here? Your grandmother too."

The orphan moved his house across the river without hesitation. They lived there and the orphan continued to get all sorts of game animals.

As for the other *umialik* who had rejected the orphan, his wealth began to decline. The *umialik* who lived downriver with a son-in-law who could catch all sorts of game got richer. The orphan had made his father-in-law richer. As for the other *umialik*, he had no such person to hunt for him. So when he became physically weak, his wealth declined.

One day the former *umialik* told his wife to go to see the *umialik's* family living downriver. He wanted his daughter to work for the orphan's wife, running errands and doing housework for her in exchange for things. The orphan rejected the request because he was earlier rejected by them. The former *umialik* felt deeply hurt. His wealth declined while the *umialik* living downriver grew rich.

And the rest of the story? They all lived a happy life.

The Young Man Who Married a Wife from Across the Sea

Flora Kuugaaq Cleveland

Storyteller Flora Kuugaaq Cleveland referred to her father as a Kuutchiamiu, a person living around Kuutchiaq River, a tributary of the Kuugruaq River, which flows into Selawik River. Flora's childhood was spent at different locations along the Selawik River, from the Kuutchiaq River to the Tagraġvik River, Katyaak, Anirullaak, and Akuliġaq. As a little girl, Flora witnessed the first white men coming up the Selawik River in their power boat. She was among the first group of students to attend the first school established in Selawik in 1909, where Leslie G. Sickles and his wife were the California Quaker Friends Church's pastor and schoolteachers.

Flora was married to Harry Supluaġniq Cleveland, a member of the Selawik Cleveland family (not related to the Kobuk Cleveland family). Both Flora and Harry had served as pastors of the Friends Church. For a time Harry also served as the postmaster of Selawik and a store owner. They had five children.

<small>Recorded in Selawik, May 18, 1976</small>

THIS IS JACK PUNGALIK'S STORY.

There was a couple. They had a child, a son.

The son was quite young but he was growing fast. The father used to take his son on his hunting trips with him. The son learned from his father what to do. They hunted a lot. His family was never in want of food.

From another place came another family. The visitors built a shelter and lived next to the couple's house. The visitors probably came from the coast. They had a daughter.

The young man was skilled in providing for his family. He was ready for marriage. When the young man was at this marriageable age, often he would climb a bluff and hunt around that area. His father advised him never to go beyond this bluff. The son would bring home the meat of the caribou he had hunted. He brought home whatever game he had hunted. During the summer, he would bring home molting ducks.

One day the son reflected on his father's words. Why did his father forbid him to go beyond the bluff? He set off against his father's advice. He climbed cross-wise up the bluff. On top of the bluff, he saw a creek on the other side.

As the young man was enjoying the countryside, he saw a grizzly bear swimming downstream. He thought to himself, "So, that's the reason why my father doesn't want me to come this way."

Nevertheless, he proceeded to intercept the bear in the river and succeeded in killing it. When he brought home some of the bear's meat, his father ate it.

The visitors' daughter grew up to the age ready for marriage. The young man was also ready. So somehow the two got married. After their daughter's marriage, the visitor couple left the area.

The young man was a good provider and his family was never in want of food. They also had food from the coast. They didn't suffer from food scarcity. The young woman was also a good worker. She worked fast and always worked with ease.

Before long, the young couple had a baby son. When the young woman was busy, helping her mother-in-law with her work, the grandfather would take care of the young grandson. The boy grew and soon he was walking around.

(There were common murres living on the bluffs near Deering. People often collected their eggs from the bluffs when the murres laid their eggs. But the place was dangerous. The murres also made strange calling sounds.)

One day, without realizing that someone else might hear him, the grandfather talked to the young child. "When you're looking at me like that, your nose looks like a murre's nose!"

The young boy's mother heard what her father-in-law said. She felt hurt. She dropped whatever she was doing and prepared to leave. Her in-laws said nothing to try to stop her. Furious, she took her son and left. She walked toward the coast in the direction of a bluff, then walked on along the beach.

When the incident happened, her husband wasn't home, but he was on his way home. When he arrived back and didn't see his wife and son, he asked his parents, "What have you done to cause her to leave?"

His parents told him about the comment. "We haven't done anything to hurt her feelings. She might have heard those words. If she did, she might be upset."

The son took off. He could see his wife's footprints, so he followed them. Along the bluff he began to lose track. Footprints, not human footprints, wider in strides, were visible. Sometimes no footprints were visible at all. Although the tracking wasn't easy, the husband kept going. The incident occurred at the time when the young ice was forming. Later on in his tracking the husband discovered that his wife had walked onto the young ice. (The sea ice can be walked on by jumping across the broken ice pieces. Sea ice is like that.) Because his wife's tracks led in that direction, the young husband, dropping all concerns for his own safety, followed her.

As the young husband was walking along, he came across a couple of hunters. They were hunting sea mammals. When he asked them, they informed him that they had seen his wife walking out into the sea. The husband told them he wanted to follow her, so the two hunters gave him something. As the story goes, they gave him a seal hide rope, either to step on or to carry along. (I can't remember exactly what it was for.) The two hunters also informed him that there was an island farther out into the sea. The young woman was heading in that direction.

The young husband followed her. (Now I'm wondering what he did with the rope? Did he step on it or did he just carry it with him?) Anyway, he took off for the island and when he approached closer, he saw people.

Once on the island, the husband walked to the village to observe. He noticed that some dwellings on the island had posts beside the house. The villagers didn't appear to be suffering from any want of food. When it grew dark, he climbed up a post and pressed close to the post to avoid being spotted.

While he was observing, he saw a boy. The boy was running around. The boy looked exactly like him. The husband thought to himself, "The boy seems to have my physical appearance. Perhaps he's my son."

The boy he saw came to the spot where the post was standing. The husband had brought along the sewing his wife had been working on before she left. The father called the boy (or maybe he beckoned the boy to come over) and told the boy to go to his mother. "Tell your mother that your father's waiting outside."

The boy did as he was told, but his mother didn't believe him.

So the boy went outside again to tell his father what happened. The husband pulled out the bundle he was carrying and instructed the boy to take it to his mother. The boy did as he was told. He told his mother to take a look at the object, and his mother instantly recognized the bundle she had made. Still, she told the boy that his father couldn't possibly have followed them. She had run away over the water. There was no way his father could follow them.

She went out to check. Her husband called her and then explained to her that he had followed her trails. His wife didn't leave him stranded outside. He entered the house with his wife and his son.

His wife had parents with whom they lived. The villagers of that island village generally went out into the sea to hunt. One day, his wife's father mentioned that he wanted to eat *aurrait*. (I wonder how they're going to translate this. It's fermented walrus.) The husband asked his father-in-law where he could get *aurrait*. He was told, "If you go out into the sea, beyond different kinds of sea mammals and then head south, there you'll find the walrus. The *aurrait* is delicious to eat."

The husband prepared to leave for the hunt. His brother-in-law went along with him to help him with the hunt. The hunters got an *umiaq* [seal-skin boat] ready. When they were all set to go, the brother-in-law was instructed to put a walrus shoulder blade into the *umiaq*. It was the shoulder blade of the walrus that was hunted down earlier. They left, passing all kinds of sea mammals. When they arrived at the hunting spot, they hunted down the walrus and filled their *umiaq* with their catch.

But when they were ready to shove off into the water, their *umiaq* wouldn't move. They worked hard to make it move, but it wouldn't budge because their *umiaq* was so heavily loaded with the catch. The husband instructed his brother-in-law to pull out the walrus shoulder blade. He used it as a paddle and was able to bring both of them back home.

The walrus meat was given to everyone. The husband and his brother-in-law knew how many walruses they were to hunt, for they knew how many people were living on the island village. Everybody in the village had walrus meat to eat.

The Fleeing Wife

Nora Paniikaaluk Norton

The following twelve stories as well as the preceding story, "The Young Man Who Married a Wife from Across the Sea," deal with different types of family relationships and family situations. They exemplify what the expected behaviors are in the relationships. In both "The Young Man Who Married a Wife from Across the Sea" and its variant "The Fleeing Wife," the wife fled from her husband because she felt insulted by an in-law. In "The Widow and the Stingy Sister-in-law," the unkind sister-in-law was punished when her husband left her. Many stories center on the issues of trust, honesty, and deceit in marital relations. In "The Woman Abducted by an Eagle," a woman was saved because she had a devoted husband and a loving brother.

RECORDED IN SELAWIK, JUNE 5, 1981

THERE WAS A COUPLE MAKING A LIVING ALONG THE COAST. THEY HAD A son. They brought up the son in the traditional ways of hunting and gathering. The father taught the son all the traditional lifeways. That's how the Iñupiat raise their children.

The boy became a young man. He would head out to sea to hunt sea mammals and soon developed into a good hunter. He would head out to the sea during spring to hunt. Everything was within his grasp. Spring was the time of the year when they hunted most of their sea mammals. He got seals, bearded seals—all sorts of animals that were possible to hunt.

The young man later married a wife. They lived together. Soon she became pregnant and after some time a son was born. The parents loved their son and the grandparents also doted on the boy. When the boy started to run around and play, he would play by himself. He was not in want for anything. His parents and grandparents loved him dearly. The storyteller didn't say if there were other people living in the area.

One day the young man left for the sea to do some hunting. His wife and his mother were both working on some kind of food, probably black seal meat stored in oil, to prepare them for storage. The boy was left on his own to play. With the boy's mother working, the grandfather was keeping an eye on his beloved grandson.

The grandfather was reclining and the grandson was beside the two busily working women when the grandfather *nuniaq* [cooed] to him, "Little baby boy, looking like that birdie in the sea." (The storyteller named the bird but I forgot its name. I tried to recall its name, but I couldn't. I know the storyteller gave the name.)

When the grandfather mentioned that his grandson had a nose like one of these birds, his mother heard him. She felt hurt that her son was told he looked like one of those birds. After all, the boy happened to have a large nose like his father's. Even though the women were at the time in the middle of working on sea mammals, the mother of the child wiped her hands, went back into the house, got ready to leave, then left the house with her son. The in-laws hadn't expected her to leave like that and expected her to return. At the time their son was still out hunting.

The woman took her little son by the hand and walked along the seashore. When no one else could see them, she carried her son on her back and, at times, on her shoulders. After walking a long way following the line of the seashore, they came across some people. Two of them took her in and asked, "What's going on? Why are you here?"

The woman replied, "My little boy's grandfather made a remark about him. I feel hurt. I want to go home to my parents across the sea."

The young woman's home was on the other side of the sea. The men told her, "You can't possibly go across the sea. You've no means to cross over."

The woman told them, "There must be a way to cross over."

She kept on asking for their assistance and the couple felt sorry for her. They finally gave her instructions. "Under no circumstances should you look back once you start crossing. We have a rope to let you hang on while crossing over, but it isn't long enough. It doesn't stretch all the way across the sea. Try to reach the other shore when the rope ends. Don't lose grip on your son. Also, you are not to look back while you're crossing."

The woman said she would follow their instructions. She was sure she could make it across the sea. She told them she had mukluks and other things she had made for herself and for her husband during her spare time. She then left with her son, walking on top of the water. She traveled in this manner for a long time until she reached the other side. She had brought her son back to her home.

The young woman had rich parents. During those days rich people were often described as having acquired surplus food supplies. Their house had a post in front. Her parents took her in and took care of her. Soon the boy grew up and became a young boy.

When the young man, the woman's husband, returned home and found his wife gone, he questioned his parents. "What happened to my wife? Why did she leave? Did you say anything harsh to her?"

"We didn't say anything harsh to her. I love my grandson dearly. I only said, 'You have a nose like one of the sea birds,'" his father told him. "Perhaps she misunderstood me and took off."

While working on his chores, the young husband would be thinking about his son and his wife. He wanted to find them. He had no idea where they went. He decided to leave and tried to follow his wife's footprints. He came upon the same couple. At first the couple tried to discourage him, but since he refused to give up, they also assisted him to cross the sea.

The husband brought along the objects his wife had made, probably a backpack. He remembered his wife saying that her house was in the middle of the village. It had a post in front of the house—the house that couldn't be missed. The young woman had said that was the place she would go to, had she decided to return home to her parents. As it turned out, that was where she went.

The husband went close to her house and stood in the shadows. He then saw a young boy come out of the house and begin to play. As the boy was running around, the husband watched him. After watching the boy for a while, he thought, "Hmm, that boy certainly looks like me. He also has my physique."

When the boy came close, he told the boy, "I believe you're my son. My son was taken away by his mother. I don't know why she left. I think you're my boy. Where is your mom?"

The boy replied, "She's in the house."

"What's she doing? You should go and tell her to come outside. You can tell her, 'My dad has arrived.' Tell her."

The boy went into the house. "Mom, my dad has arrived!"

"Ah, your dad can't possibly come here no matter how hard he tries. He can't possibly make it here."

The little boy went outside again and told him, "My mom doesn't want to come out. You must be someone else. She said there's no way her husband could make it across the sea no matter how hard he tried."

Despite that answer, the father told the boy to go back to tell his mother, "'He's out there with the object she made.' Tell her to come out and take a look." The man was insistent because he recognized his son.

The boy dashed in again and told his mother what he was told to say. Finally she came out. Seeing her walking toward him, the husband recognized his wife instantly. He showed her the backpack that she had begun to make back home. "Here's what you haven't finished and have left behind." He told her he had brought it along with him in case she doubted him.

"Finally you are here! Come on in."

The man entered the house. He became another member of the family. He had come home.

They lived there who knows for how long.

One morning the wife's father didn't look too happy. He appeared to be deep in thought. After a while he said, "Wouldn't it be nice to have young walrus to eat? After having eaten all sorts of sea mammals, it'll be so good to have young walrus. I think it's time we have a taste of this food."

When the son-in-law heard this, he asked, "Where do you catch these animals?"

"The animals I talked about are across the sea," the father-in-law replied.

They prepared the boat for traveling. The young woman had two brothers. The boat had a paddle made from the shoulder blade of a walrus. When the son-in-law was ready to leave, he asked the two brothers to go along with him. The son-in-law did all the paddling. When he paddled, the boat moved fast and far across the water. He paddled several times and before you know it, they came across the animals his father-in-law wanted.

"These are the animals my father wanted!" his two brothers-in-law said.

They began selecting the animals they wanted. The young man must have counted the houses in the village before he left. They got enough animals for cutting and for sharing with everyone in the village.

When they were trying to launch the boat to head back home, however, they found that the boat wouldn't budge—it was so full. They worked the boat until it was dislodged and moved out onto the water. The young man told his in-laws, "Sit and be comfortable. Hold onto the boat." He told them he would do the paddling himself.

They made it into deep water. With each paddle stroke, the boat moved fast—so fast it took your breath away! The boat barely touched water! And before you know it, they beached back in their home village. The man told the people who were on the lookout for them, "Go ahead, take a walrus home—one for each household. There is enough food for all of you."

They took their food home. That evening the village was quiet as everyone was home enjoying the walrus meal.

The Goose Maiden

Nora Paniikaaluk Norton

This Iñupiaq version of "The Swan Maiden" depicts the heroine as the prettiest of the three goose maidens swimming in a lake. The story has an Iñupiaq cultural setting, with Iñupiaq social organization and subsistence lifeways.

At the end of the story, the husband of the goose maiden lost his chance to be reunited with his wife because he failed her test.

RECORDED IN SELAWIK, DECEMBER 9, 1971

I'M GOING TO TELL ANOTHER SHORT STORY.

There was a young man traveling down the river. He was brought up as the only child by his parents. As he was traveling downriver, he decided to make a stop and go ashore.

Stepping ashore, he saw what looked like a lake. He walked closer to the lake to see what was around. There in the lake he saw three young women in the prime of their youth and beauty swimming. He stopped to observe them and was careful not to be seen.

After watching the young women for a while, the young man thought, "I wonder how I can locate their clothes." After giving it some thought, he began to search through shady spots. He skirted the lake and finally found their clothes.

As the young man continued to observe the three young women, he noticed that one of them was the prettiest. He thought how nice it would be to have her as his wife. He thought of ways to fulfill his wish. "I hope I can pick out that young woman's clothes correctly."

After thinking some more on the strategy, he took one set of clothing.

The young women continued with their swimming and having their fun. After a while, they came out of the water and went for their clothes. Two of them found theirs, but the one he had his eyes on a few minutes ago, the one he desired to be his wife, didn't. The young man was holding the clothes of the beautiful woman he wanted to marry. (*Aanna*! I wonder what kind of a man this guy was!)

The two women put on their clothing, but the third was still in the water because she had no clothes to wear. The young man watched her for a while, then came out and told her, "I'll give back your clothes if you'll marry me."

The young woman was probably so cold that she consented.

She went ashore and put her clothing back on. The young man left with her and took her home. He had parents. The storyteller didn't say that he had brothers and sisters. He was probably the couple's only child. He took the woman home, married her, and made a living.

After some time, they had a child, a boy. The boy followed his mother around. He followed her when she was carrying water. He followed her when she was carrying wood into the house. His grandfather and grandmother loved him dearly. So did his parents.

One time during winter, the young woman decided to go out to get some water. While she was getting ready, as usual her son wanted to follow her. So the young woman got her son ready too for going outside. She took the water bucket, ready to walk out of the house. Her son was already outside the house, but she was still in the entrance tunnel called the *tuqsruuk* (in the old days the house was differently constructed. Where I grew up on the Kobuk, the entrance tunnel is called *ivrulik*, but around here, it's called *saulik*) when she heard her mother-in-law talking, "Phew! This young woman smells like old grass!"

Everybody, including her husband, was in the house. She heard her father-in-law reply, "I can smell it too, but I don't mind. I don't care how she smells. It's her natural scent."

The young woman stepped outside. She walked down to the water hole, but she was shattered, sick with her mother-in-law's comment on her bad odor. (Her mother-in-law had commented that she smelled—that was something for her to be upset about.) She took the water bucket to the water hole, filled it with water, but didn't carry it back to the house. She was probably upset. She grabbed her son's hand and took off. She took off downriver.

They had just rounded the bend when the husband came out of the house. He walked toward the water bucket his wife had been intending to carry the water inside, but no one could be seen. Instead he discovered her footprints showing her walking with her son down the river.

The husband probably didn't tell his parents what happened. He simply took off after his wife and his son. However, he wasn't able to catch up with them. He was so exhausted that he had to stop and rest for a while. When he woke up, he set off after them again. The next day he walked until he was exhausted, but he kept on going.

When the husband finally arrived at the mouth of a river, he saw a group of people. It was the location where the river drained into a drinking water hole. He approached the group and found his wife and his child among them. But she was ready to set off again.

"What are you doing here?" she asked. "I am not going back! I will not take my child back to your place. I overheard your parent criticizing me, saying that I smell. You yourself were in the house when your parent talked like that about me!"

The wife probably felt hurt when she heard those words. Her husband tried to calm her. "They won't say things like that to you again. I won't let them. Let's just return home."

But his wife adamantly refused. Her feelings were truly hurt. The husband, failing to convince her to return home, finally told his wife that he wanted to follow her wherever she intended to go.

His wife told him, "You can go with me if you follow my instructions to the letter. You won't be able to go on your own. I have to take you along with me."

The husband agreed to follow her instructions.

The wife instructed him to get two caribou skins and sew them together. This was to prevent him from seeing where he was going. She stressed that he had to follow every instruction. "If you just follow all my instructions, you can come home with me. You can come to live with us."

"I promise to follow your instructions."

The wife sewed her husband into the skins. Once he was inside the skins, he felt he was moving. After several bumps on the ground, he realized he was airborne. His wife flew away with him. He realized then that his wife was a goose. The three young women swimming in the lake were three female geese. (The game animals of long ago would become human, just like in the story of Qayaqtauġiŋñaqtuaq. All of the game animals Qayaq met turned into human beings. That was how it was in our land we're living on. Animals lived like people and behaved just like people. They lived in an environment that was so cold and so hard to live in. That was how God made them live.)

As his wife was taking him on the journey, the husband began to think. He could hear people having great fun. *Nanaa*, how he wanted to look out! But he didn't have a place from where he could look out. After traveling like that a while longer, he began to search for a larva pocket in the caribou hides. (All women and men who work with caribou hides know that caribou have larvae on them. The reindeer have them too.)

The husband found a larva pocket, scratched it, and made a small hole in the skin. He scratched harder to make the hole bigger. After a while, he was able to look out. That encouraged him to scratch even harder.

From the larva hole he saw a group of people. He and his wife were flying above these people who were all having a lot of fun. They were dancing and blanket tossing. He arrived near a large group of people, and they all were enjoying themselves. All the while, his wife was flying, carrying her husband and her child with her.

The young man and the wife were about to descend when he heard a voice from down below. "Oh-oh, our *ninua* [male in-law] is peeking!"

Twice he heard the voice.

The young man didn't know what happened next. But when he came to, the young man found himself on the ground.

He wondered what he should do next. Although there were skins and trees all around him, he felt vulnerable. He consoled himself that at the very least he didn't die when he was dropped from the sky. He was at a loss of what to do. He didn't know which direction he ought to take. At that instant the young man regretted what he had done.

Then he saw someone approaching. The man was tall. He had with him a sled with all of his meager possessions in it—probably his food. He was walking in his old *putyugiak* (which is a type of snowshoes). He had a pole too. He appeared to be in a hurry, muttering to himself, "I probably won't get there in time! I probably won't be able to catch up with the people who are having fun over there!"

He kept going, ignoring the young man's presence.

The young man, the husband, suggested, "We should be traveling together to that place you're heading to. I'll go with you."

The other person replied, "Oh, no, no. I don't travel with anyone else. I always travel alone. If I can, I'll reach the people who are having fun. I wonder if I'll arrive there in time for the fun." (This is a good phrase. One does travel alone. No one can do it for us. One is traveling alone. No other persons, his children, his parents, or his relatives, can do it for us.)

Hearing that reply, the young man jumped up, seized some pieces of dried wood, probably alder or willow, and ran after the other man. When he caught up with him, the young man spiked a couple of sticks down on the other man's old snowshoes. (Why didn't the other man just take off his snowshoes and leave?)

The big, tall man jerked his feet but found that he couldn't move. It was there that the big man had to stop. (In the same way, a small sin will tempt a person and cause him to stop. It can stop him from being a believer. This is similar to what is said in the Gospel, if you'd think about it.)

So, both of them didn't reach their destination. The young man broke his promise to his wife. As for the man who always traveled by himself, he refused to take the young man along, so the young man prevented him from going any farther.

This is the end of the story as I had heard it. The story is probably longer, but I didn't pay sufficient attention to it at the time I heard it. I'm not able to remember the rest of the story. This is all I can remember of the story.

The Woman Abducted by an Eagle

Nora Paniikaaluk Norton

RECORDED IN SELAWIK, SEPTEMBER 6, 1968

I DON'T KNOW MANY STORIES, BUT I'LL TELL YOU A SHORT STORY.

There was a couple living by themselves. They had a small son.

When summer arrived, the wife decided to go to pick berries. By that time the little son had already learned how to walk. Her husband and her child went with her. While the wife was picking the berries, the husband went to check on something.

The wife, in the meanwhile, didn't know that above her there was an eagle hovering. The eagle swooped down, then flew away with the wife. The child was left behind. When the husband returned, he found his wife gone. He looked for her all over the place until it turned dark and he had to take his son home.

The husband, all the while grieving for his lost wife, continued to make his living.

The son grew up to be a young man, but he was without his mother. Father and son continued to live in that place by themselves. For many years in the wilderness, the poor man continued to work hard to raise his motherless son, all by himself.

The eagle took the man's wife to a place with dreadful people. There was already a woman in the place where the wife was taken to. The man in the house liked to hunt. He usually went hunting whenever the weather was good for hunting. If he left early in the morning, he would return home before it turned dark.

One day, after the man left, the woman in the house told the abducted wife to begin tanning summer hides. After the tanning, the hides were to be made into mukluks that made no noise when one walked in them. She was told that when the hides were ready for sewing, she would be given assistance. The wife did as she was told. Together the two women made a parka and a pair of mukluks. When they were finished, the wife was told to put them on and then told to flee. For a long time, that woman in the house had been feeling sorry for the captured wife. The man of the house who went hunting in the morning after he got up didn't suspect that the women had been planning an escape. When he got his travel food ready, he left.

The woman in the house gave the wife food to take along on the trip. She helped the wife put on the new clothes and then helped to tie a belt around her waist. The wife was also instructed to travel all day, as long as she could, then seek shelter when it turned dark and sleep for the night. When daylight came, she was to start traveling again.

The wife left. She didn't walk only part of the day, but walked all day, as fast as she could, as she was told. When darkness fell, she found a tree with long branches to hide in and give her shelter. There she spent the night. Probably she didn't sleep much, but whatever brief sleep she had seemed to help.

When daylight broke, she started off again. She had no idea which direction she ought to take. Her advisor had told her that she could go wherever she wanted to go. Again, she walked all day and when evening arrived, she followed the same procedure as she did the day before. She camped for the night and ate a small portion of her food when she could no longer withstand her hunger.

I don't know exactly how many days she walked. One day she came upon a river. She thought that it looked like the place where she used to live. She kept on following the river. As evening arrived, she heard people talking. She heard also the sound of someone working on some chores. When she reached closer to the place where the sound came from, the sound of the person working could be heard distinctly. She crossed the river at the spot closest to the sound. Finally she arrived at a place where evidently there was someone living.

Cautiously, she scrutinized the place. She didn't rush in to show herself. As she moved along, she came upon a trail cutting through the brushes. She sensed its familiarity. It looked so much like the place that used to be her home. She hadn't entertained the thought that the two persons she had left behind might still be alive.

She walked closer and closer, then started up a path. At the end of the path, she saw a young man. He was chopping wood. He was the person who was making the wood-chopping sound she had heard. As she was standing there, a man came out of the house. His hair was white.

The woman thought to herself, "My husband didn't have white hair like that while I was living with him. Who is this man?"

Then she began to recognize her husband. He had been so devastated by the grief of having lost her. And the young man was actually her son. He was still a child when she was abducted. He had now grown up to be a young man. As her husband's hair had turned white, her son became almost a young man.

There was no longer loneliness when the husband and the wife recognized each other and were reunited.

The woman was taken away by an eagle, taken away to a different place where she had to dwell for a long time.

The Widow and the Stingy Sister-in-law

Nora Paniikaaluk Norton

RECORDED IN SELAWIK, AUGUST 28, 1968

I'VE NEVER DONE THIS [TALKING INTO A MICROPHONE] BEFORE. I FEEL kind of strange. I'm going to tell you a story. I heard this story more or less more than once.

The story is about a poor woman. She was a widow with children. She didn't have any means to survive since her husband left her. He had passed away.

The widow used to go across the sea to obtain food from her relatives and packed it home. Her sister-in-law was probably stingy because when the widow went back for more food, her sister-in-law didn't give her much. She didn't give the widow sufficient food even to last a short while.

After going back and forth to obtain food, the widow one day made another trip. She left her children behind at home and was gone all day. Usually she returned home from such a trip when the children were already in bed asleep. That day her sister-in-law had given her something heavier than usual. The widow thought she was given a bit more food this time. As she was crossing the sea, the wind began to pick up. The widow decided to check her backpack. Why was it so heavy? She looked inside and found only rocks!

The widow threw away the rocks for she saw no reason to continue carrying them. As she continued to walk home, she saw a light.

Back home the widow was accustomed to seeing two birds flying overhead. At the time the widow thought, "How wonderful they're together—a pair." She used to envy them, for she on the other hand had lost her husband.

The widow walked toward the light she saw and entered a house unannounced. She wasted no time entering the house. Inside she saw an old couple. The husband welcomed her, telling his wife, "Serve her some food."

The old lady who was busily working at her task stopped abruptly and blurted out how lucky they were to be living together as a couple.

"You shouldn't have said that to this poor woman. Do give her some food to eat," the husband told his wife.

The widow told them that her sister-in-law had given her rocks to carry. The couple pulled out a poke made from the stomach. (I don't know what kind of stomach membrane it was.)

[John Brown, a listener: "It's the stomach membrane of a sea mammal."]

They gave her this sea mammal stomach full of oil and instructed her to be careful, not to drip any oil on the ground. When she had to procure oil from the bag, she was not to let the oil drip.

The widow returned home and, without checking, put the poke away in her storage cache. She immediately went to sleep. Her children were already fast asleep.

The next morning she got up long before her children woke up. When she left the day before, they were still asleep. When she returned home, they were already fast asleep. She took out a plate—whatever kind of plate she had—and went to her cache. She opened the cache and found that the big poke she brought back was full of food. She had been given food stored in oil. Reaching into the poke, she was extremely careful not to let the food drip. The woman who gave it to her had instructed her so and had emphasized that if she observed her instruction, she would never run out of food.

The family survived on that poke of food. She used the food to feed her children. She didn't go any more to the woman who gave her rocks to carry.

Wondering why his sister no longer came over to his house, the widow's brother was concerned. After worrying about her for some time, he set off from his house to go to check on his sister.

Arriving at his sister's house, the brother told her, "I've been so worried about you. Why don't you come back any more to our place? I thought you might be sick. I'm here to check on how you all are doing."

The widow, his sister, told him that her sister-in-law had given her rocks to carry back.

Her brother was sad. He felt lonely. He felt deep pain at the thought that his sister was given rocks to carry home by his own wife.

After visiting with his sister for a while, the brother returned home. When he arrived home, his wife gave him food to eat. But the husband was sullen. (She didn't even remember! She didn't remember that she made her sister-in-law carry rocks.)

The husband went to check his caches. He had several caches because he was a good hunter. He knew he was also supporting his sister. He found that his caches were still full of different kinds of food, every kind of game animal he had caught. Seeing that, he returned to his house and began to collect his belongings. As he was packing, his wife inquired, "What am I going to do when I run out of food? Why are you leaving me? I'll be out of food."

For a long while the husband remained silent. Then he answered, "Use the rocks. Your food supply won't run out!"

He got ready and crossed the sea to his sister's place. He lived with his sister and hunted for her. He brought back food to his sister's family. From then on, the poor widow woman's life became easier.

The Mother Who Made Her Son Blind

Nora Paniikaaluk Norton

RECORDED IN SELAWIK, SEPTEMBER 9, 1968

THERE WERE A MOTHER AND A SON LIVING BY THEMSELVES. THEY SOME-
how managed to make a living. The boy's father passed away while he was still
young. They strived to survive on their own.

The boy soon became a young man. He was capable of going hunting and
harvesting all the needed subsistence supplies for both of them. When he went
hunting, he caught many, many animals. His mother was exhausted from having
to work so hard on so many game animals. But the orphan loved hunting and he
had built many caches to store his food supplies. His mother dried everything
that could be dried. On her own she picked berries and wild plants that grew
during the summer. They were without want while making a living there.

When several caches of supplies had been accumulated, the orphan's mother
began to develop a negative attitude. She thought her son was hunting too much
and had made her work too hard. After thinking of ways to stop him from hunting, one day she began to wish her son would go blind. "I wish I could make
my son have bad eyesight!"

When the mother thought like that, her son gradually lost his eyesight. *Aanna*!
Very soon he actually became blind. The young man couldn't understand why
he could see no more.

The whole winter went by and as spring approached the blind young man
grew restless because he used to go out hunting a great deal. He had become so
blind that he could no longer hunt.

They spent the winter in that manner. Finally summer arrived.

The young man came outside. He could hear geese, ducks, and other summer
birds, but he couldn't see them. He asked his mother for specific kinds of food
he wished to eat. He knew what game animal he had hunted while he still had
his sight. He knew what animals his mother had worked on and preserved. His
mother would prepare food and cut it up for him because he couldn't see.

His mother asked, "Son, how did you happen to lose your sight? I didn't want
you to lose your eyesight. I hope you can regain your sight somehow."

His mother informed him that it was time for her to go to pick berries. Soon she left the house to pick the berries. Before she left, she prepared food and water for him to drink while she was gone. While he was living in this manner, the water no longer tasted sweet. He sensed the difference in its taste. Even food was no longer appetizing to him.

One day his mother was again gone berry-picking. When she returned home, he told her, "*Aakaan* [mother, coastal dialect], I'd like to have some berries."

He could hear his mother preparing berries. She gave him some to eat. He ate the berries, but they didn't taste like good berries. But since he wanted to have the berries, he ate them anyway.

The whole summer was spent in this manner—his mother would be out picking the berries all day; the young man would be home; and after spending the day picking berries, his mother would return home. The young man would see in his mind's eye the nice berries his mother had picked.

One day after his mother had left for berry-picking, he went outside and stayed out for a while. He knew a lake some way away from their house. The loons and ducks used to land there. He knew where the little lake was and could hear the loon calling.

When the mother returned home after her berry picking, the son asked again for some berries. Like before, the mother mixed the berries and gave him something unappetizing to eat. The berries tasted different. He felt that the food was different from what he used to eat when he still had his eyesight.

One day when his mother left to go berry picking again, he stepped outside. Once again he heard the loon calling. The young man took off toward the sound of the loon. He was moving along when he came upon a bush. He actually bumped into it since he couldn't see it. He realized then that he was quite close to the lake. He could tell that the edge of the lake wasn't too far away.

All of a sudden, the young man heard a loon calling. The loon spoke. "I'll try to cure you if you can endure and follow my instructions. I'll carry you if you'll climb on my back. I'll dive into the lake if you'll hang onto me and not let go. I'll resurface, but you are not to open your eyes underwater."

The young man had no other choices. He was so tired of staying home. He was in a sad shape. He didn't have to live this kind of life when he had his sight, so he agreed. The loon emphasized, "Never, never open your eyes."

When the young man got on the loon's back, the loon told him, "I'm going to make a try now. I'm going to dive with you. Don't let go of me. Hold your breath and try your best to keep your eyes closed."

The young man followed the loon's instructions even though he was running out of breath and was finding it difficult to hold on. The loon was diving with him on it. He could hear a loud roar in his ears. He tried hard to hold on and, just as it became unbearable, they surfaced.

When they surfaced, the loon asked, "How are you doing?"

When he was told he could open his eyes, he struggled to see and discovered that he could see some shadowy outlines.

"When you've caught your breath, we'll give it another try," the loon said.

The loon gave the young man the same instructions and dove. This time they only resurfaced when the orphan really suffered under the water. The loon asked again, "How did it go?"

The young man replied that he could see more than the first time. He could now see as if through a thin veil. The loon waited for the young man to catch his breath, then told him, "I'm going to dive now. This time I'll stay down longer. Try as hard as possible to hang on. Don't open your eyes underwater."

The loon dove with the young man on it. They were this time underwater for a long time. The young man had a hard time holding his breath. When they surfaced, the loon asked again about his eyesight. The young man told him, "Yes, I can see—all around me! I can see far away. I can even see bushes a long way away."

The young man thanked the loon for his good deed. "Why did you do this for me?"

The loon swam toward the shore with the young man. When the young man stepped off the loon's back, the loon stopped beside him near the shore.

"Your mother did it to you. No one else did. No other people did. Your mother did it and you've never realized it. Go home. Act as if you're still blind. Find out for yourself what your mother has been doing to you."

The young man's mother was gone for the day gathering berries as usual. She arrived back home after her son did. The young man sat as if he was still blind. He saw that the water his mother gave him was not good water. When his mother finished her work, he asked for food. "Mother, I'm hungry. Give me some food please."

Who knows what his mother took out, but obviously she took out some old food. She cut it up, and gave it to him. After chewing on the food for a long time, he asked for berries. "Mother, I'd like to have some berries."

She prepared some berries and gave it to him. He took a spoonful, but it didn't taste like good berries. His mother wasn't watching him so he inspected the berries she gave him. Opening his eyes just a little, he saw that the bowl of berries was full of maggots and worms. She put in only a few berries and oil. He stared at it for a while, then spoke. "Mother, these don't look like good berries at all."

His mother asked, "Son, can you see now?"

"These berries are no good," he said.

"Son, can you see now?" his mother kept asking.

He asked for some water. His mother gave him bad water, the water she got from a puddle. When he inspected the water, he saw that the water was murky. No wonder it didn't taste good when he drank it while he was still blind.

"Mother, this water is no good!"

His mother called out, "Son, can you see now? *Aarigaa*! How did you get back your eyesight?"

She pretended to be thankful. She thought he had no knowledge of what she had done. But he had already found out the truth because the one who had cured him had already told him.

His mother started to beg her son for mercy. The young man did nothing to her outright. After they continued to live together for some time, he invited his mother to go out with him for a boat ride. He planned on taking his mother out to the sea and throwing her in. The mother sweet-talked her son and tried to beg for mercy. The young man felt great anguish. He was so deeply hurt by what his mother had done to him. She had made him blind.

The young man went out to the sea and dropped his mother into the sea, alive!

The Two Loving Brothers

Minnie Aliitchak Gray

~~~~~~

Storyteller Minnie Aliitchak Gray was born above Mauneluk at Qala, about ten miles upstream from the present Kobuk village. She is a daughter of Robert and Flora Cleveland of Shungnak. Minnie's first marriage was to Teddy Jack, son of Happy Jack, one of the earliest settlers on Ambler Island, now Ambler village. Minnie's second marriage to Arthur Gray, pastor of the Friends Church, expanded Minnie's role in subsistence and as a skilled tanner and maker of mukluks

and birch bark basketry to include activities of the Friends Church.
For many years before her retirement, Minnie worked as an Iñupiaq
language and culture teacher in the Ambler school. Minnie has three
daughters and a son.

Stories from Minnie's repertoire were taped during the summer
of 1967 when her husband, Arthur, worked as a crew member of the
Brown University Archeological Expedition. I often visited Minnie
at her summer tent to photograph her skin sewing. Aware of my
interest in recording Iñupiaq stories, she kindly told me four stories
in this collection.

RECORDED AT ONION PORTAGE, AUGUST 18, 1967

THIS IS A STORY ABOUT TWO BROTHERS. I HEARD THE STORY FROM MY
late husband, Teddy Jack.

Two brothers were living together in a house. The older brother had a wife.
There were no children in the family. The three of them lived by themselves.
No one was living nearby.

They lived happily together and had a good time together. The two brothers loved each other and always hunted all sorts of animals together. The older brother's young wife always stayed home.

One time, however, the younger brother didn't want to go along. That was in the fall during freeze-up when the ground had already frozen. So he stayed behind and the two of them, the wife and her brother-in-law, remained at home.

The younger brother was lying on his back while his sister-in-law was busily cutting fur. At one point, the boy pointed his finger, but he happened to touch his sister-in-law under her arm. The sister-in-law, startled, jerked her *ulu* and accidentally cut his throat. The young boy died.

The sister-in-law started to cry, at a loss of what to do. She cried for him because what happened was really an accident. She cried for a long time. Then it occurred to her that somehow she had to hide her brother-in-law's body before her husband returned home. She dressed him, wrapped his body in a skin, tied it with a rope, then placed it in a cache. They had two caches, one for storing food and the other one for storing skins and clothing. She put her brother-in-law's body in the cache that was not for storing food. She then cleaned up the blood stain from the floor and waited for her husband's return.

Her husband returned home from hunting. He waited for a while, waiting for his younger brother. When his younger brother didn't show up, he asked his wife, "Where is he?"

"He left right after you did," his wife quickly answered.

Her husband kept expecting his brother's return. They slept. But the younger brother didn't come home.

The next day the husband waited and waited, but again nothing. When his brother whom he loved dearly still didn't show up, he decided to search for him. During the whole winter he did nothing but search for his younger brother. All winter long he remained hopeful as he continued to search.

Soon it was close to spring.

One day, the snow began to melt outside. The husband noticed a pool of blood underneath the cache with no food in it. Right away he suspected there was something amiss. He climbed up the cache to check and found there a bundle, wrapped in a skin and tied with a rope. He unwrapped the bundle and there it was—his brother's body, with his throat cut. For a moment he didn't know what to do, then he climbed down and asked his wife what happened to his brother whose body he found in the cache.

His wife told him, "I was cutting the fur and stretching my arm when he jabbed me under the arm. I was so startled that I accidentally slashed his throat. I didn't do it on purpose. He did it to himself and got slashed. I didn't know what to do with him and, because I was afraid of you, I didn't tell you. I put him away in the cache."

The husband said nothing and didn't do anything to his wife. There was nothing he could do. His brother was already dead. So they continued on with their life.

They put the brother's body away by wrapping him and giving him a new set of clothing. Then they put him in a grave close to their house where it could be seen.

After the body was put away, husband and wife continued to live without any marital disagreement.

Summer arrived.

The husband went hunting again. He would be gone all day but he brought nothing back home. His wife said nothing when her husband behaved like that.

One day, as soon as the husband left the house and the wife was home by herself, someone showed up at her house. It was a woman, about the same age as the wife. The woman told the wife, "*Uuma*, your husband has something in store for you. He wants to kill you. He's been raising maggots. I've come to warn you about it. When he drops you to the maggots, the maggots will devour you."

She added, "Start making a tiny pair of toy mukluks. When your husband says, 'Let's go over there,' when he takes you out, be sure to take along the toy mukluks. Hide them and don't let your husband know about them. Put these mukluks inside your parka. When you reach the lake with caribou-eating maggots in it, your husband would try to seize you to throw you in to those maggots. When he tries to seize you, run away as fast as you can. And take out the little mukluks, raise your arms, and shout."

When her *uuma* left, the young woman wasted no time making a tiny pair of mukluks as she was instructed. She finished making the mukluks while her husband was still away.

She finished making the mukluks. She waited.

Her husband returned home. He behaved as if nothing out of the ordinary had happened. He really loved his wife. He said no bad words to her. She continued to live the way she wanted.

But one day, upon arriving home he invited her to go with him.

"Let's go for a walk."

His wife didn't turn down his invitation. They left the house, walking together, and were having a good time talking to each other. Finally, they arrived at a deep lake. Peering down from the edge of the lake, the wife saw giant maggots wiggling in the lake.

The husband halted for a while, then he seized a caribou, skin and all, and tossed it into the lake. The maggots devoured it instantly. They finished the caribou till there were only bones left.

As fast as she could, the wife ran away from her husband. But he was fast catching up with her.

"Don't think I can't get you!" he shouted as he reached to seize her.

The wife reached into her parka, took out those tiny mukluks, raised her arms, and then shouted.

She floated upward and stayed afloat in mid-air, beyond her husband's reach. He tried to seize her, but she dodged to the other side. The husband began to plead with his wife. He began crying. He could see her, but he couldn't reach her. But his wife ignored her pleading, crying husband.

Who knows how long the young husband waited. Finally he died of starvation. He must have died. His wife, on the other hand, was not hungry because she was up there, in the air, in suspension. And the story ends there.

Pisiksuġliq and Suġli Suġli

Minnie Aliitchak Gray

RECORDED AT ONION PORTAGE IN ENGLISH, AUGUST 9, 1967

A MAN AND HIS WIFE LIVED WITH THEIR TWO CHILDREN. THEY LIVED BY themselves near a village. The village was situated higher up, above their place. There were a lot of people living up there above them.

I learned this story from my dad when I was twelve years old.

One year during the fall the husband got sick and passed away. His wife cried and cried and put his body up on the scaffold outside the house the old way. She gave him the fine clothing she had made and had stored away in the cache for storing new clothes. She gave him fur parka, mukluks, mittens—everything new. They had been living all by themselves and had never traveled anywhere.

Spring arrived. The snow began to melt and the birds began to arrive.

The two children went outside of the house to play. They heard the birds singing:

Suġli Suġli
Your husband got another woman,
Paniyavik's daughter, in the village
As his wife.
After he died, he went to another place and had a new wife!

The birds were singing about the children's father, Pisiksuġliq, and the children's mother, Suġli Suġli. When the children heard the song, they went to tell their mother about what they had heard. At first their mother didn't believe them, but when she came out of the house to listen, she heard the birds singing again:

Suġli Suġli
Your husband got another woman,
Paniyavik's daughter, in the village
As his wife.
After he died, he went to another place,
And had a new wife!

Suġli Suġli went to the grave and checked the scaffold where she had placed her husband's body. The body was gone. Maybe her husband had pretended to be dead and ran away.

During the fall, before the husband got sick, he had hunted down a mother bear and her two cubs. Suġli Suġli went out to the cache and brought these bear skins back into the house. She wet the cub skins, put them over her two children, sewed up the skins, and then asked the children to stand up. The two children started to walk in the skins. They became bears. She then wet the skin of the mother bear and put it on herself. They all walked off as bears. They walked together toward the village.

When the three of them arrived near the village, they heard people playing. It sounded like they were playing football. While the three of them were swimming across the river, the villagers happened to look up and there they saw in the river—three bears. They immediately went after the bears. (In the early spring, the bears leave their winter dens and people always go after them to hunt them.)

Suġli Suġli swam closer. She didn't flee from the hunters because she was looking for her husband. Her husband was also running toward them with other hunters. Suġli Suġli could recognize her husband.

The hunters first killed her children, the bear cubs. They then tried to kill the mother bear too, but she wouldn't let them. She ran fast, chasing after her husband who screamed with fright. She ignored his fear and finally caught him.

Suġli Suġli lifted the bear skin off her head. She talked to her husband who instantly recognized his wife.

"Did you take that woman to be your wife? You've let me work hard all by myself all winter. I've cried and cried for you. You've deceived me. Because of that, you will die! And I will die too!"

She then killed her husband. And she also killed other men who were trying to kill her. But in the end, the wife and her children were all killed.

The Old Man Who Loved Blood Gravy

Nellie Qapuk Russell

FIGURE 13 ~ *Nellie Russell weaving a coiled basket, Selawik, 1988.* PHOTO BY DOUGLAS D. ANDERSON.

Nellie Qapuk Russell, a daughter of Jim Kakiñiq and Alanmik Stoney, was born in 1908 at Aksik, the older village along the lower part of the Kobuk River before Noorvik was established. Nellie was very innovative. Besides being a creative storyteller, she was the last person in the area who knew how to make coiled baskets and clay pots. She created a new basket style combining the coiled basketry technique and the use of marsh grass, an Iñupiaq basket-making style, with a new material, two-color woolen yarn, to make them look "more colorful."

Nellie was married to Irvin Siiqaa of the Russell family, who used to live at Kuutchiaq. Irvin was a freighter for the Rotman's Store, one of the earliest stores on the Selawik. They had three children. Nellie passed away at the age of eighty-five.

RECORDED IN SELAWIK, JUNE 5, 1981

THERE WAS A MAN WITH SIX SONS. ALL THE SONS HUNTED CARIBOU. THE father would follow them whenever they went hunting. But he was growing old.

When the sons got a caribou, they would put the caribou blood into the membrane of the caribou's heart and then make a special food for their father. When the campfire was lit, they would roast the blood-filled heart membrane. When it got slightly cooked, it became his meal. That was how the sons traveled with him.

The old man was slow in his travel because he was getting old. After cooking the food for their father, the sons would dig into the snow and place the cooked food into the hole to cool it. When the father arrived, he would untie the string around the blood sack and drink it. He drank it all.

Every day when the sons got a caribou, they would fill the caribou's heart membrane with blood and make the blood gravy mixed with fat for their father. They slowly cooked it. In the meantime the father would still be walking somewhere along the way because he was weak and old.

Every time, the sons would roast the heart sack over the fire, and when it looked done, they dug a hole in the snow to cool it and turned the sack around from time to time. Finally when the father arrived he would untie the string around the blood sack, drink the blood, and drink it all up.

That was what kept the father going even though he was weak and old. He loved to eat the caribou blood gravy. When he was young and strong, that was also what he had for food.

After some time, one of the sons began to feel uneasy. He spoke to his brothers: "Our father is getting old and weaker, but still he tries to follow us everywhere when we go hunting." He sounded somewhat annoyed when he said that.

When the time came to prepare food for their father, they prepared it in the usual manner. When the father arrived closer, the sons turned it a few times in the snow to cool it. As before, the father untied the string and gulped down the blood. It was probably delicious. But because he tried to gulp the food down while it was still too hot, he burned his throat and fell on the ground. He died.

When the father died like that, I wonder what the son who made that comment thought!

The Floating Food Platter

Nellie Qapuk Russell

RECORDED IN SELAWIK, JUNE 5, 1981

THERE WAS A COUPLE LIVING BY THEMSELVES BY THE SEASHORE.

They made a good living. The husband would catch sea mammals. He would set his seal net under the ice when the sea ice froze. He loved the feel of the tug on the anchor line when a seal was caught. That's how he spent evening after evening out on the ice. Always he would hold onto the anchor line. Whenever he felt the tug, he would pull in the line, and he would catch a seal.

He would reset the net and wait. Again he felt the tug. Sometimes he was able to catch two seals. He kept track of the time and knew when he was supposed to return home. It is said that people long ago knew how to tell the time by looking at the Pleiades constellation and other stars. When the time came for the hunter to return home, he returned to his wife. There were many seals scattered on the ground and their platform cache was also piled high with seals. His wife worked on cutting them up.

The husband really liked the feel of the tug on the anchor line. That's why he enjoyed catching seals under the ice. Each time he was ready to return home, he would pull up his sealing net. He pulled his net up during the night.

Other evenings, he would reset his net under the ice. He held fast onto the anchor rope. Sometimes he had to wait a long time because it sometimes took a long time before a seal got caught in the net. When he felt the tug, he would pull up the net. And there it was—a seal.

One night, as he was sitting there waiting, holding onto the anchor rope, he saw a platter floating by him. The platter was full of all kinds of hot, steaming food. The husband was beginning to feel chilled. The platter floated by him, quite close to him, but he was unable to take or taste the food.

As he remained sitting there, another platter floated by. Again it was full of all kinds of food. He ignored it. This time the platter floated just close enough for him to be able to pick up some food. There were all kinds of sea mammal meat, caribou, and other types of food. The food looked as if it had just been dished up from the cooking pots. There was, however, no one to be seen. The platter just floated by.

When the time came for him to head home, as usual he did. Because he didn't tell his wife what had happened on the ice, his wife knew nothing about his strange encounter. He kept quiet about the whole thing.

From then on, every time he went down to the coast, the platter would float by him. He ignored it. But one time when another platter came by, he took a piece of the meat and ate it. When it was time for him to head home, he returned with the seals he had hunted.

The next night he went down to the ice again. He hung onto the anchor rope. When he felt the tug, he pulled it up and there it was, a seal. As he sat there and was beginning to feel chilled, a platter again floated by him. This time he snatched a bigger piece of meat and ate it. When he returned home to his wife, again he didn't tell her what had happened.

After some time, the husband no longer felt hungry when he returned home. His wife would cook him different kinds of food. She even cooked his favorite food. But the husband would no longer eat at home. He ate nothing. He didn't feel hungry despite the fact that plenty of food was served.

He continued to wait for that particular feel of the tug. Whenever he felt it, he would pull up the net, and there again was a seal. Then a platter of food would float by, and he would reach for some meat.

After some time, he no longer felt hungry. He stopped going down to the ice to set his net. He began to be nasty to his wife. She tried very hard to give him food to eat, saying, "You haven't eaten anything. Here, there's food for you."

But whenever she tried to feed him, he would be offensive. Then he started to beat her.

One day he decided to go to the ice to set his seal net. His wife began to dread the hour he was expected back. She had been beaten, but she didn't want her husband to starve. She continued to prepare food he wouldn't eat. He wasn't hungry any more. He didn't want any food his wife had prepared. Whatever food he had eaten down at the ice made him feel full.

One day when the time came for the husband to return, his wife contemplated hiding from him, but she had no place to hide. She thought that if she left on foot, she would have left her footprints in the snow. The best strategy for her was to hide. She dug a hole between the cribbing of the house. She dug and dug. She removed one log. When the hole was big enough for her, not too tight, she squeezed into the hole and carefully placed the log back in place. She packed the sod back in carefully so that it looked as if nothing had been disturbed. She packed it down, and that was where she hid.

The husband returned home. He looked for his wife, but he wasn't able to find her. He kept on looking. He was still looking when the sun came up. He didn't eat. He wanted to find his wife. He wondered if she had run away, but he saw no footprints.

He took out a knife and began to stab between the cribbing of the house. He went around the house, missing no spots. When he reached the spot where his wife was hiding, he lingered for a long time. Each time he stabbed his knife into the sod, he would sniff its blade. For a long time he continued to stab with his knife and didn't move away from the spot where his wife had hidden. He didn't discover that she was there, but he could smell something from his knife blade.

The husband looked for a long time. Then he got hungry because he hadn't eaten that day on the ice. He built a fire. The fire pit was in the middle of the room. People say that in those days the fire pit was directly under the skylight. He took off his belt, pulled down his trousers, and cut a chunk of meat off from his buttocks and placed the meat over the fire to roast.

Soon the wife who was watching him from her hiding place saw him keel over. She thought to herself, "He has been providing for me. Even though he might harm me, I still ought to try to help him."

With that thought, she removed the log and went out of her hiding place. Then she went over to her husband who was lying on the ground.

"The roast is cooked," she told him.

But her husband didn't respond. He had died.

After the wife found out that he was dead, she probably didn't stay on in the house. And she probably didn't remove the body from the house either.

I heard these two stories from Atlugauraq (Emma Skin). The stories are Qaniqsiruaq's stories, John Wright's stories. Panitchiaq (Tommy Skin), Atlugauraq's husband, often told stories. The time would pass till midnight and they would still be telling stories in a manner of one person telling a story and the other person telling another one in response. Those were Qaniqsiruaq's stories.

The Man Who Ate Mysterious Food

Leslie Tusraġviuraq Burnett

RECORDED IN SELAWIK, FEBRUARY 11, 1972

I'M GOING TO TELL A STORY. I DON'T KNOW HOW WELL I CAN TELL THIS story. The person from whom I heard this story said that he had forgotten certain parts of the story. I'll tell it like I had heard it.

There was a couple living along the coast. They had several children. They had a house with a window at the top. That was the house type of long, long ago; we called it a *saulik*. The house was braced with timber and covered with sod. There was a window on top of the roof.

The husband would go in the evening to the sea in front of his house to set his net for sea mammals. I don't know how the coastal people call the net, but the storyteller called it *nusruksiġiaq*. When a sea mammal was caught, he could feel the tug on the net and he would pull in the catch. He had been able to accumulate a lot of sea mammals on his rack.

One evening as he was sitting by his net a marvelous smell floated by him. As he was sitting there, a meal, already cooked and steaming, floated by him. The food smelled scrumptious!

After the husband spent some time watching his net, the food floated by him again. This time he tried a small portion. After eating at the beach, he wasn't hungry when he returned home. His wife's cooking was no longer appetizing to him.

As it happened, he was just waiting down at the beach, watching his net. He was eating the cooked food that apparently appeared from nowhere. When he returned home afterwards, he didn't eat what his wife had cooked. He lost his appetite for her cooking. He was eating well down at the beach.

One day he began to think, "I've a lot of sea mammals on my rack."

(The storyteller told this story when he was leading a Wednesday church service and said that sin tempted us with temptations. When a person yielded to sin, it was like eating good food. That's the way he made the reference.)

The husband contemplated what he should eat when he returned home. One evening, after watching his net, he thought about his two small children. He thought about peering down at the children from the window on the top of the roof and asking his wife for one of them because his wife's food no longer tasted good. He had been eating delicious food down at the beach when that delicious food floated by.

With this thought, he returned home. From high up the skylight window, he peered down at his family. Then he told his wife to give him one of their children. With no hesitation his wife gave him what he asked. When the child was given to him, he killed and ate the child outside the house, then entered the house.

The next day he went down to the beach and began watching his net again. Again the same happening occurred. He called for another child through the window and ate his second child too. He ate both of his children.

When he left to watch his net again the next day, his wife was filled with terror. She thought carefully, then came up with a plan. She took off one of the house cribbing and dug a hole behind it. (Do you know what the house cribbing is? It's the part of the house that is layered with sod.) After removing the cribbing with a knife, the wife made a space big enough for her to hide in, then crawled in and hid. She figured that her husband might be home any time, so she hid behind the cribbing.

Sure enough, when her husband reached home, he called for his wife, the only person left, from the skylight window, but his wife didn't answer. Hearing no replies, the husband, returning home after the seal-netting, burst into the house, but his wife was gone.

He methodically stabbed his knife between the cribbing of the house. He stabbed all around the house. The wife was hiding behind one of the thicker cribbing and was leaning sideways. For the longest time, the husband lingered at the spot where she was hiding and the thrust of his knife almost touched her.

After a while, the husband got discouraged. (I think he wanted to eat his wife.) He began to be upset because he couldn't locate his wife. He was unhappy. Certainly there was something going on. He built a fire, cut a piece of his thigh with his knife, and roasted it in the fire. Probably he didn't cut just a small portion, but a big chunk. All the while, he was watched by his wife. When the thigh piece of meat was cooked, he ate it. After all he had already eaten his children. Who knows what he was going to do to his wife. But when he couldn't find her, he cut off a piece of his flesh and roasted it.

After the meal, the husband was in agony. The cut was probably bleeding and hurting. After suffering a great deal of pain, something else occurred. Maybe he did something to himself. Anyway, he died.

His wife had anticipated the event correctly and she was able to escape.

The wife left her house after her husband's death. She knew there were people living nearby. While walking over, she heard a dog bark. It sounded like a Laplander's herd dog. She walked over to the place where the sound came from, but no one was there. Then she saw a grave. That was how that place enticed travelers. When a person died, he made noises as if someone was actually living there. (It is said that long ago people would have ghost encounters when weird people died. People would hear things from the land we are living in nowadays.) The wife, discovering that no one was living there, left again. She later found other people.

Her husband had done himself in. After eating his children, something evil possessed him. After eating something delicious, he turned to eating his own children. He finally did himself in.

One time we went by boat to Kotzebue to attend the Quarterly Meeting. We stopped at a shelter cabin along the Kobuk River. I started to pick some twigs. I had heard before that this shelter cabin was haunted and I was afraid. My back was turned when I felt five fingers touching my knee. I turned to look but saw no one. When I told my wife what happened, she scolded me. "You're afraid! When you're afraid, you can experience a ghostly encounter. If you're not, it won't happen. It's all your own fault." When I was scolded with those words, my fear subsided somewhat. Thinking about that encounter later on, I concluded that when someone died at a particular spot, that place could become a haunted place.

On another occasion, we were again boating on the Selawik Lake. There were many of us in the boat. Then there came a loud whistle from above, above the person who was manning the boat. It was a shrill sound. Not too long afterwards, the person manning the boat began to whistle more or less that sound. He was trying to whistle the sound we had heard, although not exactly the same. I thought to myself that the person who manned the boat must have heard that sound too. We heard the haunted sound all the way out to the sea.

We stopped at a point because the wind turned quite strong. We beached our boat. Then I heard something rattling our gas cans. I walked around the boat and looked, but saw nothing. My son-in-law asked me what made the noise. I told him I didn't see anything—maybe it was a ghost. I thought that my son-in-law had probably heard it too.

When we returned home, I told my aunt Kisik about the incident. When I told her the name of the place, she exclaimed. She told me that one time a group of people had left a sick person at that place. They took her up a hill and left her there even though she was still alive. My aunt said that when they went by that place later on, the sick woman was calling out for a drink of water. They didn't stop to help her because they thought she had a contagious disease. There she died. "Maybe that's what you heard," my aunt told me.

Nobody has told me this, but I think this is what happened. When a person dies, perhaps his or her soul haunts others, just like in the story I just told you. The woman, the wife, went to the location where a dog was making a noise, but found only a grave. That's what happened in the story.

Our land hasn't changed, although the Gospel has changed our ways. The Bible has changed us but our land hasn't changed. When you travel around in this country, there are still places that are haunted.

The Husband Who Ate Rock Blubber

Flora Kuugaaq Cleveland

Recorded in Selawik, May 18, 1971

There lived in a place a couple. To make their living the husband used snares to catch game animals. His wife always stayed home.

Whenever the husband snared game, they would eat whatever he caught. After some time, the husband stopped eating what his wife was serving. His wife began to wonder what went wrong. Her husband didn't eat the cooked food she served even though it was time to eat.

Trying to find out the fact, his wife one day, without her husband's knowledge, followed him. She followed him when her husband left to check the snares.

The husband checked his snares. He was at a place where there were small rocks. He kicked the rocks away, swept off the snow, and reaching down, pulled up a piece of blubber and ate it. When the husband went home, he brought back the animals he had snared.

His wife, who was hiding and trying to find out what her husband had been doing, hurried home ahead of her husband. As usual she waited for his return. She cooked. When her husband returned, she invited him to eat, but he again didn't eat the food. But by now his wife knew that her husband had turned white, clear rocks into blubber and ate them.

Later on the husband was in pain. He had the pain because the blubber he had eaten had turned back into rocks inside his stomach. She had seen him eating those rocks with her own eyes. The husband died.

People who lived through evil spirits could not see the whole picture. The husband did not exactly see what he ate. His wife however saw it from her hiding place.

The Husband Who Took Seals to Another Woman

Nellie Qapuk Russell

RECORDED IN SELAWIK, JUNE 6, 1981

IT IS SAID THAT THERE WERE TWO PEOPLE LIVING ON THE COAST. THEY were man and wife. The husband would go hunting every day for sea mammals. He would bring home hair seals and bearded seals. His wife would work on whatever mammal he brought back from the hunt.

They continued living this kind of life for a long time before things began to change. One day the husband didn't bring back anything. The day before when he brought home his catch, he brought back only one or two seals. He didn't bring back as many seals as he used to. His wife didn't question him. She didn't question him why he no longer caught as many sea mammals.

Finally when the husband stopped bringing in any mammal, his wife decided to follow him down to the sea without her husband knowing. She wanted to watch him. She waited until her husband left home for the sea, then followed him.

The husband was at sea all day. After some time, the wife could see her husband pulling in some seals. The woman was hiding and she could see him pulling his load. She saw a trail that ran in a different direction from their home. As she was watching, she saw him turning from his usual trail toward a small house and set down his seals near the house before entering. When she saw that, she quickly ran home and waited for her husband's return. She continued with her chores as if nothing was amiss, waiting.

The husband came home. "No seals! Nothing!"

His wife didn't make a fuss. She didn't say a word. And she didn't speak crossly to him.

Night came and they slept. The next morning the husband again went hunting toward the sea. The wife followed closely behind him. She knew he would stay out a long time when he was out hunting at the sea. She wanted to find out for herself what was in the small house. So she went there again and entered the house. Inside she found a large woman cooking blubber to render it into seal oil. She was cutting the seal blubber into strips. As she was stirring the seal oil the large woman told the wife, "This is how I make the oil." That was all she had to say.

Since the woman told her to watch how the seal oil was made, the wife peered at the oil. As it was being stirred, she noticed that it was boiling. All of a sudden, the wife seized the large woman and dunked her head into the oil. The large woman was badly burned, but the wife didn't try to pull her out. She simply left the place and ran back home.

Once home, the wife continued to work on her chores, waiting for her husband to return. After some time she heard someone at the entryway of the house. The person didn't enter the house right away. Nevertheless, the wife could tell by his movements that the person was her husband. After a while he entered. The wife mentioned nothing about the day's event. Neither did her husband. He didn't say, "You did that to her!" But she noticed that he had been crying a lot. Evidently he had been mourning. Without asking, his wife understood what happened.

But she didn't question him—simply kept quiet.

The Woman Caught on a Fishing Line

Nora Paniikaaluk Norton

~~~~~~

This story is the first of a set of stories that Iñupiaq storytellers consider short stories. They are all single-episode stories. The central theme varies. Some stories have human characters; in others we see humans interacting with animals. To interact with humans, the animals appear in human form at one time or another.

RECORDED IN SELAWIK, AUGUST 10, 1969

~~~~~~

THIS IS ANOTHER SHORT STORY.

A man was paddling his qayaq. He was by himself. After qayaqing for a while, he decided to fish. He took out his fishing hook and set it. He was fishing from his qayaq.

After waiting for a while, he felt something tugging at the line. When he pulled it up, he found a pair of mittens on the fishing hook. He removed the mittens from the hook and reset the fishing line.

Again he caught something. When he pulled up the line, he found on the hook a pair of mukluks with long fur.

He reset the line. This time he hooked up a parka, a woman's parka. He removed the parka from the hook and reset the fishing line. As before, he felt the line tugging. This time it was something real heavy. As he was pulling up the line, he could see a person emerging. It was a woman!

The man took the woman ashore and she put her clothes back on. (*Iikii*, if the clothes weren't already dried by then, they were probably dripping wet!)

When the woman got all dressed, the two of them climbed up the bank of the river. The woman began to pick berries. Immediately she started to pick the berries. (My, what an ambitious woman!) During all of this the man who caught her on the fishing hook didn't help her at all. She didn't like his behavior and he began to notice her negative attitude. After picking the berries for a while, she told the man that she needed to relieve herself, somewhere at the back of some trees.

The man told her, "Go ahead. Just do it around here!"

But the woman didn't want to. "I'll go over there, behind some trees."

As soon as she was out of sight, she quickly ran.

The man waited and waited. Since she was gone for quite a while, he decided to go to look for her. At the top of the hill, he could spot her a long way away. He ran after her, running as fast as he could, but she kept gaining on him. He kept pursuing, but she was always a long way away from him.

Then, he saw a house. (The people of long ago seemed to come across a house whenever they needed it!)

Inside the house, he found a large woman.

The woman told him, "The woman you've been following is heading toward a dreadful place. The person who lives there will never let her leave once she arrives there. Go back. I'll give you food to eat. After you've eaten, I want you to go back, wherever you came from. The person living up there is a bad man. If he catches you around here, he won't let you live."

The man decided to do as he was told. After the meal, he headed back home.

The large woman was living there because the bad man had made her stay there and be there when people stopped. She liked the young man, so she advised him to leave. Had he followed the woman, he would have been dead.

The House of Three Brothers

Nora Paniikaaluk Norton

RECORDED IN SELAWIK, AUGUST 10, 1969

THERE WAS A YOUNG WOMAN WHO DECIDED TO LEAVE HER PARENTS. Something must have happened to make her decide to leave.

She traveled all by herself. The trek took her to a river which she followed, up the river. As she was beginning to feel exhausted, she saw a house with smoke curling up from the smoke hole. She walked straight to the house, then entered.

Inside she saw a large woman sitting by herself, calmly working on her household chores. There was a lot of bedding in the house. The large woman, at the time the only person in the house, welcomed her and made her comfortable.

"Go and sit for a while on the bedding at the far end of the room. You'll have something to eat soon. I'll serve you some food," the woman said.

The young woman didn't resist. She complied with the instruction. She walked to the far end of the room and sat down.

The woman later gave her food to eat. After finishing her meal, the young woman went back to the bedding she was sitting on earlier. Just as she was sitting down, she heard someone outside the house. A young man entered the house and sat down. Another young man then followed.

As she was sitting there, another young man came in.

Three young men came into the house. One of them went to the bedding on which the young woman was sitting. It turned out that was his bed that the woman of the house had given her. All the young men were the woman's sons. The large woman then told the young woman that she thought the young woman would make a good wife for the son on whose bedding she was seated. That was why she was seated there. The young man took the young woman to be his wife.

The way things occurred, the young woman had left her home because her parents sat her down and were about to give her advice and a good talking-to for whatever reason that might be. But she had left her house, her relatives, and ended up in that situation instead.

The Goose Feather People

Flora Kuugaaq Cleveland

~~~~~~

This story demonstrates the importance of seeing storyteller-audience interaction during the storytelling event. Here John Brown, an audience member and widower, was teased. The storyteller, Flora, and John Brown were good friends. Flora was born at Kuutchiaq, Lower Selawik, and John had lived there when he first resettled on the Selawik.

RECORDED IN SELAWIK, MAY 7, 1972

~~~~~~

NORA TALKED ABOUT AN OLD WOMAN. I'M GOING TO TALK ABOUT AN old man.

There was a man living alone. (How did he happen to be living alone by himself? He was probably a Kobuk River man.)

One day the man went hunting. It was at that time of the year when the geese were molting. When geese are molting, they have their new wing feathers. The man picked these feathers off the geese and when he returned home, he stuck them into the ground outside his house. After that he went to bed.

He had been sleeping for a while when he either heard something outside, or maybe he just woke up on his own. When he went out to check, he discovered that all of the feathers had become people, many, many people. He was living among them. What he had stuck into the ground had turned into people. He saw them busily working on their regular chores.

The man had been living alone. After that he had many people living with him.

The Hungry Boy

Flora Kuugaaq Cleveland

RECORDED IN SELAWIK, MAY 7, 1972

THERE WAS AT ONE TIME A YOUNG BOY WHO WAS RAVENOUS. HE ASKED his grandmother if he could have something to eat, but his grandmother told him to wait. She told him that if he ate then, later on he would have nothing to eat.

The boy started to cry because when his grandmother told him that she was in the middle of cooking. He could smell the delicious aroma of the food she was cooking.

When the boy's father came home from hunting, he told them that he hadn't been able to catch any game animal that day.

When the grandmother finished cooking, she served only tiny portions of the cooked food to her family. The hungry boy was so dissatisfied with the portion of food he was given that he made a promise to himself. "When I'm old enough to hunt, I will eat and eat to my heart's content."

The Girl Raised by a Grizzly Bear

Nora Paniikaaluk Norton

RECORDED IN SELAWIK, SEPTEMBER 8, 1968

I'M GOING TO TELL ANOTHER SHORT STORY. I'M TELLING IT AS I KNOW IT.

There was a family making a living. The couple had two sons and a daughter.

The parents went out fishing with the two sons. (They were probably doing the summer fishing.) The girl was left behind at home. When they returned home, they discovered that the little girl had disappeared.

When they left the little girl behind, someone came unannounced. It wasn't a human being. The storyteller said it was a bear. The little girl noticed that the thing that came into her house had a different kind of skin, not like her mother's skin. It also smelled different. She noticed that the person who put her on her back was different. The grizzly bear took the girl to the grizzly bear den and put her down on the floor. Again, the little girl noticed that the house she was in was different, the woman in the house also looked different. But she had no choice. She couldn't return home by herself. (This girl was probably old enough to walk around and could understand her surroundings.)

The woman living in the house cooked really delicious meals. There were all kinds of food including berries. There were also dried fish in oil. There were all kinds of prepared food and the girl had good food to eat while living there. The girl was raised by a grizzly bear. It is said that creatures can turn into humans because they lived like humans.

They lived together. Winter came, but the lifeways of the woman of the house remained unchanged. She had no difficulties making a living. In the meanwhile the girl grew up.

When the days finally grew long, the little girl began to stay outside the house. The person who raised her got her ready for going outside, but she told the little girl not to wander for fear that she might be taken away.

One day, the weather was beautiful. The woman who took care of her allowed her to go outside again. Inside the house the woman could hear the little girl singing. She wondered what the little girl was singing about. She listened and heard the little girl sing:

U-ka, Hu-ka-nii-nii,
My older brothers have come to get me.
U-ka, Hu-ka-nii-nii,
My older brothers have come to get me.
One of them is Qunuyulik.
The other is Piksiksalik.

She sang like that. From inside the house the woman who had raised her heard her song and asked, "My dear daughter, what are you singing about?"

The girl outside replied, "Nothing! I'm just watching a gull and a raven sparring with each other."

Every time she sang the song, the woman would ask, "My dear daughter, what are you singing about?"

And her daughter would answer, "Nothing. I'm just watching a gull and a raven sparring with each other."

The woman inside the house thought nothing of it. The little girl sang all day. She sang the song over and over again.

One day while she was outside the house singing, she saw two men approaching. When the two came closer, they turned out to be her older brothers. Her brothers grabbed her, took off, and brought her home.

When the one who raised her realized that the little girl wasn't outside the house, she wondered, "I wonder who has taken her away? Or has the little thing returned home?" She hadn't forgotten from where she got the little girl, so she returned to the place. But the family didn't say anything. The grizzly bear missed the little girl very much.

The two young men afterwards told the bear, "When she grows up, she'll go and visit you. We aren't taking her away from you permanently. We too miss her and want to see her."

They told the bear that was why they went to take her back. They had been wondering where she was and had suspected that she was abducted by that bear.

When the girl grew up and could do things for herself, she went back to visit the place she had lived earlier with the bear. She would spend some time there before returning home to her parents. Who knows how long she spent her life like that, traveling back and forth between her two places.

Kunuuksaayuka

Minnie Aliitchak Gray

Recorded at Onion Portage in English, August 9, 1967

A MAN NAMED KUNUUKSAAYUKA TOOK OFF FROM HIS HOUSE, FOLLOWING the course of the river. He arrived at a slough branching off from the river. Walking along that slough, he saw a man busily digging with his adz. He watched the working man and saw that the latter dislodged the adz blade from his adz. The snowstorm was blowing so hard at the time that one couldn't see through the blizzard.

Kunuuksaayuka went closer to the working man and hid. He didn't want to be spotted. The working man began working again with his adz, but again he dislodged its blade. This time when the blade was dislodged, Kunuuksaayuka quickly snatched it and ran away with it in the midst of the blizzard. When the working man wasn't able to find his adz blade, he searched and searched for it.

He caught a glimpse of Kunuuksaayuka as Kunuuksaayuka was bolting down the slough.

Kunuuksaayuka returned home with the adz blade he had stolen. He had his meal, then lay down to rest. While he was resting, a man climbed up his house and peeked at him from the top of the skylight window. The man sang:

Kunuuksaayuka, I want my adz blade.
If you give back my adz blade,
In the morning you'll see caribou hooves.

Kunuuksaayuka, who had just started to take his rest, didn't see the man on top of his house.

A while later, the man cried again for his adz. He again sang his song:

Kunuuksaayuka, I want my adz blade.
If you give back my adz blade,
In the morning you'll see caribou hooves.

Kunuuksaayuka's mother was so tired of hearing the song of the man crying for his adz blade that she told her son to give the blade back. Kunuuksaayuka got up, took the adz blade, smashed it against the rock by the fire, and broke it. He then threw it out the skylight window. The man on top of the house laughed happily, then ran down from the housetop.

They didn't hear from him for a while, but later on they heard him again, walking up to the skylight window on top of the house. The man sang:

Kunuuksaayuka
Who broke the blade of my adz,
In the morning when you wake up,
You'll see many, many caribou hooves.

And in the morning when Kunuuksaayuka woke up, he heard the clamorous sound of the caribou hooves. He neither had to leave his house nor go on a hunt. Even from inside his house he could hear the sound of caribou hooves.

Kinnaq and the Caribou

Nellie Qapuk Russell

~~~~~~

Kinnaq, the fool, is a well-known Iñupiaq character type. The story, told as a humorous story, is much loved by the Iñupiat. Two more Kinnaq stories can be found in Unipchaallu Uqaaqtuallu: Legends and Stories *(1979), edited by Tupou L. Pulu and Ruth Ramoth-Sampson.*

Recorded in Selawik, June 5, 1981

~~~~~~

Kinnaq was qayaqing down the river. It is said that Kinnaq always traveled downriver.

As Kinnaq was traveling down the river, he spotted a caribou. Kinnaq was a strong and capable man, so he grasped the caribou by its antlers and took out his little knife. He was about to stab the caribou behind the head when the caribou said, "Ah, ah, ah, the water is too deep here. You should stab me when you arrive closer to the shore."

Kinnaq put away his knife. The caribou swam across the river with Kinnaq holding on from his qayaq by its antlers. When they were closer to the shore, Kinnaq again took out his knife to stab the caribou.

"Ah, ah, ah, it's still too deep here. When you reach the shallow part of the river, you can stab me," the caribou told him.

The caribou was also towing along the qayaq. He told Kinnaq, "Kinnaq, why don't you throw away your fishing net. You'll soon be able to make a brand-new net of sinew."

Kinnaq grabbed his net and threw it away. He threw away his only net into the river.

When the shore appeared closer, Kinnaq seized his small knife. He was about to finally stab the caribou when it told him, "Wait till we get close to the shallow part of the river. There you can stab me."

They arrived at shallow water. Suddenly the caribou shook off Kinnaq's grasp and took off. And then there was nothing!

(I wonder what happened to his qayaq. He had already thrown away his only net. The qayaq probably broke apart. Kinnaq had absolutely nothing left. At least he had been lucky enough to get hold of the caribou, but he was too easily fooled. And that's how Kinnaq ended up—empty-handed again.)

How the Caribou Lost Their Teeth

Nora Paniikaaluk Norton

RECORDED IN SELAWIK, MAY 8, 1972

~~~~~~

THIS STORY IS ABOUT A GRANDMOTHER AND HER GRANDSON. WHEN THE boy lost his parents, his grandmother worked hard on raising him the best she could.

While the child was growing up, his grandmother gave him some advice. In those days the caribou had teeth. (God had created them, but they weren't right, so he changed them. He even changed our weather.) The grandmother advised her grandson to beware of caribou that could bite like wolves.

Although he heard her advice, the grandson, without telling his grandmother, started to wander around the countryside. His grandmother had also advised him not to stray too far from home. The boy was wandering around when some caribou got him and tore him to pieces.

When the boy didn't return home, his grandmother was worried. She went out and looked for him. She called aloud his name. (I didn't ask the storyteller what the orphan's name was.) She called him, but there was no sign of the boy. Getting no reply, the old woman got ready to leave to search for him, and then left the house.

The grandmother searched in all directions but she couldn't find him. She realized that her grandson was probably dead. She continued searching and finally found her grandson, dead. He was all chewed up and she thought the caribou probably did it.

The poor old woman grieved her grandson's death. She probably took her mauled grandson home. The old woman grieved. Then she got angry. She wanted to avenge her grandson's death. She wanted to take her revenge on the caribou. She thought about ways to do it when she came upon the idea of cranberries. She would crush cranberries and layer them in her clothing.

The old grandmother didn't simply think about it. She proceeded to crush the cranberries and fold them into her clothing. (She was probably not just a little old lady, but had a helper.) When she finally went out into the countryside, sure enough the caribou charged at her.

The old woman wasn't afraid. She had a mission.

Two caribou that wandered ahead of the rest of the herd got to her first. They bit her, but then they began shaking their heads. They took off, shaking their heads. They weren't able to bite into her. As they were running, their teeth dropped. The other caribou that came later also tried to bite her, but they too took off, dropping their teeth.

From then on, biting into the cranberries, the caribou lost their teeth. They suffered from the sour taste of the cranberries which caused them to lose their teeth.

(I'd thank the old woman if she is sitting right here. The caribou sustain our lives, but if they still had their teeth, maybe caribou hunters wouldn't be able to make the killing as they do now.)

And that's where the story ends.

Raven Who Brought Back the Land

Robert Nasruk Cleveland

Recorded at Onion Portage, August 15, 1967

WHEN WATER WAS EVERYWHERE AND THE SEA AND THE LAND WERE ONE, a group of people was living on top of the mountains.

A tussock surfaced in front of these people who were all flooded out.

Seeing the tussock, the people consulted with each other about the lore they had heard. They had heard that if someone touched the tussock with a spear or an arrowhead the water would recede.

When the tussock drifted close, some men went after it in their qayaqs, but the tussock drifted away. When it drifted back out into the sea, the men, too afraid to follow, returned to land. When the tussock drifted in again, they pursued it again, but as before, it drifted back into the sea.

After watching them for some time, Raven told the people that he would go after the tussock himself. He told them not to follow him and that he would try to get close to the tussock. The people should simply watch.

When the tussock resurfaced every once in a while, Raven set off in a qayaq. The rest of the men waited on land. Raven had a throwing board with a cocked spear in one hand while paddling with the other hand. Going after the tussock, Raven sang a song. This is how the song goes:

Make it surface close by.

Make it surface close by.

Angiyaa yang-ŋaa yang-ŋaa

The tussock didn't drift away. It surfaced close by.

Raven moved closer, all the while singing, until his spear was within throwing range. He didn't paddle hard, simply kept the qayaq moving because he wanted people to see what happened as well as hear his song.

The tussock didn't drift away. It kept its distance from Raven, and then it dove under.

Raven kept singing. The tussock didn't surface for a long, long time. With Raven still singing and people watching, the tussock slowly resurfaced—in front of the bow of Raven's qayaq. Raven speared it. He hit it dead center because it was right in front of his qayaq. The tussock didn't move again because Raven had hit it dead center. It shivered.

Rapidly the water began to recede. Raven struggled, paddling hard against the torrent of receding water. The water level had been high, up all the way to the mountains. The water left with a roar. The people were left on top of the mountains since they had been living on top of mountains during the flood.

That's how people talked about Raven who got the land back for people.

When the water receded, the big worms and the sea monsters were left behind because they had come into this area with the flood. There were lots of big worms. Those worms wiggled their ways through the water puddles. As they wiggled toward the sea, they left behind them deep trenches. The rest of the floodwater flowed after them in these trenches. When the worms reached the sea, the water kept on using and flowing through these trenches. The trenches became rivers.

How the Mudshark Created Himself

Robert Nasruk Cleveland

~~~~~~

The last twenty-two stories are all animal stories. Iñupiaq storytell-ers imbued these stories with the physical forms, characteristics, and behaviors of animals they had observed from their environment. Their keen observations of detail and the humor they interjected into animal characters make these stories loved, told, and retold to adults as well as to children.

Through these stories, the children are taught about animals in the Iñupiaq environment. The simple structure of the story and the charm-ing songs embedded into many stories make them especially suitable and appealing to children. See the discussion on animal stories in the introductory chapter, "Iñupiaq Oral Narratives: Collection History and Narrative Culture."

RECORDED AT ONION PORTAGE, AUGUST 23, 1967

~~~~~~

I'M GOING TO TELL THE STORY OF THE MUDSHARK. PEOPLE HAVE BEEN telling the story of its different parts.

Mudshark took its different parts from all sorts of animals. He also took some parts from a human being. It wasn't until he had assembled all these parts to be parts of him that he swam off and became known as the mudshark. By then he had prepared himself well for swimming in the water.

These are the many parts that Mudshark took from human beings, birds, and also fish. I'll try to name all the parts. But to be able to remember all of them, one has to look at the actual pieces of the mudshark parts. It's hard to name all the parts without having all these parts in front of you. There are so many parts in a mudshark.

When Mudshark was ready to start assembling the parts, he took the back-bone of a beluga. He took its backbone and added it to his body. The mudshark's backbone looks like the backbone of a beluga.

After he got the backbone, he took the hair of a young woman with long hair to form his dorsal fin. He took her long braided hair.

After that, he took an old woman's braided sinew for his front paddles [fins].

After he got his paddles, Mudshark took a tree swallow for his mouth. The bone that looks like a tree swallow is in the upper jaw of his mouth.

For his bottom jaw, he took the handle of a bucket.

After Mudshark had all of these parts, he took wood chips for his flesh. When you shave a cottonwood branch, the shavings are soft. That's what he took for his flesh. If you look closely at the mudshark's meat, it looks like wood chips.

Mudshark took the body of a little old lady with a shawl and her two little legs. He took these to be his head.

The *qutummak* is the kingfisher. Mudshark took it to be a bone in his head, known as *qutummak*.

For the joint of his fins, he took mukluks.

From this point on I'm less sure. Unless I can see the mudshark in front of me, it's difficult for me to say this belongs here and that belongs there. However, I'll try to name them. I wonder how this will come out.

The body of the porcupine is somewhere in the mudshark's head. That part in his head looks like a porcupine. He has a lot of parts. He took all sorts of things, but I won't be able to name them all.

The beak of a raven is also in his head.

Inside his skull, he put in two flints that we use for starting a fire. That's why we can see two small rocks sitting in his skull.

I cannot name all the parts, but if right now I'm eating the cooked mudshark I can name them all for you. There are parts that I remember and those that I have forgotten.

There is also the tail of a big fish in his head.

There are lots of parts in the mudshark, but I've forgotten some of them. When I am eating and enjoying a mudshark, I can name each of its parts while placing each part in front of you. When you see it, you would believe me because these parts look so real, so much like what I referred to.

I had learned about them from my parents and my grandparents, but I've forgotten some of them. "This is what this part is," they told me when I was learning from them.

Without looking at them, I cannot name all of them. I've named the parts that are more common. The mudshark took all kinds of parts from other animals. It looks just like different animals. It has its liver, intestines, and stomach from different animals. It has its stomach from a beluga.

I think I got nearly all of its parts. I may have forgotten some parts. They aren't easy to keep track of unless one is eating it.

The Caribou and the Blackfish

Nora Paniikaaluk Norton

Recorded in Selawik, August 28, 1969

I'M GOING TO TELL A SHORT STORY.

One summer when the weather turned warm, there was a caribou, a bull, who felt that it was too warm for him to be lying on a mountain. When the heat became too unbearable, he left. He probably knew where to go at this time of the year.

He arrived at a lake and galloped straight into the water. At the depth where he was standing, he caught sight of a fish. It was a blackfish.

The blackfish swam closer and closer to the caribou, then asked, "What's that enormous thing on top of your head? What do you use it for? Why do you keep it on your head, burdening yourself with extra weight? Also down there, at your feet, you have rocks. What are they for—those rocks you're carrying on your feet? Also that thing on your head—what is it for? I wonder what that thing is that stretches and stretches so long!"

The blackfish pointed out the things the caribou had, insulting him loudly.

Hearing the blackfish's insult, the caribou lunged with his antlers and hooked the blackfish. He then galloped up on land, carrying the little blackfish along with him. It was hot that day. The sun was shining brightly. After traveling some distance, the caribou set the blackfish down at the place he lived on the ridge of a mountain. He shook his head and dropped the blackfish on the ground.

The blackfish could do nothing. He was drying up. He turned from side to side, but he felt very hot lying between the tussocks. There was no water there. The caribou had left the blackfish at the spot because he had no idea what to do with the blackfish either. The blackfish struggled, trying to survive.

Lacking other options, he began to sing. (I didn't hear the song. The story-teller didn't sing the blackfish song while telling the story. If he had sung it, I'd have asked him what kind of song it was, but he didn't sing it.) The blackfish closed his eyes and sang. He wished for bad weather, for the rain to come, for he was getting dried. If it rained and his skin became moist again, it would be good again for him.

He sang for a while. But when he opened his eyes again, there were no clouds in sight.

The blackfish didn't give up. He sang again. He sang and sang. (Unfortunately the storyteller didn't sing this song. I'd have sung it even though it might be inaccurate.) This time when he opened his eyes, he saw a small cloud.

So he sang again, calling for the rain clouds. He was desperate for a little water.

The blackfish was still lying there when the big sky soon turned dark with clouds. Then it started to rain. After raining small raindrops, it began to pour. The small ditches between the tussocks began to fill up with water. Blackfish enjoyed the weather tremendously. After a while there was running water between the tussocks. Little by little, the blackfish swam bravely between the tussocks and inched his way back down. Soon he reached a large lake. As he was very thirsty, he drank the water—all the water in the lake. (Did he really do that?) After drinking all the water in one lake, he was still thirsty, so he drank the water in another lake. (I doubt if he drank all the water in the lake!)

After doing all of this, the blackfish became the son-in-law to the beluga. That's why the blackfish spouts water like a beluga. Who knows for how long the blackfish was the beluga's son-in-law. This is as far as I heard the story.

The Raven and the Loon

Nellie Qapuk Russell

RECORDED IN SELAWIK, JUNE 6, 1981

〜〜〜〜〜〜〜〜〜〜〜〜〜〜〜〜〜〜〜〜〜〜〜〜〜〜〜〜〜〜〜〜〜〜

MY NAME IS NELLIE RUSSELL, QAPUK. I'M GOING TO TELL A STORY ABOUT the raven and the loon.

One day, probably out in the countryside, Raven and Loon ran into each other.

"We should paint each other," Loon suggested to Raven.

So Raven began to paint and painted Loon very nicely. He made Loon wonderful to look at. It is said that Loon was painted and designed by Raven.

When Raven was finished, Loon began to paint Raven in different patterns. Unfortunately Loon made a mistake, so he repainted Raven all over with very dark color.

Loon was about to dive into the water when Raven grabbed some ashes and threw them at Loon. Nowadays the loon has ashes on top of his head because Raven had thrown it there.

(I wonder what design Raven would have had if Loon hadn't made the mistake.)

Wolf, Fox, and Raven Brothers

Beatrice Anausuk Mouse

~~~~~~

Beatrice Anausuk Mouse, born in the Upper Kobuk in 1891, was a daughter of Kanauq of Wales and Saiḷaq of the Upper Kobuk. As a young girl she lived with her parents and grandmother, Ullaaq. Beatrice lived traditional Iñupiaq subsistence lifeways in a sod house, did her seining and gathering, and witnessed her mother giving birth to her younger brother the traditional way in a snow house. Beatrice had a good recollection of the transition period when the white man's food and Christianity were introduced into the area (see D. Anderson et al. 1998:94–101).

Beatrice, living in Noorvik, visited Onion Portage in 1967, the same year Robert and Flora Cleveland visited and camped at Onion Portage. The visit occasioned the telling of this animal story with Robert, his wife, Robert's grandchildren, and me as her audience.

Beatrice's version of "Wolf, Fox, and Raven Brothers" was narrated in a lively style with very close imitations of animals' calls, which delighted everyone, especially the children.

Beatrice passed away in 1980 at the age of eighty-nine.

Recorded at Onion Portage, August 28, 1967

~~~~~~

There was a family living in a house.

One day the parents didn't return home. The brothers, Wolf, Fox, and Raven, were left by themselves. High above them they could see the skylight. They continued living in the house for some time, but then they felt lonely. As they couldn't go out to obtain more food, they began to run short of food. After contemplating on their situation, Wolf, the eldest brother, started to sing a song:

I wish I were something else and could go out of here.

I wish I were something else and could go out of here.

I wish I were a wolf and could go outside.

Wolf!

Wolf left the house.

The two brothers left inside the house began pacing. After a period of trying to withstand his loneliness, Fox, the next brother, thought, "By singing a song, my older brother was able to leave this place. I'll do the same."

I wish I were something else and could get out of here.

I wish I were a fox and could go outside.

Vaaa!

Fox left the house too.

When Raven was the only one left, he cried and cried. His clothes were in rags and he was lonesome. He was also filthy. He hadn't bothered to practice the song his older brothers had sung. When what he could remember finally came back to him, he sang:

I wish I were.

I wish I were.

I wish I were.

Raven started singing these words. He was practicing his song. After some more practicing, he sang again:

I wish I were something else and could get out of here.

I wish I were something else and could get out of here.

Wolf!

Raven forgot to make the correct animal call of the animal he wanted to become. Nothing happened. So he began singing again:

I wish I were something else and could get out of here.

I wish I were something else and could get out of here.

Caw, caw.

Raven flew out.

But when he looked at himself he saw that his clothes were really filthy. He was happy to be outside anyway.

Wolf, Fox, and Raven Brothers

Robert Nasruk Cleveland

RECORDED AT ONION PORTAGE, AUGUST 28, 1967

THIS STORY IS TOLD FROM WAY BACK ABOUT THE THREE BROTHERS: Wolf, Fox, and Raven. They had become orphans. (That's the way things happened in the story. Certain parts of the dialogue are missing, but I'll tell it the way I heard it. It's different from the one told earlier.)

After living in the house for some time, the older brother said that they should become something else and leave the house.

When the older brother was ready to try to leave the house, he told his younger brothers, "When you're ready to leave, don't forget to take the *agamiga* [small knife]. Whoever is the last person to leave the house, he should carry it with him." (The older brother was talking about a knife. He called it an *agamiga*.)

After giving his advice to his younger brothers, the older brother prepared to leave. He sang:

I wish I were something else and could go out from here.
I wish I were something else and could go out from here.
I wish I were a wolf and could leave.
"Vu-uu!"

He howled like a wolf and left the house. He left his younger brothers behind.

The two brothers wanted to leave too, but they just stood there. They stayed there with their ears perked, listening for their older brother. When dawn arrived, they heard a howl. They knew that their older brother had caught something because he had told them that he would howl when he did.

The two younger brothers wanted to go outside too. Fox started to sing the same song his older brother had sung:

I wish I were something else and could go out from here.
I wish I were something else and could go out from here.
I wish I were a fox and could leave.
"Vaaq!"

And he dashed off.

There was only one brother left. His two older brothers had already left. Raven too wanted to leave, but he was having a difficult time at it. He thought about

OLD STORIES · 265

becoming a raven and then leaving, but something was not quite right and he couldn't leave. After a while he began singing a song:

I wish I were something else and could go out from here.
I wish I were something else and could go out from here.
I wish I were a raven and could leave.
"Caw!"

He sang "caw, caw" and left. He flew around, looking for his two brothers who were howling earlier. Then he saw them with a dead caribou between them. He landed. His two brothers had been waiting for him and hadn't even touched the caribou. They thought Raven might have a knife with him.

"Where's the knife?"

"Oh no, I've forgotten it!"

For a while the brothers didn't know what to do because they had no knife. Then the oldest brother told the others, "Oh, go on. Eat whatever you'd like to eat." He slashed the belly of the caribou and ate the liver. Raven landed on the head of the caribou so that he could eat its eyes. He ate the caribou's eyes, stabbing at them with his beak. Fox ate what he wanted. And that's the way I heard it.

The Raven and the Fox

Sarah Qiñuġana Goode

~~~~~~

Sarah Qiñuġana Goode, the storyteller, was born Sarah Qiñuġana in 1902 at a place called Inuruk on the Tagraġvik River, Upper Selawik. She spent part of her childhood in the vicinity of Aksik, Lower Kobuk. When Sarah was twelve years old, her family moved to resettle at Akuliġaq, the island part of the present Selawik village, so that Sarah could begin her schooling. Sarah was married to Luke Tuttuġruk Goode. On her ninety-second birthday in 1994, when I was in Selawik, I heard birthday messages for her all day on the CB radios, a tribute to the oldest person in Selawik.

Sarah Goode had three children. She lived in her traditional Iñupiaq house on the upriver end of the island with her adopted son, Elwood Goode, until her death in 1997 at the age of ninety-five.

Recorded in Selawik, July 21, 1994

~~~~~~

RAVEN AND FOX WERE MAKING A LIVING TOGETHER. THEY WERE CROSS-cousins. When Fox went hunting, he would bring something home. When Raven went hunting, he got nothing.

One day Fox went hunting. He came upon a house. A very large woman came out of the house. She had lots of sores on her face. The woman with the sores asked Fox, "How do I look? Am I beautiful?"

"Yes, you are beautiful," said Fox.

Upon being told that she was beautiful, the large woman gave Fox a string of dried fish. Fox brought the food back home to his cousin, Raven, who lived with him.

Raven too decided to go hunting toward the woman's house.

Fox advised Raven, "If a large woman comes out and asks if she is beautiful, say 'Yes, you're beautiful' even though she has sores on her face and isn't at all beautiful."

Raven accepted Fox's advice and went on his way, following his cousin's direction of how to get there. Sure enough, a large woman came out of the house. "How do I look? Am I beautiful?"

"*Iikii*! You are an ugly woman!" Raven said. Seeing how dirty she looked, Raven completely forgot his cousin's instruction!

Because Raven had told her she was ugly, the woman gave Raven nothing. She just went back into her house.

"*Aanna*!" Raven suddenly remembered his cousin's instruction to praise the woman. "I didn't praise her, so she gave me nothing," he lamented. He returned home empty-handed. He had no luck because he had told the woman she was ugly.

The Raven and the Fox

Nora Paniikaaluk Norton

RECORDED IN SELAWIK, SEPTEMBER 6, 1968

I'M GOING TO TELL ANOTHER SHORT STORY TO ADD TO THE ONE I JUST TOLD.

There were two cross-cousins, Raven and Fox. This story tells about Raven and Fox who were making a living together.

One time the two of them ran short of food, so Fox took off to the seashore to look for some food. Most likely, he was looking for animal carcasses that might have drifted ashore.

Walking along the shore, Fox saw a small house, so he decided to check what sort of house that was. As he was standing at the door of the house, he heard someone coming to the door. Then he saw a large woman who didn't appear to have suffered a hard time as he had.

The woman came out of the house. When she saw Fox standing at her door, right away she asked, "How do I look? Am I a beautiful woman?"

Fox answered, praising the woman, "Oh yes, you are beautiful."

The woman invited Fox inside her house. Then she went outside and came back with dried fish in fish oil and berries. The woman wasn't beautiful at all, but the cunning Fox told her what she wanted to hear. He gave her a good answer and he had a scrumptious meal. He ate till he was no longer hungry. He left after the meal and returned home to his cousin, Raven.

"Cousin, where have you been all day?" Raven asked.

"Yonder. I walked along the seashore," Fox replied.

"While you were over there, what did you do?" Raven asked.

"Nothing really! But I'm not hungry. I had a big meal."

Raven too was ready to leave and have a look. He wanted to find the place where his cousin had eaten so well. On his venture he also found the house.

Raven was standing in front of the door when the same woman came out to greet him. She asked him the same question she had asked Fox, "How do I look? Am I a beautiful woman?"

"*Iikii*, you are ugly!" Raven replied.

Too bad! Raven wasn't as crafty as told in other stories from way back. In all of the other old stories he was a liar and more.

The woman didn't invite Raven into the house because of his "*iikii*" comment about her. After standing by the door waiting for a long time, Raven left and returned home. (Poor guy, he didn't have anything to eat.) He told his cousin that he hadn't had his meal and then asked his cousin how he managed to obtain his food.

Fox asked, "What did she ask you when you were at the door?"

Raven said, "The woman who was ugly asked me, 'How do I look? Am I a beautiful woman?' I said, '*Iikii*! You are ugly!'"

Tricky Fox laughed gleefully. As was so characteristic of Fox, he didn't tell his cousin what to do if he happened to see this woman. Fox was crafty and had a scrumptious meal. Raven wasn't crafty and didn't get any food to eat.

The Ground Squirrel and the Raven

Robert Nasruk Cleveland

~~~~~~

This set of three versions of the story "The Ground Squirrel and the Raven" is a good example of differences among versions. Compare the first version told by Robert Cleveland to the second version told by his daughter, Minnie Gray, who said that her father told her the story when she was a little girl. The storyteller of the third version, Maude Cleveland, was Robert's sister-in-law. Her version has variations that mark her style of storytelling.

RECORDED AT ONION PORTAGE, AUGUST 28, 1967

~~~~~~

I'M GOING TO TELL YOU ABOUT THE RAVEN AND HIS SONG.

At one time a ground squirrel was picking berries. She was beside her burrow, picking the berries. As she was busily picking the berries, she heard a sound. "Hah, I've blocked her entrance! Ground Squirrel, I've blocked your entrance, hah!"

Ground Squirrel darted home. But there, standing above her burrow, was Raven. Raven told her that he had blocked the entrance to her home. There was no way she could get into her burrow.

For a while Ground Squirrel was at a loss of what to do. Then she said, "Cousin, if you sing, I'll dance. If you sing, I'll give you half of my *qatlisiq* [belly fat] as oil. If you'll just let me dance to your song, I promise to give you some oil."

Raven replied, "All right, I'll sing for you."

"Start singing. When I'm through with dancing all the dances, I'll give you half of my belly fat."

Raven got ready to sing. Then he sang:

Bow your head haa, ha.
Bow your head haa, ha.
This is a burrow, huh?
This is a burrow, huh?
Burrow!

"Hey, what are you trying to do, Cousin?" Raven asked.

"Cousin, a blade of grass was stabbing my eye. I was just trying to remove it. Now, start singing again," Ground Squirrel answered.

Raven was motivated to sing again:

Bow your head haa, ha.
Bow your head haa, ha.
This is a burrow, huh?
This is a burrow, huh?
Burrow!

Ground Squirrel was about to dash into her burrow when Raven asked her, "Cousin, what are you trying to do?"

"That blade of grass is trying to stab me in the eye. Why don't you just close your eyes again and sing hard because I'm going to give you some of my belly fat," Ground Squirrel replied.

Raven started to sing again:

Bow your head haa, ha.
Bow your head haa, ha.
This is a burrow, huh?
This is a burrow, huh?
Burrow!

Raven wasn't able to catch Ground Squirrel as she darted into the burrow. She exclaimed, "*Siisiq!*" [burrow] and then rushed into her burrow.

Raven got nothing. He called down the burrow, "Cousin, let's play together outside. The sun is shining brightly."

"I've blocked her entrance, huh?" Ground Squirrel, quoting Raven's words, answered from inside her burrow.

"Cousin, come on outside. The sun is shining brightly. Come out and play with me."

"I've blocked her entrance, huh?" Ground Squirrel, quoting Raven again, replied from inside her burrow.

Ground Squirrel refused to come out.

What happened to Raven? I think he died there. The way people tell this story, I think he starved out there, outside the burrow. He died keeping watch over the entrance of the burrow. It is said that he died of hunger at the entrance.

The Ground Squirrel and the Raven

Minnie Aliitchak Gray

RECORDED AT ONION PORTAGE, AUGUST 10, 1967

A GROUND SQUIRREL WENT OUT TO PICK BERRIES. WHILE SHE WAS PICK-ing berries, Raven went to the little burrow and blocked her from entering. Ground Squirrel told Raven, "If you bend your head, I'll give you one side of my fat."

Raven believed her and started dancing. Ground Squirrel started singing:

Bow down your head.
Bow down your head.
A home, a home
Home!

Ground Squirrel tried to enter her burrow, but Raven saw her. He stood in front and stopped her from going in.

"What's the matter?" Raven asked.

Ground Squirrel answered, "The grass was stabbing my eyes." She started to sing again:

Bow down your head.
Bow down your head.
A home, a home
Home!

Then Squirrel darted into her home.

Raven, left outside alone, started to call her. "Let's play together outside. The sun is shining brightly."

Ground Squirrel answered, "You've just blocked me."

Raven waited for Ground Squirrel, then left Ground Squirrel alone. Ground Squirrel didn't come out of her burrow.

The Ground Squirrel and the Raven

Maude Kanayuqpak Cleveland

RECORDED AT ONION PORTAGE, JULY 5, 1967

GROUND SQUIRREL LIVED IN A BURROW.

One day she went berry picking. She went away from her burrow to pick some berries. As she was busily picking her berries, she heard a noise from the direction of her burrow. She could hear someone saying, "Ground Squirrel, I've blocked her entrance! Ground Squirrel, I've blocked her entrance!"

Hearing this, Ground Squirrel darted back home, spilling her berries along the way. When she reached her burrow, she saw a raven blocking its entrance. Raven wouldn't allow her to enter her burrow. Realizing her situation, she talked sweetly to Raven, calling Raven her cousin.

"Cousin, you really should do a dance. If you dance, I'll give you one side of my belly fat."

Ground Squirrel began singing for Raven and Raven started to dance. This is the song Ground Squirrel sang for Raven:

Bow down your head, haa, ha.
Bow down your head, haa, ha.
This is a burrow, huh?
This is a burrow, huh?
Burrow!

Ground Squirrel tried to dart into her burrow, but Raven was blocking it. So Ground Squirrel told Raven, "Cousin, you should dance more lively this time. You should raise your furry tail and also close your eyes. Dance again and I'll give you some of my belly fat you want to eat."

Ground Squirrel began singing again. This time Raven danced wildly. He lifted his furry tail. During the singing, when Ground Squirrel sang the word "burrow," she dashed into her burrow. She slipped by Raven and was able to enter her burrow.

Raven thought to himself, "Why was I dancing madly like that?"

He called down to Ground Squirrel, "Cousin, we should be outside and enjoy. The sun is shining beautifully."

He kept calling down to Ground Squirrel, but Ground Squirrel replied, "Surely, you'll block me!"

Raven tried to entice Ground Squirrel to come out several times that day, but Ground Squirrel's reply was always the same.

After spending several days in her burrow, Ground Squirrel decided to go out to check what occurred outside. She came out and found her cousin dead beside the entrance of the burrow. When Raven was dead, Ground Squirrel began to make a living again. (Maybe after two or three days!) [Laughter.]

The Redpoll and the Fox

Sarah Qinuġana Goode

Recorded in Selawik, July 21, 1994

There was a common redpoll. She was sitting in her nest in a willow bush when a fox came and stood underneath her nest.

Fox told Redpoll, "Drop me a small bird to eat. If you don't, I'll cut down the willows and eat every single one of your little birds."

Arii, Redpoll didn't want all her young children to be eaten, so she dropped one of them down to the fox. Fox ate the little bird, then took off.

The redpoll had tears streaming down her cheeks when Raven flew by.

"What happened? You look like you've been crying!" Raven asked.

"Fox came under my nest and told me to drop him one of my baby birds. That's why I'm crying and have tears in my eyes," she replied.

"Oh, he's always lying!" said Raven, who was always given a Kobuk accent. "He really doesn't have anything to cut the willows with."

But Redpoll had believed Fox.

The Ptarmigan and the Crane

Minnie Aliitchak Gray

~~~~~~

"The Ptarmigan and the Crane" is one of the most well-known Iñu-piaq animal stories. I obtained two versions of this story. The birds have been portrayed here as having families and emotions, likes and dislikes, love and anger. Note the variations between the two versions and the metaphor of the ptarmigan's new head coloring in spring.

RECORDED AT ONION PORTAGE IN ENGLISH, AUGUST 9, 1967

~~~~~~

THERE WAS A PAIR OF PTARMIGAN. THEY WERE HUSBAND AND WIFE. The ptarmigan husband one day got caught in the snare. The ptarmigan wife cried and cried for her husband. She sang:

My husband got caught in the snare.
My husband got caught in the snare.

From a long way away, the crane heard her song. He sang back to her:

Will you be my wife?
Will you be my wife?
I have a big forehead.
I have a big head.
I have a big neck, big neck, big neck.

The ptarmigan sang back to the crane:

Who would want you as a husband?
Who would want you as a husband?
You with a big forehead!
You with a big forehead!
You with a big head!
You with a big neck, big neck, big neck!

The crane sang in response:

Why did you cry then for the dead one by the willows with their tips removed?
Why did you cry then for the dead one in the willows with the tips removed?

And the ptarmigan answered him:
I will make a hood for you.
I will make a hood for you
With beautiful red tassels.

The Ptarmigan and the Crane

Nora Paniikaaluk Norton

Recorded in Selawik, September 6, 1968

I'M GOING TO TELL A VERY SHORT STORY ABOUT THE PTARMIGAN. I HAD heard stories from my husband, but I've forgotten so many of them.

There was a ptarmigan couple making their living. (From the time way back, God's creatures lived like humans. But humans have set their snares to catch the ptarmigan.)

While feeding, the ptarmigan couple came upon an area where a snare was set. The husband unfortunately got caught in the snare. He thrashed about, trying to free himself. His wife didn't know how to free him. After a while, the husband died. He was suffocated in the snare.

The poor wife started to grieve. (How pitiful! I know this can happen. I have snared animals too. It hurts. But God's creatures have been caught by humans from time immemorial.) This incident probably occurred during spring because when the female ptarmigan looked across the river, she saw a crane. The crane was strutting around and making his calls.

The female ptarmigan, upon seeing the crane, thought that the crane would make a good husband for her. She began to sing for him:
I wonder what he's hunting, the one over there across the river.
I wonder what he's hunting, the one over there across the river.
I'll have a hood,
I'll have a hood, a very beautiful hood.
In these words the female ptarmigan sang her song.

The insensitive crane, the ungrateful creature, replied with a song:
Things like that!
I hardly think they are beautiful!

From the crane's point of view, the ptarmigan's hood was not considered beautiful. The ptarmigan has a brown head in spring.

The female ptarmigan was furious at the crane's reply song. Her patience snapped. She sang:

Who would have wanted you as a husband?
Who would have wanted you as a husband?
You, with a big forehead!
You, with a big hump on your back!
You have a long neck! Long neck!

Sometimes people say nasty things to each other, but I don't think anyone can outdo the ptarmigan. She was so fast with her retort. It is said that during this exchange between the ptarmigan and the crane, the ptarmigan stood tall, looking as if she had long legs like the crane.

The Porcupine and His Qayaq

Willie Panik Goodwin, Sr.

RECORDED AT ONION PORTAGE IN ENGLISH, JULY 3, 1966

AT ONE TIME A MAN WAS WALKING ALONG THE EDGE OF A ROLLING HILL. He noticed that the land around there was quite beautiful. But after walking back and forth for a while along this rolling hill, he got bored and decided to push on, go elsewhere. When he reached a river, he noticed another rolling hill on the other side of the river with thick growth of trees and beautiful scenery. He wanted to go across, but he couldn't fly and he couldn't swim.

So he waited, thinking to himself, "Maybe someone will come along. Before long someone should be coming along this way."

Toward the evening, looking downriver, he saw something making waves down the river. The man watched for a while. Sure enough, a qayaq was making its way up the river. He waited and waited. When the qayaq came closer, the man began to sing and whistle.

When the qayaq came close enough, the man shouted to the other person to let the other person know that he was there. The qayaq landed close to the spot where the man was sitting. They sat together, talked together for a while, and asked each other questions. The man told the qayaq man, "I'd like to go across the river, but I've nothing to carry me across."

The qayaq man said, "Well, I'm not sure I'd be able to take you across because my qayaq is so small." He added, "Soon there should be someone else coming after me and he might have a bigger qayaq than mine."

The man said, "It's okay." And the qayaq man left.

The man sat and waited. Soon he saw bigger ripples in the water downriver.

Sure enough, another qayaq was coming. The man was so happy that he had another chance to ask the qayaq man to pick him up and carry him across the river. When the qayaq arrived closer, the man let the qayaq man know where he was. The qayaq man stopped, talked to him, and asked questions. The man told him, "I'd like to go across the river. The land over there on the other side of the river looks real good."

The qayaq man answered, "We can try. I think I can take you across."

They both got ready. They went across and barely made it. When they landed, the man was very happy.

"Thank you, Friend. The only way I can thank you is this—there'd never be any fat at the spot where you and I touched while we were coming across."

The qayaq man said, "Thank you," and then took off.

The man got to the place he wanted to go. He felt very happy.

The man who was walking on the edge of the rolling hill was a porcupine and the first qayaq that came along the river was a land otter. The next qayaq was a beaver. The beaver's back has no fat at all. And the porcupine's belly also has no fat.

I heard this story from my grandpa when I was a young boy living in Selawik. His name was Panik. He had no last name. In the old days people didn't have last names. My Eskimo name is also Panik.

The Porcupine and His Qayaq

Minnie Aliitchak Gray

RECORDED AT ONION PORTAGE, AUGUST 9, 1967

~~~~~~

PORCUPINE WAS SITTING BY THE RIVER. HE WANTED TO CROSS THE RIVER
to the other side, so he started to sing:

> *I kaa yai, i kaa yai*
> *I kaa yai, i kaa yai*
> *Su ġu taa ni kai, a yaa ni kai*
> *kaa yai*
> *Across, across,*
> *Hey, qayaq, can you take me across?*

But the qayaq, the little canoe that went by, told him, "A bigger boat will take
you across."

So Porcupine sat down and waited. As another qayaq was passing by,
Porcupine sang again:

> *I kaa yai, i kai yai*
> *I kaa yai, i kaa yai*
> *Su ġu taa ni kai, a yaa ni kai*
> *Across, across*
> *Hey, qayaq, can you take me across?*

The second qayaq told him, "A bigger boat will take you across." It passed
him again.

Then the third qayaq came. It was a bigger qayaq. Porcupine began singing.
The big qayaq stopped, took in Porcupine, and carried him across the river.

When he arrived at the other side, Porcupine told the big qayaq, "No matter what
happens in the future, your back and my belly will never have any fat on it."

That big qayaq was a beaver. The beaver's back has no fat on it. Neither has
the porcupine any fat on its belly. And the first boat, the little qayaq, was a mink.
The second boat was an otter.

The Man in the Lake

Willie Panik Goodwin, Sr.

RECORDED AT ONION PORTAGE, JULY 3, 1966

THIS LITTLE STORY I HEARD FROM MY GRANDMOTHER, MY FATHER'S mother.

At one time my mother talked about the dream she had. Another man who was also there in the house talked about his dream too. That's when my grandmother began to tell this story she knew, what I would call a "dream comes true" story. So, this is the beginning of the story of the man who lived in the lake.

A man had been living in a little lake for a long, long time.

One day he thought, "Tomorrow I should perhaps venture downstream. During my whole life I've never been anywhere downstream. All I know is this place, this lake."

He decided to set off the very next day, early in the morning. He went to sleep, and then began to dream.

He dreamt he was traveling down the stream. The first thing he saw in his dream was flowing water, crashing downward. The farther he traveled, the more downward the watercourse flowed. At one place where he finally fell into the water, he saw maybe a big mouth. Since he couldn't get away from it, he went into the mouth.

At that point, he woke up.

"Ah, I've only been dreaming! I'm now wide awake. I should leave as I planned anyway. Why not? I wonder if my dream will come true."

The man was worried somewhat, but he had already made up his mind about going. So he left. Anyway, he wanted to go away from the place where he had been living. He traveled a long way and came to a place where the water was running swiftly. He came to a waterfall and wasn't able to turn back. He kept going and the first thing he knew was that there was something just right in front of him. He couldn't get away from it, so he went in. The thing looked just like a gigantic whale to him.

That's the end of the story.

My grandmother told me this story. She told me that the man going down the stream was a little blackfish and when he went through the slough he ran into a mudshark.

Little blackfish stay in the lakes during the whole winter. Many times we found frozen blackfish in a lake. If you find them frozen, don't break them into pieces. Just put them into the water, then heat the water, and you'll see the blackfish starting to swim again.

The Mouse and the Man in the Qayaq

Minnie Aliitchak Gray

RECORDED AT ONION PORTAGE, AUGUST 10, 1967

A MAN WAS TRAVELING IN HIS QAYAQ. AFTER DARK, WHEN HE ARRIVED at the end of a steep riverbank he heard a man singing from the willow bush:

At night I sleep and I rest
Pii-hi-hai!

The man stopped and tried to find the singing man but wasn't able to find him. He went back to his qayaq, intending to continue on his trip. When he started to paddle his qayaq, he heard a man singing again:

At night I sleep and I rest
Pii-hi-hai!

Again, the man stopped and went up to try to find the singing man. When he went through the willows, he found the house of a little mouse. He tried to find the one who did the singing just like a man, but could find no one.

The man went back to his qayaq and when he looked back toward the house of the mouse, he saw a mouse coming out and sat on top of his house. Then the mouse began to sing real loud the same song.

The man went up, stomped on the mouse's house, and returned to his qayaq. He didn't want to hear that singing mouse again.

The Mouse Bridegroom

Andrew Nuqaqsrauraq Skin

RECORDED IN SELAWIK IN 1972

~~~~~~

A MOUSE STARTED TO SWIM THROUGH THE RIVER. HE FOLLOWED THE river. He swam and swam.

A man saw that mouse swimming. He noticed that the mouse didn't bother to take even a short, little rest on land. Loudly, he called out to the mouse, asking, "Mouse, Mouse, where are you going?"

"I'm going to Kotzebue—to get married," the mouse answered.

"Stay real close to the beach. And when you reach the ocean, do stay really close to the beach or else the pike will eat you," the man told the mouse.

The mouse was so eager to reach his bride that he disregarded that man's warning. He crossed the ocean to Kotzebue by swimming right through the middle of the ocean. When he reached the deepest part, a pike ate him up. So the mouse didn't reach his bride-to-be.

(A man who doesn't think before going into the marriage is short-sighted. His marriage might end in a divorce. Or after the marriage, if he isn't providing for his family he would end up with no food to feed his wife and his children.)

The Hard Worker and the Lazy Neighbor

Kitty Qalutchuq Foster

Kitty Qalutchuq Foster was a Selawik woman born in 1892. She was married to Jimmy Urgiiḷiq Foster. One of her relatives, Matulikkaaq, is remembered as a community leader who organized the last Selawik potlatch with the Koyukon Indians in 1911. Kitty's father, Omokatuk (Aumaqutuk) Knox, used to live in a settlement named Ikaaġiaq. Her brothers were John Knox and Joe Knox. Kitty had three children.

RECORDED IN SELAWIK IN 1988

THERE WERE TWO PEOPLE LIVING BY THE RIVER, ACROSS FROM EACH OTHER. One man worked laboriously, but the other didn't. The working person worked all the time until he was totally exhausted. He was getting ready for the coming winter. The other man, on the other hand, couldn't be seen, even during the day. The hard-working man kept his eyes peeled for the other person, but the other man couldn't be seen.

Whenever the hard-working man wanted to leave his house, he would get ready and then take off. Even when it was dark outside, he would still leave his house to go to work. The working man was so exhausted from working so hard that he wasn't able to keep his eyes on the other man all the time.

One day the working man finally saw him coming out of his house. He told the other man, "Be very, very careful! The nighthawk enjoys eating mice."

But the other man didn't listen to him. He didn't say a word. He just left.

Waiting, the working man later heard a cry asking for help. He knew then that the other man living across from him was dead.

The working man was a camp robber and the other man was a mouse.

The Raven at Kuugruaq River

Willie Panik Goodwin, Sr.

This is one of the four stories told by Willie Goodwin, Sr., in English to entertain members of the Brown University Archeological Expedition at Onion Portage on the Kobuk River one evening. He began his storytelling session with the narration of this short, funny, real incident. It was enthusiastically received by his audience. Encouraged by the audience response, he proceeded to tell other stories. Despite the new context of storytelling, a good Iñupiaq storyteller like Willie was resilient and never failed to rise to the occasion.

RECORDED AT ONION PORTAGE IN ENGLISH, JULY 3, 1966

THIS IS A REAL STORY. IT HAPPENED NOT TOO LONG AGO. IT HAPPENED during the time when people were hunting muskrats.

While sitting around taking a rest from the hunt, one of the men in the group enjoyed telling stories to make others laugh. One time he told this story:

One spring we were coming down the river, the Kuugruaq. The current wasn't too swift at that time of the year. The water level was however quite high and we were out, hunting muskrats.

When morning arrived, we found nice weather. By that time we were ready to camp. When we were hunting muskrats, we always stopped to camp when the sun came up, around four o'clock in the morning, sometimes five o'clock or six o'clock.

Just before we were ready to put up camp, we went toward the riverbank where there were clumps of trees. There we saw a tree bending down toward the bank. It was bending so low that it almost touched the ground. On that tree sat a raven. It looked like he was sleeping.

We started to flap our arms, trying to frighten him. The first time we did that, the raven didn't even wake up. On the second try, one person managed to wake him up.

The raven was so startled and groggy that he fell—straight into the water! [Laughter.]

Everyone had a big laugh.

Index

Page numbers in italics refer to illustrations.

Burnett, Leslie
  and Christian influence, 16–17
  and gender differences, 14
  and haunting, 243–244
  and teasing, 12
  vocalization style, 16

CAA building, 108
cache, platform, 162
California Quaker Friends Church. *See*
  Quakers
cannibal (specific characters)
  arm, 114–115
  child, 112–113
  father-in-law as, 108–111
  head, 186–191
  manslayer as, 177
cannibals (in general)
  in the bad lands, 27
  female, 71
  and use of sticky ball, 70–71
categorization, narrative, 19–20
childbirth, natural, 24, 63–64
  introduced by Qayaq, 25, 26, 63
children
  nursing, 91
  as prize, 162–163
Christianity, 244
  and storytellers, 16–17, 179
  and textual interpretation, 17
  and textual variation, 45, 48
classification, 19
Cleveland, Flora, *9, 10*
  family history, 211
  and story ownership, 13
  and teasing, 11, 250
Cleveland, Lois, 186
Cleveland, Maude, 6, 171, *171*
  and gender differences, 14
  and material culture, 17
Cleveland, Robert, 6, 9, *9, 10, 121*
  Christian influence on, 179
  family history, 121
  and Foote, Don, 4
  and gender differences, 14, 15
  and narrative categorization, 19, 20
  Native Educator's Conference, 121
  and story ownership, 13
  and tape recording of stories, 47
  and textual variation, 15
  and transmission authentication, 12–13
cliffs, crushing, 66
Cloud Man, 168–169

Coalmine, *54*
coastal
  subsistence living, 32
  vocal distinctions, 17, 18
conflict resolution method, song as, 84–86
contact period. *See* time frames
cosmology, 3, 26–29, 78
  man from moon in, 81–83
  sky people in, 78–80
cousins, 41. *See also* social structure
crazy man, 60
creamed fat (*akutuq*), 18, 52
culture. *See also* post-contact period
  expressive, 7
  interplay with narratives, 31–48
  and language in text, 33–34
  material, 33–34
  narrative, 3–48
  and reconceptualization of identity, 46
  revitalization of, 45–46
Curtis, Edward, 19
  folktale collection of (Kotzebue Sound), 3
  and the Qayaq cycle, 23, 24
Custer, Charlie, 4

Dall sheep, 59–60
dance, 10, 91
daughters, roles of, 38
DeBree, Susan Towne, 4
Deering, *2, 54*
devices, narrative, 31, 32, 34. *See also*
  narrative technique
didactic themes, *170*, 191, 259
Downey, Gladys, *8*
Downey, Shield, Jr., *8*
drum, small, 94–95

Earth world, as parallel world, 26
ecology, and identity, 12
Elders' Conferences (NANA), 5, 23
Elephant Point, 4
emic categories, 19
emigration, Indian, 22
endearments in song, 186
Eschscholtz Bay, 4
Eskimo-Indian conflicts, 21, 22, 130–131,
  138–139
Eskimo stories hour, 46
Evil One, the, 175
exclamations, *52*

Family. *See* social structure; transitions, life
  stage (men/women)

menstruation, 36. *See also* transitions, life
stage (women)
and birch bark hats, 173
mermaids, 27
messenger (*kivgaq*), 42
metacommunication, 10, 11
metanarration, 15–16, 17
as narrative shift, 10, 11
metaphor, killing as, 44–45
Mitchell, Jenny, 4
Mitchell, Mark, 4
Monroe, Paul, 4, 17
moon, man from, 81–83
motif-by-motif narrative technique, 14
Mountain Man, 169–170
mouse
bridegroom, 280, 281
gigantic, 92–93
Mouse, Beatrice, 15, 16
biographical information, 263
Mouse Man, 170
Mudshark, 259–260

Nakasruktuuq
in animal stories, 30
and laziness, 38–39, 191–194
zoomorphosis of, 27
nalukataq (blanket toss), 107, 136–138, 140
names, absence of, 24
NANA, 5, 12, 103
narrative categories, 19–20, 21
narrative technique
and Christianity, 16–17
devices in, 31, 32, 34
and gender, 14–15
metacommunication, 10, 11
metanarration, 10, 11, 15–16, 17
motif-by-motif, 14
regional characteristics, 17–18
and social organization, 39–42
and vocal distinctions, 17–18
vocalization style, 16, 17
Nasruk. *See* Cleveland, Robert
National Bilingual Education Development
Center, 5
Native Educator's Conference, 121
Nelson, Edward William, 19
and cosmology, 26
folktale collection of (Kotzebue Sound), 3
Nida, Eugene, 7
Niġlaaq River, 10
Niġlaaqtuuġmiut, 125–126
Niyuk. *See* Johnson, Charlie

Noatak, *2, 54*
Noatak River region, *2*, 3, 4, *54*
stories from, 3, 4, 17, 44, 45
Noonagak, 4
and story ownership, 13
Noorvik, *2*, 5, *54*
Northern People (Siḷalliñiġmiut), 146–147
Northwest Alaska, villages in, *2*
Northwest Alaska Native Association, 5, 103
Northwest Arctic Borough, 14
Northwest Arctic Borough School District,
5, 25, 46
Norton, Edward, and the Qayaq cycle, 23
Norton, Emma, 10, 11, 78
Norton, Nora, 10, 11, 23, *55*
and anthropomorphosis, 28
and Christian influences, 17
family history, 55, 153
father as *umialik*, 40–41
and gender differences, 14, 15
and hospitality, 78
and humility, 43
Indian raids, tales of, 21
and location of Qayaq's home, 24
and metanarration, 15
and narrative categorization, 19, 20
and the Qayaq cycle, *25*, 25–26
and vocal distinctions, 17
vocalization style, 16
Nunachiam Sissauni (Buckland) high school, 48
nuniaq. See song
nursing, of children, 91

Old story category (*unipchaaq utuqqaq*), 19,
20, 21
Oman, Lela, 4
Onion Portage, 5, 6, *9*
Oquilluk, William, 4
orphan story complex, 20, 43–44, 194–211
orthography, modern, 7
outsiders (*iksiak*), fear of, 21
ownership, story, 13–14

Pah River, 6, *54*
Panitchiaq. *See* Skin, Tommy
people, little, 27
peregrine falcon, 75–77
performance
contextual, 6, 13
narrative, 9–10, 11, 12
Piñaqtuq, 103–104
platform cache, 162
Point Hope, 4, 5, 78

Siktagvik, 126
Siḷalliñiġmiut (Northern People), 146–147
Sisaulik, 4
skills, mastery of, 32. *See also* hunting
Skin, Andrew, 103
  and topic transitions, 16
Skin, Emma, 198
Skin, Tommy, 9
sky world, 3, 26, 78–80
  and Uqaqtoqaiyaq (chief of sky people), 83
social structure, 10, 40. *See also* legends;
    stories, old
  ataniq (head of village), 52
  and ideal behavior, 87, 215
  iḷagiikpaurat (family units in), 39–40
  networks, 39, 41
  and non-kin relationships, 41–42
  and norms, 117–120
  aŋaayyuqaq (chief), 40
  qaukḷiq (top man/manager), 40
  and siblings, 179–186
  suunaaq (male friends), 42
  uumaa (female friends), 42
song, 5, 10
  in animal stories, 259
  blackfish, 261–262
  blanket toss, 10, 137
  and conflict, 84–86, 135–136
  and education, 259
  and endearments, 186
  lullabies, 29
  nuniaq (to sing endearments), 52, 186
  for safety, 66
  and suicide, 91
  sung by sky people, 80
  in warfare legend, 135–136
sons, role of, 37
Spencer, Robert, 4
staff, magic, 174–179
sticky ball, 70–71
stinginess, 225–227
stories. *See also* legends; stories, old
  categories of, 19–20, 21
  as children's literature, 4
  dramatic performance of, 47
  at funeral gatherings, 46
  horror, 20
  and identity, 10, 11
  and language study, 5
  length of, 20
  ownership of, 13–14
  Western counterparts of, 47

stories, old. *See also* legends; social structure
  child as prize in, 162–163
  consequences in, 170
  didactic theme in, 170, 191
  foresight in, 157–165
  laziness in, 191–194
  revenge on mother, 228–231
  stinginess in, 225–227
  wind in, 152–157
story collection
  and mass media, 45–46
  methodology of, 5–7
  taping of, 6, 7, 46
  translation of, 6
storytellers
  Christian influence on, 16–17
  and empathy with animal characters, 30
  at funeral gatherings, 46
  and gender differences, 14–15
  and memory recall, 81
storytelling
  commencement of, 31
  contexts of, 7–13, 45–48
  as contextual performance, 7, 13
  cultural influences on, 16–17
  as event, 7–13, 24
  at funeral gatherings, 46
  and gender differences, 14–15
  interactive, 9, 16, 166–170, 206, 250
  and mass media, 45–46
  and modern technology, 6, 7, 45–46
  regional, 17–18, 45–46
  as seasonal performance, 7–9
  and story ownership, 13–14
  as transformative communicative event, 47
  and vocal distinctions, 17–18
  and vocalization style, 16
structure, narrative, 18–21
subsistence, 26–27, 29, 32
  and fishing rights, 125–126
  and gender, 35–39
  and the hero, 35, 42
  and hunting, 27, 32, 35–36, 37, 38
  and life stages, 35–39
  and riverine life, 32, 37
  sites in legend, 125–126
  of sky world, 26
  unpredictability of resources, 41
  women's roles in, 36–38
sufficiency, self, 35, 179–186
suicide, 90–91
Sun Man, 168

Wright, John
  as Quaker preacher, 45
  and story ownership, 13

Zoomorphosis, 25, 27–29